Chris Nixon • Sportscar Heaven

Chris Nixon
Sportscar Heaven

Aston Martin DBR1 V Ferrari Testa Rossa

Foreword by Tony Brooks

THE BATTLE FOR THE
WORLD CHAMPIONSHIP
1957-1959

Transport Bookman Publications

Published by Transport Bookman Publications Ltd,
8, South Street, Isleworth, Middlesex TW7 7DH, England

Copyright © Chris Nixon 2002

All rights reserved. Apart from any fair dealing for the purpose of private study, research, criticism or review under Copyright, Designs and Patent Act 1988, no part of this publication may be reproduced, stored in a retrieval system or transmitted by any means electronic, electrical, chemical, mechanical, optical, photocopying, recording or otherwise, without prior written permission.
All enquiries should be addressed to the publisher.

ISBN 0-85184-067-1

Layout: Chris Nixon
Production: Uwe Kraus GmbH
Printed in Italy

SPORTSCAR HEAVEN

"Give me Goodwood on a summer's day," said Roy Salvadori "and you can keep the rest of the world."

I have no idea just when Roy uttered those words, but they captured my feelings precisely as I knelt behind the Aston Martin DBR1 he was to drive in the Tourist Trophy on September 5th, 1959. I was kneeling because the race was about to begin with a Le Mans start and I wanted to photograph Stirling Moss (sharing the Aston with Roy) making one of his famous lightning getaways. I was surprised to see that Stirling, poised like an Olympic sprinter on the other side of the track, was not looking at the official starter, but at his wrist. With his usual thoroughness, he had synchronised his watch with those of the timekeepers and on the stroke of midday he was off and running - while the starter was still raising the Union flag!

Luckily, I pressed the shutter release just as Stirling blasted into action and I also caught the starter with his flag held high (see page 172). Moss was almost into the middle distance before anyone else was moving and as the field of Astons, Ferraris, Jaguars, Porsches, Lotuses and Lolas streamed away from the pits in an absolute kaleidoscope of national racing colours, one of the greatest races I have ever witnessed was under way.

It was my good fortune to be reporting the TT for *Autosport* and during the next six hours I watched with mounting excitement and disbelief as Stirling proceeded to destroy the Ferrari and Porsche opposition. With one of the most remarkable drives of his remarkable career he snatched victory from the very jaws of defeat in a manner that is just not possible now. And he did so against the toughest opposition, for in those days the world's greatest drivers did not restrict themselves to Grand Prix racing, so I was priviledged to watch many of my heroes - Moss, Tony Brooks, Roy Salvadori, Phil Hill, Olivier Gendebien, Taffy von Trips, Carroll Shelby - and a promising lad named Jim Clark - in action. This was Goodwood on a summer's day - and I was in Sportscar Heaven.

I fell in love with sports rather than GP cars not only because Aston Martins, Jaguars, Ferraris and Maseratis were so beautiful to look at, but also because I knew - in theory, at least - that I could step into any one of them, turn the key, press the starter and go for a thrilling drive on our then unrestricted country roads. All were street legal, with two seats, windscreens, lights and proper ground clearance and looked similar to cars one could buy in a showroom.

The Aston Martin DBR1, Ferrari Testa Rossa and Maserati 300S were big boys' versions of the Austin-Healey 3000, Triumph TR3A and MGA. Technology had not yet forced them off the public roads, as it would by the early seventies, so I could relate to the cars of Scuderia Ferrari, Officine Maserati, Aston Martin and Jaguar in a way that is not possible today. Imagine just trying to get into a modern Le Mans Audi, Panoz or Bentley. And as for driving on country roads with that zero ground clearance and minimal steering lock, forget it! However, although clearly beyond my skills in terms of racing, all those fifties racers were eminently driveable in an everyday manner.

So this book is essentially a celebration of two of the outstanding sportsracing cars of the 1950s, the Aston Martin DBR1 and the Ferrari Testa Rossa (not forgetting the men who raced them). Beautiful, driveable cars, they captured the imagination of all who saw them in their pomp. Sportscar Heaven, indeed!

Chris Nixon

CONTENTS

SPORTSCAR HEAVEN	5
ACKNOWLEDGEMENTS	8
INTRODUCTION	10
FOREWORD by Tony Brooks	11

1956

CHAPTER ONE
Working Towards a Winner - The Design of the DBR1 — 12

CHAPTER TWO
Brief Encounter With a Redhead - The 24 Hours of Le Mans — 16

CHAPTER THREE
All Change for '57 - Teams and Drivers — 21

1957

THE CONTENDERS 1
The Aston Martin DBR1: Specification and Cutaway Drawing — 26

CHAPTER FOUR
The Last of the Big Bangers - The Buenos Aires 1000 Kms;
the 12 Hours of Sebring; the Mille Miglia — 28

CHAPTER FIVE
Aston Martin's Greatest Triumph - The Nürburgring 1000 Kms — 37

CHAPTER SIX
Reunion at the Ring - Brooks, Cunningham-Reid and
the DBR1 38 years on — 49

CHAPTER SEVEN
Luckless at Le Mans - Failure for Ferrari and Aston Martin — 56

CHAPTER EIGHT
Ferrari: Champions Again - The Swedish GP; the GP de Belge
and the GP of Venezuela — 63

RESULTS — 69

CHAPTER NINE
Spa Spectacular - Tony Brooks reminisces — 70

1958

THE CONTENDERS 2
The Ferrari 250 TR, Specification and Cutaway Drawing — 74

CHAPTER TEN
The Maranello Marvel - The Design of the 250 TR;
the Buenos Aires 1000 Kms — 77

CHAPTER ELEVEN
First Blood to Ferrari - the 12 Hours of Sebring — 81

CHAPTER TWELVE
Testa Rossa Supreme - The Targa Florio — 87

CHAPTER THIRTEEN
Meister Moss - The Nürburgring 1000 Kms — 93

CHAPTER FOURTEEN
Triumph and Tragedy for Ferrari - the 24 Hours of Le Mans;
the Deaths of Luigi Musso and Peter Collins — 107

RESULTS — 115

CHAPTER FIFTEEN
Winter Moves - Teams and Drivers   116

1959
THE CONTENDERS 3
The Ferrari TR59, Specification and Cutaway Drawing   122

CHAPTER SIXTEEN
Ferrari's Flying Start - the 12 Hours of Sebring   125

CHAPTER SEVENTEEN
A Setback for Astons, A Shock for Ferrari - Le Mans
Test Day; the Targa Florio   130

CHAPTER EIGHTEEN
Moss, the DBR1 and the Greatest Drive -
The Nürburgring 1000 Kms   135

CHAPTER NINETEEN
Such a Stunning Car!
Moss on the DBR1, the 300SLR and the Nürburgring   146

CHAPTER TWENTY
Astons, at Long Last Le Mans - Falling into Victory   149

CHAPTER TWENTY-ONE
Post Mortems - Le Mans Afterthoughts   161

CHAPTER TWENTY-TWO
Goodwood on a Summer's Day: The Tourist Trophy
The Championship goes to Feltham   169

RESULTS   179

CHAPTER TWENTY-THREE
The End of an Era - Aston Martin withdraw from Racing   181

CHAPTER TWENTY-FOUR
Bouquets and Brickbats - Roy Salvadori tries the Cars   189

BIBLIOGRAPHY, PERIODICALS, PHOTO CREDITS   192

INDEX   195

ACKNOWLEDGEMENTS

First of all, 'Sportscar Heaven' is a tribute to my friend, the late Frank Stroud. My very first book, the two-volume 'Racing With the David Brown Aston Martins' came about after a brief conversation with Frank in his bookshop more than 20 years ago. The deal was done on a handshake, which was to see us through another seven books. This would have been our ninth together, as he had agreed to publish it shortly before his untimely death in November, 2001. Happily, his wife June and their son Clive are carrying on the good work at Transport Bookman and I am very grateful for their continuing support - still on a handshake.

When planning this book I decided that I really ought to visit the Nürburgring, as it was acknowledged as the greatest road circuit in the world in the 1950s and one of my protagonists - Aston Martin - had dominated the 1000 Kms race in the three years I was writing about. The more I thought of it, the more the grandeur of the Ring produced delusions of the same in me and I hatched a plot to reunite the winners of the 1957 race - Tony Brooks, Noel Cunningham-Reid and DBR1/2 - at the circuit.

This was the stuff of dreams, of course, but thanks to the generosity and enthusiasm of Brandon Wang (a Ferrari man!) I was able to realise mine and, to prove it, photographer Richard Newton was on hand to record the occasion.

Also present were a 1958 'pontoon' Testa Rossa (0718, then owned by Brandon) and a replica TR59. The latter and the Aston are owned by someone who insists on remaining anonymous, but whose generosity must be gratefully acknowledged, nonetheless. Both cars are maintained by Tim Samways whose company, Sporting and Historic Car Engineers, completed a ground-up restoration of the DBR1 in 1994.

Our trip to the Ring was facilitated by Gerry Moroney, who invited us to join his splendid Wheeltorque tour and we were also helped by my friends Bernd and Helga Schneider, of Cologne. Bernd was born within earshot of the circuit, knows it better than many racing drivers and has proved invaluable in identifying the location of many of the archive photographs taken there.

The fact that the fabulous Spa-Francorchamps circuit is only a couple of hours' drive from the Ring made it imperative that we pay it a visit, as Tony Brooks had won two races there for Aston Martin. Unlike the Ring, the original circuit is made up of public roads, so we would need official permission to drive our cars around. Another friend, Jeff Ward, had put me in touch with Francois Olivier in Belgium and he introduced me to Yvan Bastin, who runs the Spa Motor Museum at Stavelot. Francois and Yvan thenz took me to meet the Chief of Police, Commissaire Arsene Francois. He proved to be a great racing enthusiast, very proud of the historic circuit within his jurisdiction and more than happy to help us.

On location in Spa-Francorchamps are (front l-r) Francois Olivier; Tim Samways; Quincy the Husky; Yolande Bastin; Alma Hill; Helga Schneider; Agent Brigadier Georges Helman (in cap); Yvan Bastin and Tony Brooks. (Back l-r) Commissaire de Police Arsene Francois; Caryn Newton; Pina Brooks; Phil Hill; Chris Nixon; Richard Newton; Jeff Ward; Ian Walker. Photo: Bernd Schneider.

Armed with these introductions we went to Spa, where we were joined by former World Champion Phil Hill, one of Tony Brooks' Ferrari team-mates in 1959. Thanks to Commissaire Francois, traffic was stopped for a few minutes at various points on the circuit so Richard Newton could photograph Tony and Phil in the cars.

All three racers were taken to the circuits by Ian Walker of Prestige Deliveries and Yvan Bastin gave them and the transporter a secure base during our stay. Yvan and his wife, Yolande, could not have been more hospitable.

A few months later I was able to reunite Roy Salvadori and DBR1/2 (in which he and Carroll Shelby had won Le Mans in 1959) at Goodwood, the scene of Astons' Championship triumph that same year. Paul Pappalardo was kind enough to bring along his Testa Rossa (0774), which started life as a 1959 works car and won Le Mans in 1960, driven by Olivier Gendebien and Paul Frère. Roy was able to drive both cars (photography by Maurice Rowe) and his comments appear in the final chapter of the book.

Many of the personalities involved with the teams of 1956-1959 were kind enough to reminisce for me and their words certainly add spice and authenticity to my story. Ted Cutting (who designed the DBR1) was extremely helpful with details of the Aston Martin racing programme and Romolo Tavoni (Ferrari Team Manager) provided some fascinating insights on working for The Old Man at the Scuderia.

My thanks to them and to the following:
ASTON MARTIN: Sir Jack Brabham, Tony Brooks, Noel Cunningham-Reid, Sir Stirling Moss and Roy Salvadori.
FERRARI: Cliff Allison, Tony Brooks, Mauro Forghieri, Olivier Gendebien, Dan Gurney, Phil Hill and Sergio Scaglietti. Brenda Vernor, formerly of Sefac Ferrari, was also very helpful.

Finding archive photographs that have not been seen before (or at least, not often) is always a challenge, but I have succeeded thanks to a number of people. In the 1950s weekly and monthly magazines were unable to use colour, which only appeared in quarterlies and annuals. However, I have been fortunate to find some really exciting colour photos by Yves Debraine (Archives l'année automobile) and Peter Coltrin (The Klemantaski Collection) and in the private collections of Brian Joscelyne, Martin McGlone and Michael Turner, to add to some of my own.

As with several of my previous books, Bill Kaye of Blowup has been most helpful. This time his expertise with computer technology has meant that a number of photographs I would not have considered using a few years ago have now been made well worth inclusion in the book.

Over the past few years Haymarket Publications has acquired the photo archives of *The Autocar*, *The Motor*, *Autosport*, and *Motor Sport*. They are now under the banner of LAT, which is run with great efficiency by Peter Higham. All enthusiasts who value the history of motor racing must be grateful for the way in which several million photographs are being stored and catalogued at LAT.

I am also grateful to the following: J-R Piccard of Archives l'année automobile; Peter Sachs of the Klemantaski Collection; Roger Stowers of Aston Martin; Walter Bäumer of the Nürburgring Collection; Ted Walker of Ferret Photos; Tony Adriaensens of Corsa Research and Pablo Vignone of Editorial Atlantida. To anyone I have inadvertently omitted, my apologies.

Through these various sources I have been able to make use of photos by some of the finest snappers of the period, including Yves Debraine, George Phillips, Bernard Cahier, Francis Penn, Pete Coltrin, Maurice Rowe, Maxwell Boyd and Ted Eves.

My historical research was aided by Jim Whyman at the AMOC, who provided access to Aston Martin Race Reports of the period, and by Simon Taylor, who gave me the run of his library of motor magazines.

Once again I have called upon the artistic skills of the remarkable father and son act that is Michael and Graham Turner for the cover of one of my books. Michael's painting of Mike Hawthorn and Peter Collins in the 1957 German GP graced 'Mon Ami Mate'; Graham's portrayal of Dick Seaman winning the 1938 German GP was a natural for 'Shooting Star', as was his portrait of Bernd and Elly Rosemeyer for 'Rosemeyer!'. Graham has now produced the cover picture for 'Sportscar Heaven' and I have also been able to include works by both artists in the book.

My thanks to all concerned.

CHRIS NIXON
Richmond, Surrey.
March, 2002.

ASTONS, PLEASE, NOT ASTON!

For the past 10 or 15 years motoring magazines have been referring to the Aston Martin company as 'Aston', in the singular. In strictly grammatical terms, this may be correct, but historically it is wrong.

In 1980 I published 'Racing With The David Brown Aston Martins'. The first volume was a personal account of the whole period by Team Manager John Wyer while the second comprised a memoir from virtually everyone in the Competitions Department, starting with Patron David Brown (not yet Sir David) himself. Without exception (and with great affection) all referred to the team and the company as 'Astons', in the plural. Keeping up with tradition, so do I.

C.N.

Introduction

There is good reason for regarding the decade 1950-1959 as a golden age of sportscar racing. During those years events such as the 24 Hours of Le Mans, the Mille Miglia, the Targa Florio, the 24 Hours of Spa-Francorchamps and the Tourist Trophy – the classic road races of old – were joined by new major endurance races such as the Nürburgring 1,000 Kms, the 12 Hours of Sebring, the Carrera Panamericana, the Swedish Grand Prix and the Buenos Aires 1,000 Kms.

In 1953 the Sportscar Manufacturers World Championship came into being and all these races were qualifying rounds at least once. Other important – but non-Championship – events included the Tour of Sicily, the Goodwood Nine Hours, the Supercortemaggiore 1,000 Kms, the 12 Hours of Pescara and the 12 Hours of Reims. In total 42 Championship races were run, with a high of seven events in 1953 and 1957 and a low of five in 1955 and 1959.

Over the years they attracted the cream of the manufacturers, large and small, the big guns including Alfa Romeo, Aston Martin, Bristol, Ferrari, Frazer Nash, Jaguar, Lagonda, Lancia, Mercedes-Benz and Porsche. All these companies produced road cars for the market place but they were joined on the circuits by entries from tiny firms run by enthusiasts who simply wanted to go racing. Names such as Allard, Connaught, Cooper, Cunningham, Elva, Gordini, HWM, Kieft, Lister, Lola, Lotus, Maserati, OSCA and Talbot litter the race programmes of the 1950s, and two of them – Cooper and Lotus – were to change the face of motor racing for ever.

In those days aerodynamics was a black art which no-one really understood properly, so few sports cars ever saw the inside of a wind-tunnel. The stylist was king, with the happy result that some of the sports racing cars of the period are among the most beautiful two-seaters ever built. In Italy, racing Ferraris were clothed in elegant bodywork styled by Carrozzeria Touring, Vignale and 'Pinin' Farina (later to become Pininfarina) and Scaglietti. In truth, styling is hardly the right word in some cases, as Sergio Scaglietti admits when recalling the first body he made for Enzo Ferrari – a Barchetta on a two-litre, V12 chassis destined for a customer named Cacciari – who drove it in the 1953 Mille Miglia.

"Nobody designed it – Ferrari gave me a chassis fitted with engine, fuel tank and wheels, and we made a frame of thin wire to fit over it and put the aluminium over that."

No doubt there were other such hit-and-miss 'designs' which emanated from Italian coachbuilders but, by and large, the bodies were built to fairly detailed drawings.

At Maserati Merdardo Fantuzzi was responsible for the 300S of 1955/56, and the gorgeous lines he drew for that looked almost as good on the larger 450S of 1957.

In England William Lyons set out to win Le Mans in 1951 with the beautiful Jaguar C-type, which was styled by the brilliant aerodynamicist Malcolm Sayer, who had joined Jaguar from The Bristol Aeroplane Company. In 1954 Sayer followed up with the sensational D-type which – in its 1955 form, with long nose and wicked-looking fin – is one of the most beautiful racing cars of all time.

Also in England, Aston Martin revived its racing heritage under the new ownership of the industrialist David Brown, who bought Astons (and then Lagonda) as a hobby. He quickly realised that racing success would reflect upon his whole David Brown organisation and so took to the circuits with his handsome DB2s.

These were styled by an ex-Lagonda man, Frank Feeley, who did himself few favours in 1952 with his next effort, the DB3, a purpose-built racing car which he clothed with what was little more than an open version of the DB2's bodywork. However, when the DB3 became the DB3S in 1953, Feeley really showed his stuff again, designing a curvaceous body with distinctive cutaway front wings for the Aston which, by 1955, he had refined into one of the prettiest sportscars ever to take the road.

However, the fact that the DB3S was a racing sportscar meant that it could not challenge the purpose-built sports racing cars of Mercedes-Benz, Jaguar and Ferrari. David Brown and his Team Manager, John Wyer, therefore commissioned a new car for 1956 – the DBR1 – and gave a relatively free hand to their young designer Ted Cutting. As Frank Feeley had decided to leave the company, Cutting found himself styling the bodywork as well, and although his first effort was rather lumpy, his 1957 version of the DBR1 was a real beauty.

In Italy Enzo Ferrari planned his new Testa Rossa to comply with the forthcoming 1958 three-litre capacity limit in sportscar Championship events and asked his friend Sergio Scaglietti to clothe it. Sergio's cutaway front wings resembled those on the DB3S Aston Martin, but whereas the Aston had been sleekly gorgeous, the Ferrari was starkly handsome – a dramatic-looking racing machine, rather than a beautiful sportscar. The works Ferraris soon abandoned the cutaway wings in favour of conventional bodywork, but the Testa Rossa lost none of its charisma.

Ferrari and the Aston Martin approached the same objective – winning the sportscar Championship – in very different ways: the former with a V12 engine in a very basic chassis with (initially) drum brakes; the latter with a straight-six in a sophisticated space-frame with discs. Each achieved its aim before the decade was out, and the cars concerned soon became uncompetitive and unwanted, so much so that the teams could hardly give them away.

Foreword by Tony Brooks

The Aston Martin DBR1 and the Ferrari Testa Rossa were the classic sports racing cars of the 1950s, the ultimate expression of the designer's accumulated wisdom and experience in one of the most exciting decades in sports racing history.

They were real sports cars which could be driven and enjoyed on the roads. They were designed and built to be raced on the limit on normal roads with challenging natural hazards, not on billiard smooth tarmac bounded by prairies, and technology had not even begun to mitigate the importance of the drivers' skills.

I was in the unique position of driving both these cars for Aston Martin and Ferrari and roads do not come any more natural than those making up the Targa Florio circuit, where I had my first experience of the Testa Rossa. Its sweet gearbox made the endless gear-changing a joy and the power sent it soaring up the hillsides like a jet taking off, but it could not match the roadholding and balance of the Aston, which could be threaded through the continuous succession of corners with a mere caress of the steering.

The Ferrari was a great car and provided its own sense of satisfaction, but despite the Aston's temperamental gearbox and power disadvantage, I will always treasure my drives in the DBR1 at Spa and the Nürburgring, where it seemed automatically to adopt a four-wheel drift attitude on medium/fast corners, and recall the ecstacy in balancing the car on a tightrope, seemingly by thought rather than conscious operation of the controls.

It is said that if a car looks right it is right and that is certainly true of these two classics, which were both very rewarding to drive. Chris Nixon's fine book will ensure that these two great rivals and the era in which they competed will be remembered long after technology renders the sport impotent.

At the Nürburgring with TR59 0768.

At Le Mans with DBR1/2.

CHAPTER ONE

Working towards a Winner

The design of the DBR1

The brand new Aston Martin DBR1/1 draws admiring glances from a number of Feltham personnel before being driven to Le Mans in 1956. Designer Ted Cutting and draughtsman Alex 'Steve' Stephens are third and fourth from left.

In May 1957 Aston Martin shook the motor racing world by taking on the full might of Ferrari and Maserati in that breaker's yard known as the Nürburgring and beating them out of sight in the 1,000 Kms race. That in itself was a remarkable achievement, but what made it all the more so was that unlike its Italian rivals which were designed by a team of engineers, the winning Aston – the DBR1 – was almost entirely the work of one man, Ted Cutting. Two seasons later his car was to secure the Sportscar World Championship for Aston Martin, the first time ever for a British team.

Until that momentous victory at the Ring the cars from Feltham in Middlesex had been regarded as good also-rans in international circles, having flattered to deceive on several occasions since Patron David Brown had begun his racing programme in 1949. The problem was that Astons were handicapped by an engine that had been designed in the 1940s and a chassis which had its origins in the 1930s.

The engine had begun life as the LB6 (Lagonda Bentley), a six-cylinder, 2.6-litre unit designed for the Lagonda company during World War Two by Willie Watson, under the supervision of W.O. Bentley. In 1952 Watson enlarged it to 2.9 litres, but it was still down on power compared with the larger engines of its competitors, and David Brown had already instigated the design of a 4.5-litre V12 in order to compete on better terms with Ferrari, Cunningham, Jaguar, Lancia and Alfa Romeo. DB planned to put this engine into a luxury Lagonda saloon of advanced specification, having proved it on the race track.

After racing modified DB2 saloons in 1949 and 1950, DB hired Professor Robert Eberan-Eberhorst to design a completely new chassis for racing – the DB3. The good Professor had worked for the legendary Professor Ferdinand Porsche at Auto Union from 1933 to 1939, a fact that was readily apparent in the chassis he drew for the DB3, for it bore a startling resemblance to that of Porsche's Auto Union, albeit with its engine in front of the driver, rather than behind him.

The DB3 proved to be too big and too heavy, and so Willie Watson came up with a smaller, lighter version of its chassis which was powered by his 2.9-litre engine and called the DB3S. Although this unit produced more that twice the 105bhp it had originally given in 2.6-litre form when David Brown had bought Aston Martin and Lagonda in 1947, it was incapable of further enlargement.

The DB3S made its international début at Le Mans in 1953, and all three cars failed to finish. After that débâcle, however, it won five events, culminating in a superb victory in the Tourist Trophy at Dundrod, the last race in the brand new Sportscar World Championship. Although Astons finished first and second and soundly trounced the Jaguars (their arch domestic rivals) on a very demanding circuit, it was a somewhat hollow victory, as Scuderia Ferrari had already won the Championship, and none of the Continental team bothered to show up.

Nonetheless, it proved that the 3S was a very fine car and – properly developed – capable of better things. In the afterglow of the TT, Astons' prospects for 1954 looked decidedly rosy, but the team's hopes were destined to be crushed by the arrival of a very large cuckoo in the Feltham nest – the Lagonda.

Team Manager John Wyer was not in favour of racing the V12, as it consumed huge amounts of time and money which he was convinced would have been better invested in the 3S. Furthermore, DB seemed to think that the Lagonda project could just be added to Aston Martin's racing programme, with no increase in the Competitions Department's staff at Feltham and, apparently, no real increase in the budget.

The result was chaos. In 1954, overstretched and underfunded, Astons tumbled to the nadir of their racing history at Le Mans, where they foolishly entered no fewer than five cars: a supercharged DB3S; a 1953 specification 3S; two brand-new 3S

Patron David Brown (right) and his Team Manager, John Wyer.

saloons, and a Lagonda. In a race that must have in no small way contributed to John Wyer's subsequent nervous breakdown, the Lagonda crashed and was forced to retire; the saloons were both written off; the '53 car went out with a broken stub axle, and the supercharged Aston blew a gasket and expired.

Afterwards, John was all for withdrawing for the rest of the season and using the remaining months to prepare properly for 1955. David Brown, however, would have none of it, insisting that his cars were back in the fray as soon as possible.

Somehow Astons pulled themselves together sufficiently to assemble three 3Ss and a Lagonda for the British GP meeting at Silverstone, where their spirits were revived somewhat by a one-two-three-four result in the sportscar race, although there was no opposition worth a damn. They then pushed their luck too far by entering the TT at Dundrod, where they failed dismally before ending the season on another low note, being soundly beaten by the Ferrari of the young American privateer Masten Gregory in a race of no importance at Aintree.

Although DB insisted on pursuing his Lagonda dream (demanding that an entirely new chassis be ready for Le Mans) a rested and recuperated John Wyer concentrated on building two new DB3S models in time for the Daily Express Silverstone meeting in May 1955. Equipped with twin-plug cylinder heads, Girling disc brakes and ZF differentials these cars swept to an impressive victory over the works Jaguars in the sportscar race.

Astons' pleasure in their fine début was tempered by the knowledge that, just a week before, Mercedes-Benz had returned to sportscar racing with a similar one-two victory. The similarity ended there, however, for the race in question was not a jolly, one-hour blast around Silverstone, but the legendary Mille Miglia and, in the drive of his young life, Stirling Moss had led Juan Manuel Fangio home by more than 30 minutes in the sensational new three-litre Mercedes-Benz 300SLRs. In a trice, Astons' 'new' DB3S was rendered obsolete.

John Wyer and David Brown agreed that they would need a new Aston Martin for 1956, one that was lower and lighter than the DB3S and blessed with better weight distribution. That meant following Mercedes-Benz down the spaceframe path and building a brand-new sports racing car – as opposed to the DB3S, which was a racing sportscar. Wyer appointed 28-year-old Ted Cutting as Racing Car Designer and told him to get on with the job.

After a brief spell with Sydney Allard, Ted had joined Aston Martin as a draughtsman in March 1949, and worked on the DB2, DB3, DB3S and Lagonda under the eyes of Professor Eberan-Eberhorst, Frank Ayto and Willie Watson.

Both he and John Wyer were well aware that the DB3S, with its rather short, 87-inch wheelbase and low polar moment of inertia, had to be fought on rough surfaces, so a longer, 90-inch wheelbase was agreed for the DBR1's spaceframe chassis, together with a transverse, five-speed gearbox in unit with the ZF final drive. This would increase the polar moment of inertia in conjunction with the longer wheelbase, and having its masses at the ends of the car would make the DBR1 easier to drive and give more warning of trouble to the driver.

"John Wyer and I decided to make as much of a new car as we could reasonably afford and which we could build in the time available, prior to Le Mans, 1956." recalls Ted. "This meant using the DB3S front suspension and steering gear virtually unchanged. The R1's track was one inch wider than that on the 3S, but we took care of that simply by altering the length of the torsion bars and track rods. I also based the rear suspension very much on the de Dion system used on the 3S, with simple parallelogram side rods, but whereas the 3S had a slider bar on the back of the differential unit I put a Watts linkage across the back of the R1. I designed the multi-tube, spaceframe chassis as a 'perimeter-type', using a one-and-a-quarter-inch by 18 gauge moly steel tube. This allowed me to produce a car that was both lower and lighter than the DB3S and gave me more freedom when it came to positioning the ancillaries."

As with the 3S, the R1 ran on off-set Borrani wheels fitted with Avon tyres and Girling single calliper disc brakes were employed all-round.

John Wyer asked Cutting to redesign the Aston's cast-iron cylinder block in aluminium, as the performance of the top half of the unit had long ago out-distanced that of the bottom. ("We were getting 240bhp on a block designed for 100!" says Ted). He also wanted a dry sump lubrication system, in order to reduce the car's frontal area.

The barrel-type crankcase of the DB3S had employed aluminium cheeses to hold the crankshaft in place. However, the block had become heavier and heavier and Astons had got to the point where, in order to fit the one into the other, they were heating the iron cylinder block in boiling water before inserting the crankshaft and cheeses, which had been stored in a refrigerator!

"And even then, the crankshaft was virtually holding the engine together," says Cutting. "I threw away the cheeses and made an orthodox block – extended four inches below the crank centreline – with four drop-in main bearing caps, studs and all the rest and we got back to the situation you ought to have, where the block holds the engine together."

The DBR1 was always destined to be a three-litre car, but the tragedy at Le Mans brought panic changes in its wake for the 1956 event. When the new regulations were announced in October 1955, they restricted prototypes to a capacity of 2.5 litres. Ted Cutting was already at work on the new, three-litre engine, but the reduction in capacity was made easier for him by the fact that Aston Martin had made a 2.5-litre version of their LB6 unit back in 1953, when they were toying with the idea of going Grand Prix racing in 1954. The arrival of the Mercedes-Benz W196 knocked that on the head and the engine was abandoned, but there were some 2.5-litre crankshafts left over.

"These had the appropriate stroke for our 83mm bore," says Ted, "so I designed two engines which could be made from largely common pattern equipment, where the three-litre block was one and a half inches taller than the 2.5-litre, with shorter conrods for the latter. They had different timing cases, but there was only one gear difference in the timing gears and that was an idler gear in the middle."

It is indeed ironic that the one main component of the DBR1 that Ted Cutting did not design (although he did some work on it) was the CG537 five-speed gearbox, for this was to bedevil the car's three-year racing career. It was made by the David Brown Gear Co, which had been designing gears for almost 100 years, so one would reasonably have thought that the company could have produced a successful unit for the new racing Aston. Sadly, it was a disaster and cost the team several victories.

The CG537 was a large unit, with its own dry sump lubrication system. The gearbox shafts ran transversely across the frame, with input via bevel gears from the propshaft. The transverse shafts gave a choice of five input and five output wheels, making 25 ratios available. It was the input gears which were to prove so troublesome for the DBR1.

The 2.5-litre engine was designated the RB6/250 and just one example was built for the R1. Its dimensions were 83 x 76.8mm (2493cc) and it was fitted with the twin-plug, 60° aluminium cylinder head from the DB3S. It first ran on the Feltham test bench in March,1956 and produced a healthy 212bhp @ 7,000rpm.

As for the body, that too was the work of Ted Cutting. The beautiful DB3S had been styled by Frank Feeley, but he was about to leave Astons, and so Ted assumed responsibility for the R1's shape, with the help of Alex 'Steve' Stephens, a very fine body draughtsman who had worked closely with Feeley.

"I had never designed a body before," says Ted, "but Steve and I drew one-tenth and then one-quarter scale drawings from three angles which we showed to John Wyer and David Brown. They suggested a few minor changes and we went ahead. We wanted to make the R1 as light as we could, so we used some very special, aircraft quality aluminium-alloy sheets of 20-gauge." (The DB3S had been made of heavier, 18-gauge metal.)

The complete regulations for Le Mans were very slow in coming through, and it was soon obvious that Astons would not be able to build three DBR1s in time for the race. John Wyer therefore decided to enter just the one, alongside two brand new DB3Ss. Any car powered by an engine of more than 2.5 litres had to be a production car, which meant that at least 50 examples had to have been 'built or provided for'. Despite this, both Jaguar and Aston Martin entered cars to full works specification and got away with it because the Le Mans organisers knew that they would withdraw if required to race their less powerful production versions.

When the 1956 regulations did arrive they required that all cars have two proper seats and doors and a full-width windscreen. This meant a redesign for both the DB3S and the DBR1, which Ted Cutting had originally drawn 1955 3S-style, with just a driver's door, single wrap-around windscreen and metal tonneau cover.

The new DB3S models were completed in time for a shakedown race at Rouen on July 8, but the DBR1 was not ready until Friday, July 20 – just eight days before Le Mans – when it ran for the first time at MIRA, driven by Roy Parnell, Astons' full-time test driver. The following Tuesday, Roy drove it from Feltham to Le Mans, crossing the Channel from Southampton to Deauville via Silver City Airways. At Deauville he was met by John Wyer in a works DB2/4 (56 DMF) who escorted him to Aston Martin's HQ, the Hotel de France at La Chartre.

Astons' test driver Roy Parnell waves farewell as he sets off for Le Mans in the 2.5-litre prototype DBR1/1.

1956

CHAPTER TWO

Brief Encounter with a Redhead

The 24 Hours of Le Mans

The Automobile Club de l'Ouest (which ran Le Mans) was a law unto itself, and as its new rules for the 1956 24-hour race were not those of motor racing's governing body – the FIA – the event did not count towards that year's Sportscar World Championship. For this reason Ferrari and Maserati announced that they would not be entering the 24-hour race. Enzo Ferrari was competing in the Championship with his 290MM V12 and 860 Monza four-cylinder models, but both had a capacity of 3.4 litres and so were ineligible for the Prototype class. As was Maserati's very successful three-litre, 300S but, unlike Aston Martin and Jaguar, the Modenese concern did not attempt to convince the Le Mans authorities that the 300S was a Production car. In truth, Maserati was strapped for cash (as usual) and preferred to prepare its GP cars for the remainder of the season and give Le Mans a miss. At the last minute, however, Enzo Ferrari changed his mind and, as a result, the new Aston Martin had its first encounter with a Testa Rossa.

Late in 1953 Ferrari had introduced the 500 Mondial, a two-litre, four-cylinder sportscar which had been built in small numbers for customers to race. It had fared none too well against the Maserati A6GCS, so for 1956 Ferrari prepared a revised version which used a more powerful, 180bhp engine. The de Dion rear end and four-speed transaxle of the Mondial were abandoned in favour of a live rear axle and coil springs and a gearbox mated to the engine. As was common practice at Maranello, the engine's cam covers were painted red, but for the first time this feature led to a name for the car: Testa Rossa 500.

The first three chassis were bodied by Carrozzeria Touring of Milan and featured cutaway front wings, as on the Aston Martin DB3S, although whereas Frank Feeley had used the cutaways to facilitate the exit of hot air from the Aston's radiator, with Touring it was purely a stylistic signature. Enzo Ferrari was mainly looking to Americans to buy and race the 500 TR, which made its public début at the New York Motor Show in April 1956.

Two months later the three cars were entered for the Supercortemaggiore 1,000 Kms race at Monza. There was a lot of prize money involved and this may have had something to do with the fact that the organisers restricted the cars to two litres and under, thus keeping out Jaguar and Aston Martin and leaving the race to Ferrari and Maserati. The former team had a field day, as Peter Collins and Mike Hawthorn won from the Maserati of Stirling Moss/Cesare Perdisa and the Testa Rossas of Juan Fangio/Eugenio Castellotti and Olivier Gendebien/Fon de Portago were third and fourth. This result did the sales prospects of the TR no harm at all, and eventually a further 12 cars were built, but this time with bodywork by Sergio Scaglietti to a design by Pininfarina.

When it came to Le Mans, Ferrari used the same three chassis which had raced so successfully at Monza, but equipped them with his 2.5-litre, 625 Grand Prix engines modified for the 24 hours by having a lower compression ratio, smaller carburettors and distributors instead of magnetos. In this form they produced a claimed 225bhp @ 6,200rpm – slightly more than the Aston DBR1, which was their direct competitor in the Prototype class.

Ferrari's three main drivers – Juan Fangio, Eugenio Castellotti and Peter Collins – were absent from his team at Le Mans. The first two were reportedly unwell and Collins was reluctantly contracted to Aston Martin for this race. (He was driving for Ferrari in F1 and had already won the Belgian and French GPs. He had also won the Tour of Sicily and finished second in the Mille Miglia for Ferrari and was thoroughly disenchanted with the lack of power in the Aston Martin DB3S. Le Mans would be his last race for the Feltham team).

Nonetheless, the Scuderia had a strong line-up, with Phil Hill/André Simon; Fon de Portago/Duncan Hamilton (the latter recently sacked by Jaguar for disobeying orders and winning the Reims 12-Hour race) and Olivier Gendebien/Maurice Trintignant.

Maserati had first call on Stirling Moss, but as they were not competing he joined Aston Martin. Feltham, too, had a very strong team, comprising Moss/Peter Collins (DB3S/9); Roy Salvadori/Peter Walker (DB3S/10) and Reg Parnell/Tony Brooks (DBR1/1).

All three Astons passed scrutineering without trouble, but John Wyer was disappointed to find that the R1 was not the much lighter car he was hoping for. With four gallons of fuel on board a DB3S weighed 2,161lbs, whereas the R1 (admittedly with 13 gallons of fuel) registered 2,073lbs. More worrying was the fact that the Ferrari Testa Rossa stood at a mere 1,810lbs.

A key point in the new regulations was the imposition of a fuel consumption limit. Cars were allowed to start with full tanks but could only take on 120 litres (26.4 gallons) at refuelling stops, which had to be no fewer than 34 laps (284 miles) apart. This meant that the cars had to average at least 10.83mpg, which the Astons found hard to do.

On the first day's practice Moss and Collins did fastest laps of 4 mins 31 secs and 4' 39"; Salvadori and Walker did 4' 36" and 4' 35" and Parnell and Brooks recorded

Tony Brooks (14) gets away from the start, just a couple of cars' lengths behind the 2.5-litre Ferrari Testa Rossa (10) of Phil Hill. Neither finished the race.

The Parnell/Brooks DBR1/1 prototype comes under scrutiny during a pit stop.

4' 54" and 4' 41" in the R1.

The next day Moss recorded 4' 26", and Collins and Salvadori each did 4' 27". On the Mulsanne straight Moss – with a 3.09/1 final drive – was reaching 5,400rpm and was officially timed at 142.6mph, whereas in 1955 the 3S – with 3.27/1 final drive – had been timed at 155mph. John Wyer reckoned that he had underestimated the effect of the new, full-width windscreen (which had to be eight inches high) and that the 3Ss would have been faster had they been equipped with the 1955 ratio.

The performance of Tony Brooks and the R1 was most encouraging, for he took the R1 round in 4' 29" and was hitting 6,200 in fifth gear on Mulsanne, equal to 144mph. The new Aston in its 2.5-litre form was virtually as fast as its three-litre sister cars and in just three laps, for on the fourth the transmission failed, and the gearbox/final drive unit was later replaced.

All the Astons were on a knife-edge where fuel consumption was concerned: in the first practice session 3S/9 was right on the limit with 10.8mpg; 3S/10 a mite to the good with 10.9 and the R1 a similar amount to the bad with 10.7. During the second day's practice the carburettor air-intake box was removed from DB3S/10 when Peter Walker was driving and although he reported that speed on the straight was reduced by 200/300rpm, the fuel consumption improved dramatically to 12.3mpg.

As there was no practice on the Friday, John Wyer decided on a drastic move to try and improve the consumption of the R1. That afternoon Roy Parnell (nephew of Reg) drove the car all the way to Montlhéry to do some high-speed testing under John's eagle eye.

"We arrived with something like an hour of daylight left," he recalled, "and John said, 'Right, Parnelli, we'll fill the tank up to the brim and you go out and do some high-speed motoring.'"

Parnell did just that, and got the fright of his life. The R1 had been completed so late that there had been no time for handling or suspension tests and although there had been no complaints from Reg Parnell or Tony Brooks during practice, Roy soon found that the bumpy Montlhéry track was very different to the billiard table smoothness of Le Mans. The first time he got into fifth gear the Aston started bottoming out and he could see a trail of sparks in the mirror – and the fuel tank was brim-full!

He stopped for some fuel to be removed and went on to lap the Piste de Vitesse at around 125mph, first with the carburettor air-intake box in place, then without it. He did 20 laps in all and showed that fuel consumption improved by a remarkable 20 per cent without the airbox. As a result, John Wyer ordered that the R1 and the

Ron Flockhart drives Ninian Sanderson to the winner's enclosure in their travel-stained D-type after their superb win.

Salvadori/Walker 3S should race without the box but that the Moss/Collins car should retain it.

Favourites for the race had to be the works 3.4-litre D-type Jaguars of Mike Hawthorn/Ivor Bueb, Paul Frère/Desmond Titterington and Jack Fairman/Ken Wharton. They were backed up by the production D-types of Ecurie Ecosse (Ron Flockhart/Ninian Sanderson) and Ecurie Francorchamps (Jacques Swaters/Freddy Rousselle).

However, the entire Jaguar team was out of contention almost at once, as Frère and Fairman crashed in the Esses on lap two in company with Portago's Testa Rossa Ferrari and the Hawthorn/Bueb car lost many laps with a blocked fuel line. This left the lone Ecurie Ecosse D-type to do battle with the two DB3S Astons for the lead, and a right battle royal it was. Sadly, Peter Walker crashed DB3S/10 under Dunlop Bridge at about 7.30 on the Sunday morning and was badly hurt. He never raced again.

Stirling Moss and Peter Collins alternately led and hounded the Scottish D-type throughout the 24 hours, and were only a lap behind at the finish after a classic race.

The performance of the DBR1 was severely handicapped by the removal of the carburettor air box and it would not exceed 5,600rpm/130.9mph on the straight, whereas it had been doing 6,200rpm/144mph in practice. By contrast the Hill/Simon Testa Rossa was timed at 144.8mph. As a result the DBR1 never got a look at the Ferraris and after six hours was down in eighth place, while Gendebien/Trintignant and Hill/Simon were third and fourth respectively. This did not bother Astons unduly, as John Wyer believed that the real race began at midnight and only got going properly at 8am on the Sunday.

The Hill/Simon Ferrari retired after some eight hours with a broken transmission, but Gendebien and Trintignant drove superbly to finish a fine third overall, a mere 60 miles behind the winning D-type and just 50 behind the Moss/Collins DB3S.

The R1 was placed as high as fourth at one stage, but it suffered from a loss of oil pressure and a broken bracket in the throttle mechanism. In all it spent more than 37 minutes in the pits and had fallen to seventh by the time Tony Brooks parked it on the Mulsanne straight with just one hour to go. It had run its bearings.

"The DBR1 handled beautifully," recalls Brooks, "but it was very much down on power. And it was very frustrating to retire after lasting so long - almost 23 hours. We might as well have retired after three!" Tony was to enjoy considerable success with the new Aston, but he came to loathe Le Mans, as we shall see.

Back at Feltham, it was found that all the R1's big end bearings had failed and that there were fewer than five pints of oil in the oil tank.

Roy Parnell later recalled that the Aston retired "for a silly reason. Inside the oil tank was a little baffle plate to show the level, and a mechanic misread this during a pit stop. No oil was added when, in fact, it was needed and sometime later the engine knocked out its bearings. It was a great shame, because that 2.5-litre DBR1 really was a fabulous car."

DBR1/1 is surrounded by curious spectators beside the Mulsanne Straight, where Tony Brooks had to abandon it with one hour to go.

CHAPTER THREE

All change for '57

Teams and drivers

After Le Mans Aston Martin and Ferrari put their prototypes away and returned to their normal racing programme. For Ferrari this meant just one event, the Swedish GP, which they won, clinching the 1956 Sportscar World Championship. Astons did not enter, preferring to bask in the domestic sunshine at Oulton Park and Goodwood rather than be blown into the shadows at Kristianstad.

When, late in the year, the FIA published its sportscar regulations (Appendix C of the International Sporting Code) for 1957, they were seen to be very similar to those devised by the ACO for the recent Le Mans race. Cars were required to have two proper seats; two doors, a full-width windscreen (but only six inches high) and a cockpit hood that could be properly raised and lowered. (This latter requirement was ridiculous, as the hood did not have to be carried on the car. Astons made only one, which fitted both DB3Ss and – just – the DBR1.) However, the big differences were that there was to be no limit on engine size and no restriction on fuel consumption.

Originally, six races were scheduled for the Manufacturers' Championship, all of which were to be of a minimum of six hours duration or 1,000kms in length. At the end of the season, only the best four results were to count. The events were: the 1,000 Kms of Buenos Aires; the Sebring 12 Hours; the Mille Miglia; the Nürburgring 1,000 Kms; the Le Mans 24 Hours; and the Swedish Grand Prix. In February it was announced that a seventh event – the GP of Venezuela – was to be added to the list, although the actual date was not confirmed.

After years of racing in the 1.5 to three-litre classes, Maserati now set out to challenge their rivals with a large-capacity engine. They had first shown their hand in Sweden when, as well as five 300S machines they had brought along their new toy, a 4.5-litre V8 which produced a thundering 360bhp at 6,100rpm. Tried in practice only, this monster was very ugly, very noisy and very fast in a straight line, but it handled like a jelly on a plate and the brakes (from a Grand Prix car) were no match for its extra weight. This prototype 450S could not equal the lap times of the three-litre Maseratis, but its promise was there for all to see. Scuderia Ferrari took note and set about making some bigger V12s for 1957.

Juan Manuel Fangio, who had an unhappy year with Ferrari, despite winning his fourth World Championship.

During the winter months there was some serious shuffling of drivers among the teams. Driving for Ferrari, Juan Manuel Fangio had won his fourth World Championship in 1956 but had not been happy with the Scuderia, feeling that Enzo Ferrari had not accorded him the respect he deserved as undisputed number-one driver in the world. For 1957, therefore, he moved to Maserati, for whom he had driven in 1952/53. Fangio was 46 and revered by all as the Old Man.

He was joined by the young man widely regarded as his heir apparent, 28-year-old Stirling Moss, who had proved himself to be the most versatile driver of the time by winning in virtually every form of racing he had tried. In Grand Prix racing he had

Stirling Moss.

Jean Behra.

driven his Mercedes in the wheeltracks of Fangio's similar car during the 1955 season and had learned a lot, but even Fangio had nothing to teach him in sportscars, and Moss had won the Mille Miglia, the Tourist Trophy and the Targa Florio that year. In 1956 he had driven for Maserati in F1 and had shared his time between Maserati and Aston Martin in sports cars, being far more successful with the former. Now he joined them full-time for endurance races, but moved to Vanwall for GPs.

Maserati backed up these two superstars with the considerable talents of 36-year-old Jean Behra, the French former motorcycle champion who had already proved himself to be extremely fast on four wheels, but a tad unlucky. He was also rather temperamental and prone to find conspiracies under every engine cover, but he was a great fighter who never knew when he was beaten. With a reliable car under him, he was a formidable threat to anyone.

Harry Schell.

Mike Hawthorn.

Another 36-year-old in the Maserati camp was Harry Schell, a much-loved character (in an era of characters) who, while not in the front rank of drivers could always be guaranteed to give of his best until he ran out of steam, which he did frequently. How much this had to do with his love of the good life is not entirely clear, but Harry (brought up in France by American parents) was known as the American in Paris, where he and his wife, Monique, ran L'Action Automobile, the bistro near L'Etoile where racing folk gathered of an evening for a drink before moving out on the town to misbehave.

Having lost Fangio, Scuderia Ferrari brought Mike Hawthorn back into the fold for 1957. Tall, blond and charismatic, 28-year-old Mike shared Harry Schell's love of alcohol, girls and practical jokes. He had been the first Englishman to drive for Ferrari and had scored a sensational victory for the Prancing Horse in 1953 when he won the French GP at Reims after a race-long duel with Fangio. In 1954 he had suffered severe burns during a crash at Syracuse and although he had won the Spanish GP he decided to drive British in 1955, joining the fledgling Vanwall équipe for GPs and the successful Jaguar team for endurance racing.

That decision to leave Ferrari was to have the most terrible consequences, for not only was Vanwall a wash-out, but when driving a D-type Jaguar at Le Mans, Mike set off the chain of events which led to the disaster there.

He moved to BRM for 1956 and, if anything, the Bourne cars were even worse than the Vanwalls. Then Jaguar withdrew from racing at the end of the year and so, when Ferrari invited him back to Maranello for 1957 Mike was happy to accept. In truth, Enzo Ferrari wasn't quite sure of his ground with the Englishman, for although he had, on occasion, shown himself to be a driver of surpassing brilliance – capable of beating even the great Juan Fangio and Alberto Ascari on his day – such days were by no means frequent. At times Mike could appear listless and downright bored with racing; he lacked the relentless drive and consistency of Fangio, Moss and the late lamented Ascari. There was a good reason for this, but one that Mike kept strictly to himself – he was suffering from an incurable kidney disease and, as a result, was seldom at full strength.

Back at Ferrari, he found himself in the company of another Englishman, 26-year-old Peter Collins, who was also blond and charismatic. Peter had made his name first in 500s, then with HWM, Tony Vandervell's Thinwall Special and David Brown's Aston Martins. He had driven for DB since 1952 and had won the Feltham concern's one and only Sportscar World Championship event, the Tourist Trophy of 1953. He shot to prominence, however, at the end of 1955 when Stirling Moss asked for him as his co-driver in the Targa Florio. The Mercedes Team Manager Alfred Neubauer agreed and Stirling and Peter scored a magnificent victory. Although Peter only did the middle third of the race he drove superbly and made a very real contribution to the win, which sealed the Championship for Mercedes.

Enzo Ferrari took notice of this, and Peter duly got the call to Maranello in 1956. He was still under contract to Aston Martin, however, and David Brown held him to it. Astons only had a limited number of international races that year, though, and so Peter was able to drive Ferrari sportscars on several occasions and to good effect, winning the Tour of Sicily and finishing an impressive second behind team-mate Eugenio Castellotti in the Mille Miglia.

He won two GPs for Ferrari as well, and was in with a chance of winning a third – and maybe the World Championship – at Monza, when he sportingly handed his car over to team leader Fangio, whose own car had expired. Juan Manuel went on to finish second in the race and thus clinch his fourth title, but Peter's genuinely selfless act made him a hero to millions.

That year Collins was very unhappy at having to share his sportscar time between Ferrari and Aston Martin. The English team's three-litre DB3S was in its fourth season and, frankly, was just not in the same league as the Ferraris and Maseratis it was up against. The Aston had always been down on power compared with its rivals, and Peter's taste of real horsepower – first with Mercedes-Benz and then Ferrari – made him realise that he was wasting his time in the green cars, something that the people at Maranello were always happy to point out. For 1957, therefore, he joined Scuderia Ferrari full-time.

Collins' move meant that at the end of the 1956 season Aston Martin had lost no fewer than four of their drivers, for Moss signed with Maserati for sportscar races; Peter Walker never recovered from his bad crash at Le Mans and retired from racing, as did Feltham's longest-serving driver, Reg Parnell. He, too, had had a bad crash, at

Peter Collins left Aston Martin to drive full-time for Ferrari in 1957. He is seen here with Stirling Moss minutes after they had finished second at Le Mans for Astons in 1956.

Crystal Palace in Rob Walker's Connaught and, at the age of 46, had decided to call it a day.

So Astons began 1957 with just two drivers, the very experienced Roy Salvadori and the supremely gifted youngster Tony Brooks. Roy had been with the team since 1953 and had made a name for himself as a very fast and forceful driver who also raced successfully for Connaught, Sid Greene's team of Gilby Engineering Maseratis and Cooper, becoming the latter's first 'works' driver.

Everyone was predicting great things for Brooks. A dental student who still regarded motor racing as a hobby, he had caused a sensation late in 1955 by driving a Connaught to victory in the Syracuse GP, beating all the works Maseratis handsomely and, in the process, becoming the first Briton to win a Grand Prix in a British car since Sir Henry Segrave won the 1924 Spanish GP in a Sunbeam.

Another youngster who had begun to make a name for himself (driving an HWM-Jaguar in British sportscar events) was Noel Cunningham-Reid and, after a test session at Silverstone at the very end of 1956, John Wyer signed him up. More drivers would join the team early in 1957.

The very fast Roy Salvadori (left) drove a record eight years for Aston Martin, but had to wait until the seventh for his big win, at Le Mans with Carroll Shelby in 1959. The brilliant Tony Brooks enjoyed more success with the Feltham équipe, winning the 1957 Nürburgring 1000 kms (with Cunningham-Reid) and the 1958 TT (with Moss), as well as two races at Spa in '57 before leaving for Ferrari in 1959.

The Contenders 1
ASTON MARTIN DBR1/300

SPECIFICATION

DESIGN ENGINEER: Ted Cutting.
ENGINE: 6 cyl, 83 x 90 mm, 2992 cc, 2 valves per cylinder, 2 ohc,
Comp ratio: 8.7:1,
Max bhp: 250@6000 rpm,
Max bmep: 195 lb/sq in@5500 rpm,
Carburettors: 3 twin-choke Weber 45 DCO,
Plugs: 12 KLG 10mm,
Lubrication: dry sump.
TRANSMISSION:
Clutch: Borg & Beck triple-plate,
Gearbox: David Brown CG537 rear-mounted, non-synchro, 5-speed & reverse.
CHASSIS:
Spaceframe;
Suspension: (front) trailing link & torsion bars; (rear) de Dion & torsion bars,
Shock absorbers: Armstrong,
Brakes: Girling disc;
Tyres: Avon (front) 6.00 x 16; (rear) 6.50 x 16,
Wheels: Borrani;
Steering: rack & pinion
BODY:
Stylist: Ted Cutting,
Builder: Aston Martin Lagonda Ltd.
DIMENSIONS:
Length: 13 ft 2.5 ins;
Width: 5 ft 4 ins;
Height: 3 ft 2.5 ins
Ground Clearance: 5 ins
Wheelbase (front) 4 ft 3.5 ins; (rear) 4 ft 3.5 ins;
Weight (dry) 1760 lbs.

The three iterations of the DBR1: for 1957 Ted Cutting smoothed out the bodywork, turning a rather lumpy shape (top) into a real beauty (centre). The bodywork extensions for Le Mans in 1959 (bottom) improved performance, if not looks.

Aston Martin DBR1/300
1957-1959

Design Engineer and Stylist:
Ted Cutting

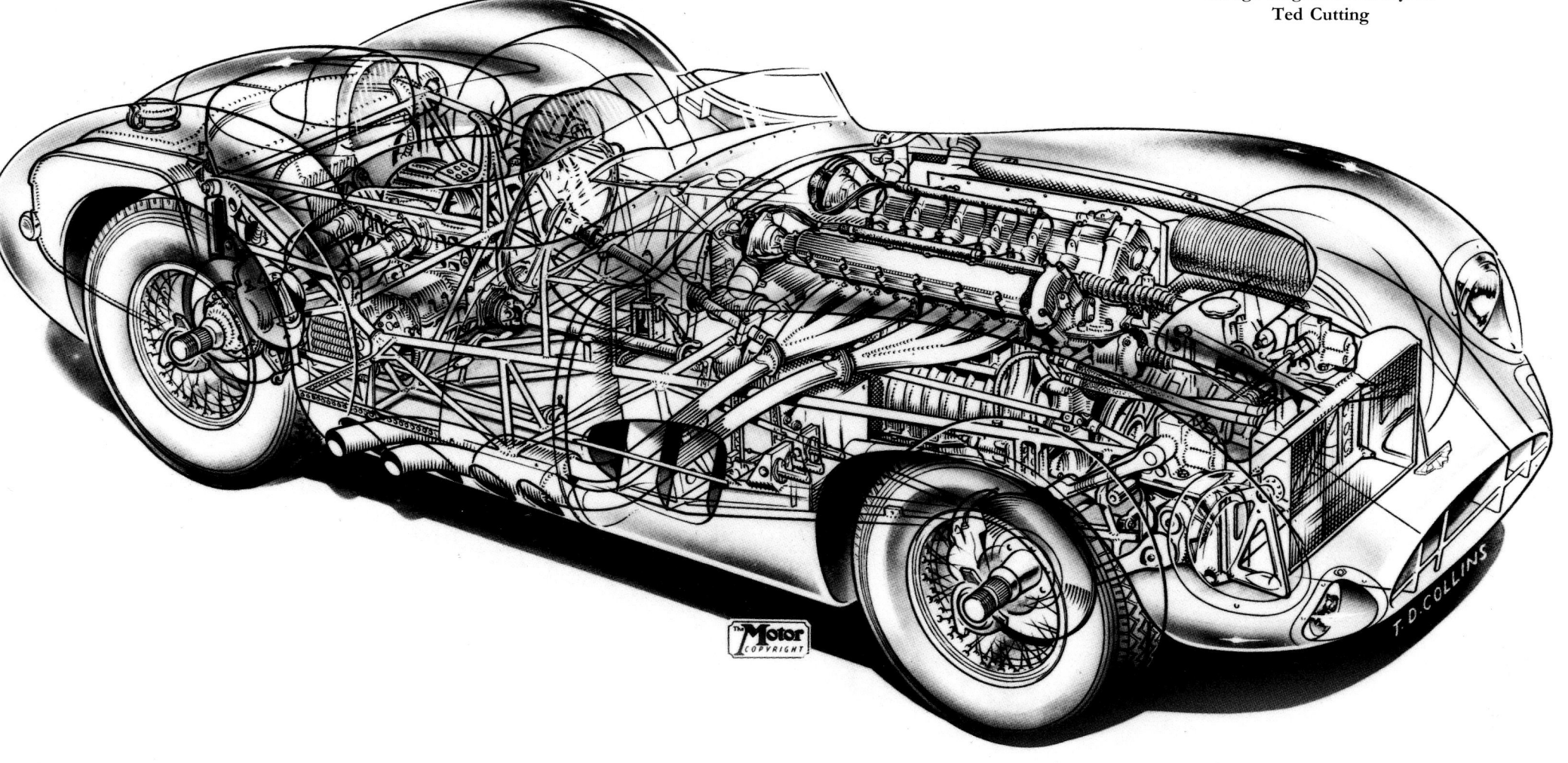

CHAPTER FOUR

The Last of the Big Bangers

The Buenos Aires 1000 kms;
the 12 Hours of Sebring; the the Mille Miglia

The late start on the new three-litre engines meant that Aston Martin would not be ready for the first two Championship events of the year – the Buenos Aires 1,000 Kms race and the Sebring 12 Hours. In Italy, however, Ferrari and Maserati were up and running.

Maserati now entered the big league with a vengeance. They had developed their twin ohc 4.5-litre engine to deliver 400bhp and dropped it into a revised, spaceframe chassis which was suspended on wishbones and coil springs at the front with de Dion rear axle and transverse leaf springs at the rear. The five-speed gearbox was in unit with the differential, and the new car was equipped with very large and powerful drum brakes. This 450S promised to be one hell of a racing car!

For their part, Ferrari added twin overhead camshafts to their 3.4-litre V12 engine, which now developed 330bhp at 8,000rpm. Three of these were dropped into 290MM chassis and sent (along with a 1956 290MM machine) to Argentina for the Buenos Aires 1,000 Kms on January 20.

Maserati entered one 450S for Fangio/Moss and a 300S for Behra/Menditeguy. Stirling simply pulverised the opposition, going away from all the Ferraris at the rate of six to 10 seconds a lap. Fangio then continued to lead with ease until the clutch withdrawal mechanism failed and eventually the gearbox packed up. Moss promptly took over the 300S and went even faster than he had done in the 450S, illustrating just how easy he and Fangio had been taking it in the big Maser. He almost caught the leading Ferrari, which was the 1956 model, driven by Masten Gregory, Eugenio Castellotti and Luigi Musso and had to be content with second place. Two of the new Ferraris failed to last the distance and the other finished third.

No doubt spurred on by the remarkable performance of the big Maserati, Enzo Ferrari increased the size of his V12s to 3.8 litres. Known as the 315S, two of these 360bhp cars were sent to Sebring for the 12-hour race in March. They had barely arrived in Florida however, when Scuderia Ferrari was rocked by the death of Eugenio Castellotti while testing a GP car at the Modena Autodrome. He had been due to race at Sebring with his friend Cesare Perdisa, but the latter now retired from racing and so Maurice Trintignant and Phil Hill replaced the two Italians.

Romolo Tavoli (in blue shirt and glasses) was Enzo Ferrari's personal assistant for seven years before his boss surprised him (and many others) by making him Team Manager for 1957. Here Ferrari talks with veteran journalist Giovanni Canestrini.

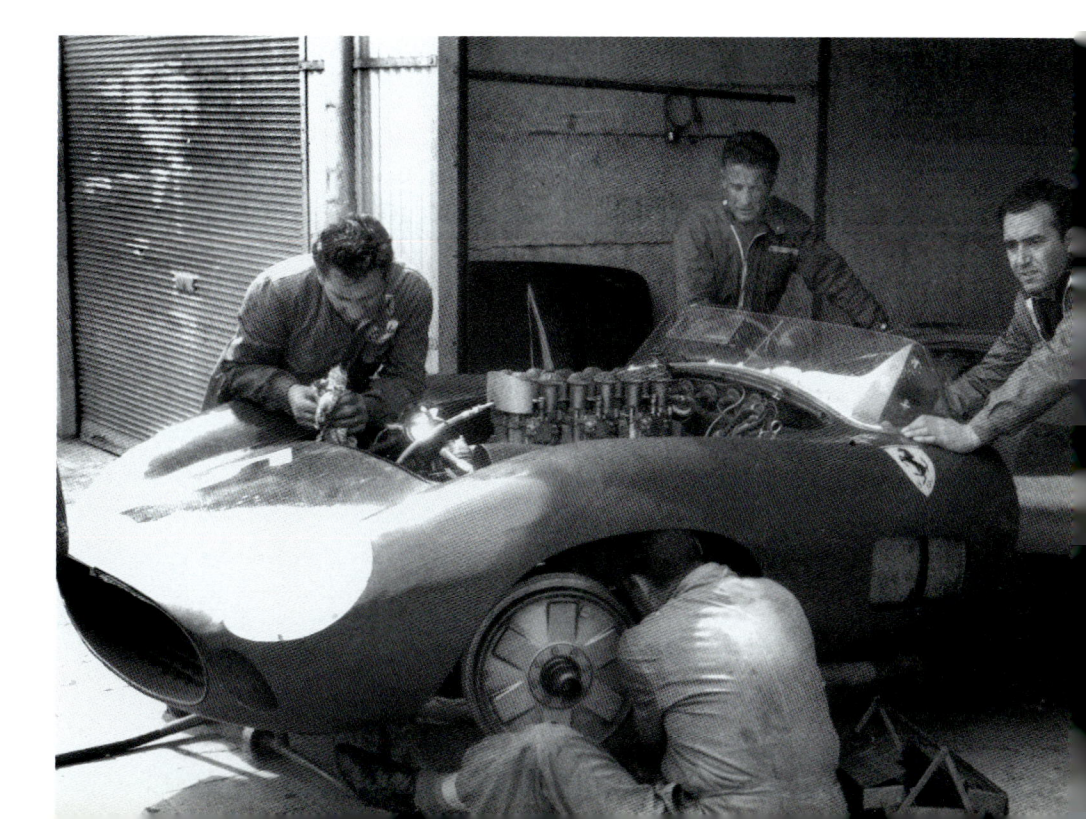

Maserati's 400 bhp, 4.5-litre V8 (above right) prompted Ferrari to increase the power of his V12 (right).

Scuderia Ferrari also had a new Team Manager. Nello Ugolini had done the unthinkable (as far as Enzo Ferrari was concerned) and joined Maserati for 1956. He had been replaced by Eraldo Sculati, but he couldn't be bothered to do one of the Ferrari Team Manager's most important tasks, which was to phone the boss in Maranello after every practice session and race. Ferrari sacked Sculati when he returned from South America and appointed his long-time assistant Romolo Tavoni to the job. Tavoni had no relevant experience, but was someone whom Enzo could trust absolutely.

Doubtless on the instructions of Enzo Ferrari himself, Tavoni allotted the 315S Ferraris to Peter Collins/Maurice Trintignant and Fon de Portago/Luigi Musso and the two 290MMs went to Masten Gregory/Lou Brero and Phil Hill/Wolfgang 'Taffy' von Trips.

Maserati sent a trio of cars: the 450S for Juan Fangio/Jean Behra; a 300S for Stirling Moss/Harry Schell and a 250S for Carroll Shelby/Giorgio Scarlatti. This time it was no contest. Although Peter Collins led the race for the first hour, the new Ferrari soon ran out of brakes and Jean Behra swept into the lead, which he and Fangio were never to lose. The 450S cruised home imperiously and won by two laps from the 300S of Moss and Schell. Once again it was the old 290MM that saved the day for Ferrari, Gregory and Brero finishing fourth behind the D-type Jaguar of Mike Hawthorn/Ivor Bueb. The 315S cars of Collins/Trintignant and Portago/Musso were sixth and seventh.

A noteworthy first and second in the up to two-litre class were two of the latest examples of the Testa Rossa. Built to the new Appendix C regulations, this was designated the 500TRC, and Sergio Scaglietti producad a very pretty body for it to a design by Pininfarina. Some 20 examples would be sold – mainly to Americans – before the model was discontinued at the end of the year. This two-litre car would play its part in the evolution of the next Testa Rossa, the three-litre machine that would become the rival to the Aston Martin DBR1.

By the end of March Ferrari and Maserati had taken part in two World Championship events, and Aston Martin had yet to turn a wheel in anger, and whereas the races in Buenos Aires and Sebring had lasted six and 12 hours, respectively, the Feltham team's first race of the year was to last a taxing 49 minutes!

In common with Ferrari, Aston Martin had a new Team Manager for 1957, although the change came about in much happier circumstances. John Wyer had done the job superbly since 1950, but in 1955 David Brown had appointed him Technical Director of Aston Martin Lagonda Ltd, and John really should have relinquished the Team Management then. However, he could see no natural

Aston Martin Team Manager John Wyer was unable to find a successor until his great friend Reg Parnell (right) decided to retire from racing at the end of 1956.

successor, so he soldiered on. At the end of 1956 he was given even more responsibility when DB made him General Manager of the company, so when Reg Parnell – his great friend and long-time Aston stalwart – decided to retire from racing, John knew that here was the ideal man to run the team.

Throughout the winter the DBR1 was being refined at Feltham and new blocks were cast for three-litre engines. Meanwhile the 2.5-litre unit was used for development. Paul Jackman ran a torsion test on chassis number 1 and found a few tubes were redundant, so they were removed, saving a little weight. Two more chassis were then built. The body was altered considerably at the front end, as John Wyer felt that the original wings were too high, and Ted Cutting abandoned the

Roy Salvadori (2.5-litre DBR1) holds a very brief lead over Archie Scott-Brown (3.4-litre Lister-Jaguar) on the first lap of the British Empire Trophy Race at Oulton Park. They are followed by Noel Cunningham-Reid (Aston Martin DB3S) and Ron Flockhart (Jaguar D-type). Archie won the race with ease.

traditional Aston radiator shape, opting for an elegant oval instead. The large and rather ugly headrest of the 1956 car was reduced in size, and all these alterations made the DBR1 a very handsome beast indeed. Girling's latest disc brakes had narrower callipers, which meant that the off-set Borrani wheels were no longer necessary.

As there were still no three-litre engines available, Parnell decided to run the 2.5-litre DBR1 in the British Empire Trophy Race at Oulton Park, on April 6. At the time, England was in the grip of post-Suez fuel rationing, and so the race comprised three 25-lap heats for cars of different sizes, but no final: the winner to be the driver recording the fastest race average. Astons took DBR1/1 and two DB3Ss to the Cheshire circuit for Roy Salvadori and newcomer Noel Cunningham-Reid. They would drive all three cars before deciding which two they would race.

DB3S/9 was a standard, works machine, but DB3S/10 (which Peter Walker had crashed at Le Mans the previous July) had been rebuilt with wishbone front suspension designed for the forthcoming DB4 GT car. It also had CAV fuel injection.

1957

Aston Martin were granted an unofficial practice session on the Thursday, and Roy Salvadori recorded 1 min 59 secs in the R1 and 2' 00" in both 3Ss. Noel Cunningham-Reid could only manage 2' 06" in the R1 and 2' 02" and 2' 03" in the 3Ss. Neither had driven the R1 before and both were very impressed with it, Roy electing to drive it in the race.

In Friday's official practice session Archie Scott-Brown was fastest in the big-car class, recording a time of 1' 56" in his 3.4-litre Lister-Jaguar – a full two seconds faster than Salvadori in the R1. Worse, Ron Flockhart was one second faster than Roy in his 1.5-litre Lotus! Cunningham-Reid was fourth fastest in DB3S/10, sharing a time of 1' 59" with Colin Chapman (1.5-litre Lotus) and Brian Naylor (2-litre Lotus).

Roy led from the start of the big-car heat on the Saturday, but by the end of the first lap Scott-Brown was ahead by two seconds and proceeded to pull away with ease. After 15 laps the Lister-Jaguar was cruising and 11 seconds in front of Salvadori, with Cunningham-Reid in third place, followed by Graham Whitehead in DB3S/6, which he had bought from the factory. They finished in that order, but both Ron Flockhart and Colin Chapman had completed Heat 2 faster than Cunningham-Reid and Whitehead had completed Heat 3, so they took third and fourth places overall.

Astons were by no means downhearted at finishing behind Archie, for the Lister-Jaguar had a litre advantage in capacity and, unlike the DBR1, had been built for sprints, not endurance races. Salvadori expressed himself well pleased with the new car, although he was lucky to finish the race, as the R1's gearbox began the year as it planned to continue – by giving trouble. As John Bolster reported in *Autosport*: 'Towards the end Salvadori was experiencing trouble sorting out his five gears, and the car came to a grinding halt immediately after the finish, accompanied by non-standard noises from the rear end.'

With one victory apiece in the World Championship series, back in Maranello and Modena Ferrari and Maserati set about preparing themselves for Italy's tour de force: the Mille Miglia. Meanwhile, in Paris the powers that be at the FIA were worrying about the size and speed of the new breed of sports racing car they had so recently sanctioned. They had got rid of the single-seater 'sportscars' of recent years, to be sure, and the 1957 machines, with their full-width windscreens and passenger seats and doors at least bore a resemblance to the two-seaters which enthusiasts could buy in the showrooms. However, the FIA felt that cars of four and 4.5 litres capacity were becoming too fast and possibly dangerous, and so the idea of a capacity limit of three or 3.5 litres was mooted, the former being the favourite.

Whether Enzo Ferrari was given advance notice of these thoughts is not known, but he had ears everywhere and it seems beyond mere coincidence that he was experimenting with his trusty three-litre, V12 GT engine as early as April 1957 and produced a competition version of his 250GT Europa for Olivier Gendebien to drive in the Tour of Sicily on April 14.

The conditions were appalling, with prolonged heavy rain, and whereas Taruffi was in an open Maserati 300S, Gendebien and Washer were in the relative comfort of the GT Europa. Eventually, with fewer than 100 miles to go, Taruffi went off the road and hit a house, damaging the Maserati quite severely but not himself. He managed to effect some repairs and finished a gallant second, behind the Ferrari. Gendebien's superb victory prompted Ferrari to do some more work on the three-litre V12, his eyes now on the Mille Miglia.

Aston Martin, on the other hand, were looking towards Germany and, early in May, announced that two DBR1s would be racing in the Nürburgring 1,000 Kms. Before that, however, the 2.5-litre R1 was entered in a 50-mile race at Goodwood.

While Aston Martin were playing around in sprints, Ferrari and Maserati were preparing for Italy's greatest race, the Mille Miglia. Despite the fact that they now had two DBR1s completed, Astons were not prepared to risk them in the Italian classic. Instead, Reg Parnell decided they would race at Spa on the same day as the Mille Miglia for a good shake-down prior to the Nürburgring 1,000 Kms.

Following Olivier Gendebien's success in the Tour of Sicily with the three-litre 250GT, Enzo Ferrari – still with his eye on a capacity limit for 1958 – ordered more work to be done on the engine in time for the Mille Miglia. He was looking for 100 bhp per litre and, with the camshaft timing from the 290MM he moved ever closer to that figure..

Ferrari's main entry comprised four V12 sportscars, two 4.1-litre 335S models for Piero Taruffi and Peter Collins/Louis Klemantaski and two 3.8-litre 315S cars for Taffy von Trips and Luigi Musso. The latter was ill, however, and so both Olivier Gendebien and Fon de Portago sought the drive. Always trying to get the most of his drivers by setting one against another, Enzo Ferrari called them together and said, "You, Gendebien, will take the GT and you, Portago, will take the sportscar – and I will be surprised if you go as fast as Gendebien in the GT."

Ferrari's attempt to wind up Portago was to have the most tragic consequences.

Mean Machine. Peter Collins (accompanied by photographer Louis Klemantaski) led the Mille Miglia for most of the way in this V12, 4.1-litre 335S Ferrari. The power and speed of machines such as this was of great concern to the FIA and Fon de Portago's fatal accident in a similar, 3.8-litre car in the same race was to lead to a capacity limit of three litres for 1958.

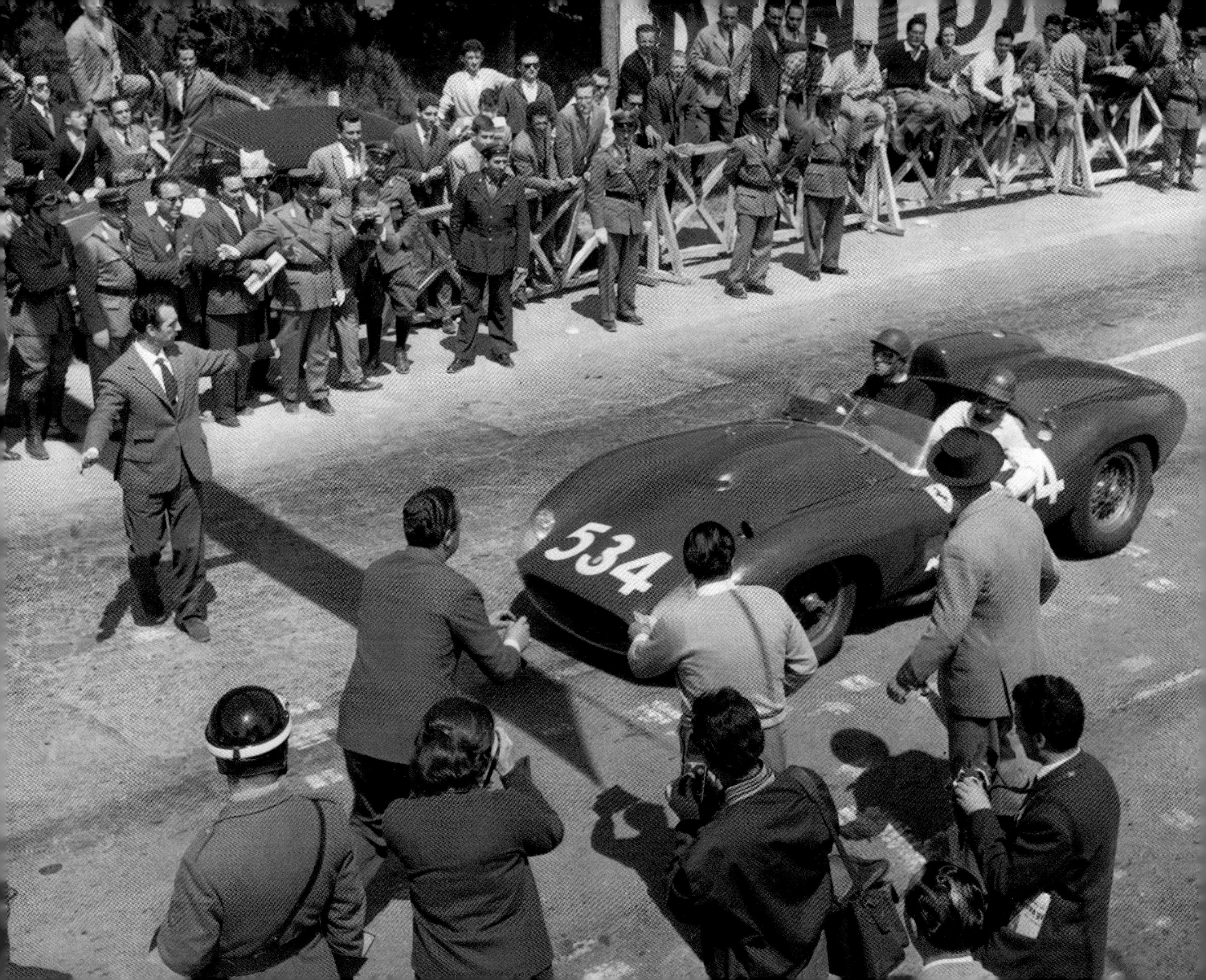
534

Maserati entered two of the fearsome 450S machines – a brand new one for Stirling Moss/Denis Jenkinson and the Sebring winner for Jean Behra. Unfortunately, two days before the race Behra was out testing his car and at around 150mph found the road blocked by a lorry. He was unable to avoid it and wrote off the front of the Maserati, being lucky to escape with a broken wrist and cuts and bruises. Both he and the car were out of the race.

Which was both a triumph and disaster for Ferrari, whose cars finished first, second and third. Peter Collins led nearly all the way and had a lead of 11 minutes when the rear axle failed with just 130 miles to go. Piero Taruffi inherited the lead and won the race to great acclaim – the first time he had finished in 13 attempts! Wolfgang von Trips was a fine second but undoubtedly the finest performance of all was that of Olivier Gendebien who, with his faithful friend Jacques Washer beside him once more, finished third in his GT car.

That was Ferrari's triumph. The disaster was Portago's crash on the road between Mantua and Brescia, caused by a burst tyre when he and his passenger, Ed Nelson, were travelling at around 170mph. Both men died, as did 10 spectators, and the tragedy was to bring the Mille Miglia to an end.

Portago's death could not diminish Gendebien's achievement, however. "I regard that as the very best result of my career," he said. "In that Berlinetta I set up the fastest-ever time for the last section of the Mille Miglia, from Cremona to Mantua to Brescia – faster even than Moss had done in the Mercedes 300SLR in 1955. I averaged 199kph for that section and Stirling's average was 198kph. To beat his time in a 250GT was really something!"

It was indeed, and that performance spoke volumes not only for Olivier's skill, but also for the power and strength of Ferrari's experimental three-litre engine. Gendebien beat the fourth man home – Scarlatti in the Maserati 300S – by no fewer than 25 minutes! And Moss? His race lasted all of seven miles – then the brake pedal on his 450S snapped off under his foot . . .

On the same day as the Mille Miglia was held – May 12 – Aston Martin were in Belgium for the Grand Prix de Spa, to be run over 15 laps of the 8.7-mile circuit.

This race marked the very first appearance of Aston Martin's new three-litre engine, which initially produced a modest 240bhp @ 6,250rpm. Designated the RB6/300, it used the 60° included-angle cylinder head of the DB3S, but a 95° head was under development. Roy Salvadori was assigned the prototype chassis and the just-completed DBR1/2 went to Tony Brooks, Roy's car having a blue nose-band, that on Tony's being yellow. The cars were tested at Silverstone on Monday, May 6 and travelled to Spa in Astons' AEC transporter two days later.

Roy Salvadori heads for the pits at Spa in DBR1/1. Note the sparcely populated spectator enclosure during this practice session.

Their opposition in the unlimited class came mainly from British entries. There were five D-types for Ninian Sanderson and Jock Lawrence (Ecurie Ecosse); Duncan Hamilton, Max Trimble and Henry Taylor; and a sixth for the Belgian, Freddy Rousselle. Graham and Peter Whitehead had brought their ex-works DB3S Astons, and there was a Cooper-Jaguar for C. Murray. Jacques Swaters entered a 3.5-litre Ferrari and there was also a Ferrari Monza and a three-litre Maserati in the line-up.

For the first practice session DBR1/1 was fitted with a 3.51:1 axle ratio, while that in DBR1/2 was 3.38:1. Tony did six laps, recording a fastest time of 4 mins 40 secs and Roy did nine, his best being four seconds slower. As the 3.38:1 axle ratio was more suited to the circuit, that on Salvadori's car was changed overnight.

Henry Taylor drove his D-type superbly in the rain and after five laps was this close to Brooks and the Aston.

The next day Brooks really got to grips with the wonderful Spa circuit, doing 11 laps, setting the fastest time of 4' 21.0" (121mph) and averaging 11.7mpg. Salvadori was second fastest with 4' 27.8", and Ninian Sanderson third with 4' 33" – all three cars beating the previous lap record of 4' 35", set the previous year by Desmond Titterington's D-type.

Heavy rain fell for most of race day, and parts of the circuit were almost underwater. Tony Brooks shot into a lead he was never to relinquish and at the end of the first lap he led Salvadori, Hamilton, Taylor and Rousselle, but after five laps he was only averaging 97.8mph, so heavy was the rain. Henry Taylor and Freddy Rousselle were driving their D-types superbly and at this point were in second and third places, with Taylor only two seconds behind Brooks. Both Aston drivers were suffering from an excess of water in the cockpits, as the undertrays had been fitted badly.

In the next few laps the rain eased somewhat, and Brooks sped away from Taylor, being almost 80 seconds ahead at the end of lap 10. Salvadori also speeded up and on lap 12 he was back in second spot. On the 15th and final lap Brooks recorded the fastest lap of the race with a time of 4' 48.8" (109.37mph). Salvadori's fastest was 4' 57.6".

It was a very satisfactory result for Aston Martin, even though their real opposition had been taking part in the Mille Miglia. However, the gearbox problems which had appeared in Salvadori's car at Oulton Park now reappeared in Brooks'. After the race he told Reg Parnell that when approaching La Source hairpin on one occasion he tried to change from fourth to third, but the gear lever moved into neutral while the car remained stuck in fourth gear. Then, under heavy braking for the hairpin the car went into neutral, and he had no further trouble. All this was to be a bad omen for the future.

1957

Tony Brooks seen from above the pits on his way to a sensational victory in DBR1/2.

CHAPTER FIVE

Aston Martin's Greatest Triumph

The Nürburgring 1000 kms

As a result of the Portago tragedy in the Mille Miglia, the Italian state and church predictably railed against Scuderia Ferrari and motor racing in general. The works Ferraris were all impounded by the authorities pending inspection, and only one – the Collins/Klemantaski 335S – was released in time for the Nürburgring 1,000 Kms.

The Scuderia arrived in Germany with four cars – the 4.1-litre 335S; a 3.8-litre 315S; the 250GT Berlinetta with which Gendebien had done wonders in the Tour of Sicily and the Mille Miglia and, finally, an intriguing newcomer, the first prototype of what was to become the three-litre Testa Rossa.

Chassis number 0666 was that of a slightly modified 1956 290MM fitted with a 240 bhp version of the Mille Miglia 250GT three-litre V12 that Ferrari had been developing so determinedly. The new car had a de Dion rear axle with the gearbox not in unit with the differential, but mated to the engine.

Sergio Scaglietti had knocked up a rough-and-ready right-hand drive body which was a cross between that of the two-litre Testa Rossa and the larger 290MM, giving it a revised bonnet with a large hump to cover the Weber carburettors.

The Scuderia had some difficulty in raising a full team of drivers at the Ring, for Eugenio Castellotti and Fon de Portago were dead; Phil Hill – surprisingly – had not been invited, and Luigi Musso was still not well enough to race, although he was originally entered to drive the 315S with Maurice Trintignant. And the previous weekend Ferrari had very nearly lost two more drivers at Monaco, when Stirling Moss had crashed his Vanwall into the chicane on lap four of the Grand Prix. Collins and Hawthorn were so close behind they were unable to avoid a pile-up, and all three cars were very badly bent. Remarkably, the drivers were able to walk away, angry but unharmed. Later, they shrugged off the crash as just one of those things but, in fact, Britain's Golden Boys had come within a hair's breadth of being badly hurt, if not killed.

When it became clear that Musso would not be fit in time, the young American Masten Gregory was invited to join the team. Mike Hawthorn and Peter Collins were paired in the 335S, and Taffy von Trips and Olivier Gendebien were allotted the prototype. The 250GT appears to have been taken along as a practice car, for it was not listed in the official programme, which showed no works Ferrari entered in the GT section of the race.

Officine Maserati brought along the four machines they had entered for the Mille Miglia: the Moss 450S had been given a new, unbreakable (it was hoped) brake pedal, and Behra's car had been completely rebuilt. Also present were the experimental 3.5-litre V12 and the 300S with 450S brakes with which Scarlatti had finished fourth. Despite the fact that Jean Behra was still indisposed with a broken wrist, Maserati's main driver line-up was formidable: Juan Fangio, Stirling Moss, Harry Schell, Hans Herrmann, Jo Bonnier and Giorgio Scarlatti. Somewhat less than formidable were Francisco Godia and Horace Gould in the former's 300S, which was entered by the factory, but this car would do better than all the others in the race.

Fresh from their one-two victory at Spa, Aston Martin were now confident that their new, three-litre DBR1 was a real threat, lacking only the sheer power of the bigger-engined Ferraris and Maseratis. That confidence had been reinforced the previous weekend when Tony Brooks had put up yet another impressive performance, driving his Vanwall to second place at Monaco, behind the 250F Maserati of World Champion Juan Fangio.

Reconditioned gearboxes were fitted to both Astons while they were still in Brussels, and the undertrays were reworked to keep rain water out. The DBR1s were then transported to the Nürburgring in company with DB3S/9 (to be used as a practice car) and 3S/10. At this point Team Manager Reg Parnell had paired Roy Salvadori with Noel Cunningham-Reid in DBR1/1 and Tony Brooks with F3 champion and Connaught F1 driver Les Leston in DBR1/2. Both cars were fitted with a 3.38:1 rear axle. The Astons were present as a team, but 3S/10 was entered by Peter Whitehead for himself and half-brother Graham to drive to avoid problems with fuel and oil contracts. There was unofficial practice on Wednesday, May 22, but heavy mist lasted until well after midday, and all six drivers used their own cars and a factory DB2/4.

The new Aston Martin (left - being checked out by Roy Salvadori and Les Leston) is in showroom condition, whereas the prototype Testa Rossa (right) has clearly been put together in a hurry.

Official practice began at 8.30am on the Thursday in bad weather with mist everywhere. It ended at five o'clock that evening with Tony Brooks (DBR1) heading the time-sheets with 10 mins 16.5 secs, followed by Stirling Moss (Maserati 450S) on 10' 32.5" and Umberto Maglioli (1.5-litre Porsche) on a remarkable 10' 37.0".

Neither Cunningham-Reid nor Leston had ever seen the Ring before, but Noel only got in two laps (best 11' 03.3") and Les managed seven in DB3S/9 (best 12' 10.0"). The next day the weather improved slightly and ended with Tony Brooks and the DBR1 the talk of Adenau. As expected, the two 450S Maseratis dominated the practice times, Moss and Fangio doing a remarkable 9' 43.5" and 9' 43.6" respectively, but Brooks was next up with 9' 48.2" in the Aston, which was giving away 1.5 litres and a good 160bhp to the Maseratis. Brooks had improved upon his best 1956 time in a DB3S by a staggering 38 seconds and had lapped one mph faster than Bernd Rosemeyer's fastest lap in the 1937 German GP, achieved in a six-litre, supercharged Auto Union producing 600bhp.

'The whole Aston Martin team were put very severely in their places by the unbelievable Brooks,' wrote Denis Jenkinson in *Motor Sport*, 'and no-one was more embarrassed about it than Brooks himself, but he just cannot help being a superb driver and even when not trying he is faster than most, so that when he does "have a go" he shakes the very top of the tree, and it will not be long before some of the accepted stars have to come tumbling down . . . The Feltham team were never more confident of putting up the best possible performance that they could, and even after the form shown in training it was difficult to imagine that any team could be so well prepared.'

By contrast, Scuderia Ferrari was in some disarray. Only one of their drivers managed to get below 10 minutes and although the official timekeepers credited Maurice Trintignant with 9' 57.6" in the 315S, most observers were sure that time had been set by Mike Hawthorn. Peter Collins was next with 10' 02.2" in the 335S and Olivier Gendebien lapped the Testa Rossa prototype in an impressive 10' 09.3", to be sixth fastest of all.

On the Saturday morning, however, Team Manager Romolo Tavoni found himself short of a driver once more when Taffy von Trips crashed the Berlinetta at Wehrseifen. The Ferrari drivers had been trying all the cars throughout practice, and poor Taffy momentarily forgot that the GT had its throttle pedal on the right, whereas the sports machines all had a central accelerator. As a result he hit the throttle instead of the brake and stuffed the Berlinetta through a hedge. The car was badly damaged and Taffy wound up in hospital with a broken vertebra, which would keep him in plaster for more than a month.

Pit stop for the Salvadori/Leston Aston during late evening practice. Watched by Roy Parnell (bottom left) Bryan Clayton is about to catch the oil pump thrown by John King as Eric Hind jacks up the rear of the car. Right: shortly before the start of the race, Juan Manuel Fangio greets Peter Collins and Louise, his bride of three months.

Tavoni now had only five drivers for three cars. After consulting his boss in Maranello, no doubt, he put the medium-sized Gendebien and Collins in the 335S; the very tall Hawthorn with the very short Trintignant in the 315S, and Masten Gregory in the prototype – but with whom? Not surprisingly, no driver of repute was available, so Tavoni felt he had no option but to withdraw the car. This decision infuriated Masten Gregory, who demanded that Tavoni find someone – anyone! – and who then retired to his hotel room convinced that the race would start without him the next morning.

Somehow, Tavoni came across an OSCA driver named Olindo Morolli and pressed him into service to drive the prototype with Gregory. Morolli had no experience of anything approaching the power of the V12 Ferrari, but Gregory wanted a co-driver, and the Italian was available. Unfortunately, Tavoni forgot to tell Masten about his new partner, and as the cars were lining up for the nine o'clock start on the Sunday morning Gregory was nowhere to be seen. He was eventually unearthed from his hotel room, unwashed and unshaven, in time to take the first stint at the wheel without, it seems, even being introduced to Morolli!

After the Friday practice session, Reg Parnell decided to change his drivers around for the race. Roy Salvadori had lapped in 10' 17.0" in DBR1/1, and Cunningham-Reid – allowed only another two laps – had achieved an impressive 10' 23.0", 12 seconds faster than Leston had managed in his four laps with DBR1/2. Reg therefore put Les with Roy in R1/1 and Noel with Tony in R1/2. It was to prove an excellent decision.

Sunday dawned bright and clear but very cold. When the cars were lined up for the Le Mans start it was seen that Maserati had decided not to run their 3.5-litre V12,

1957

Left: Tony Brooks makes a superb start and Aston Martin 14 is on its winning way. Cars 2 and 1 are the Maseratis of Harry Schell and Stirling Moss; 6, 5 & 7 are the Ferraris of Mike Hawthorn, Peter Collins and Masten Gregory; 3 is the Maserati of Jo Bonnier; 12 the Aston Martin of Roy Salvadori; 21 the Porsche of Umberto Maglioli; 16 the Jaguar of Henry Taylor;

4 the Maserati of Francesco Godia; 22 the Porsche of von Frankenberg; 11 the Jaguar of Ninian Sanderson and 15 the Aston Martin of Peter Whitehead. Right: Moss (1) and Hawthorn (6) have stalled, as have the Porsches of Maglioli and von Frankenberg. Schell (2) has made a fine start and sets out after Brooks, who is almost halfway to the South Turn. The pattern of the race has been set.

but that the Harry Schell/Hans Herrmann Maserati No 1 was in pole position, despite the fact that its time had been set by Juan Fangio, who was sharing 450S Number 2 with Stirling Moss. The Brooks/Cunningham-Reid Aston Martin was third, with the Ferraris of Hawthorn/Trintignant and Collins/Gendebien next. Then came the Testa Rossa prototype of Gregory/Morolli; the Bonnier/Scarlatti Maserati 300S; and the Salvadori/Leston Aston DBR1.

As usual Stirling Moss was the first to get his car going, but the Maserati moved about three feet and then stalled. Mike Hawthorn leapt into the 315S, pressed the starter button and, hearing an engine roar into life, let in the clutch. The Ferrari went nowhere, for the engine he had heard was that of Peter Collins' car next door! Tony Brooks meanwhile made a copybook start and was 100 yards down the road almost before anyone else had moved. At least 30 cars had gone by before Moss persuaded the Maserati to get going and Hawthorn was stationary for almost 20 seconds before the Ferrari would start in 60th position.

'For the whole of the long, seven-and-a-half-hour race, the tension in the pits could hardly have been greater than on that first lap,' wrote Maxwell Boyd in *Autosport*. 'Would Brooks be able to hold the lead gained by his magnificent start? The minutes ticked by while the Aston's progress round the circuit was traced out on the illuminated scoreboard. Then, suddenly the green car shot over the hump under the bridge at the end of the straight and slammed through the pits. Its lead and engine note inspired confidence and seemed somehow even then to foretell the final outcome.'

Brooks covered that first, standing lap (of 44) in 10' 09" and was two seconds ahead of Harry Schell, the sheer power of the 4.5-litre Maserati enabling it to make up huge amounts of time on the Ring's three-kilometre straight. Third was Peter Collins (Ferrari) followed by Salvadori (Aston Martin) and Moss (Maserati). A lap later Moss had passed Salvadori, and Mike Hawthorn was eighth, having passed 52 cars in two laps!

After five laps Brooks was 23 seconds ahead of Schell, with Collins a further six seconds back, and Moss seven seconds behind him and gaining fast. Stirling repeatedly broke the lap record as he hauled in Collins and Schell and went after Brooks, his fastest lap of 9' 49.9" (86.43mph) demolishing Fangio's 1956 Ferrari

Having negotiated the Karussell (background) the Ferraris of Olivier Gendebien and Maurice Trintignant head for Wippermann in their vain chase of the Brooks/Cunningham-Reid Aston Martin.

1957

The 450S Maserati squats down on its haunches (above) as Stirling Moss powers out of the South Turn. After stalling at the start, he was chasing race leader Tony Brooks (right), whose Aston Martin dips its nose under heavy braking as it passes behind the pits, heading for the North Turn.

record of 10' 05" (84.26 mph). Brooks was averaging just over 85mph, but on lap seven Moss was only 12 seconds behind, and next time round the Aston was once again overhauled by the sheer power of the big Maserati, as Moss blew past Tony on the straight, to lead him across the line by two seconds.

Two laps later, and Maserati's hopes were dashed when Brooks came by in the lead once more. Stirling's 450S had shed a rear wheel on the approach to Schwalbenschwanz. Moss brought the car safely to a halt, but Maserati's most powerful weapon was silenced. So, after 10 laps Brooks was 40 seconds ahead of Harry Schell (Maserati) and 62 seconds ahead of Peter Collins (4.1-litre Ferrari). Then came Mike Hawthorn (3.8-litre Ferrari) and the remarkable Masten Gregory in the three-litre Testa Rossa, who was now ahead of Roy Salvadori in the second DBR1.

On lap 11 Harry Schell came in for his first scheduled pit stop, but it was Juan Fangio who took over the car, not Hans Herrmann. Collins and Hawthorn went by in second and third places and at the end of lap 12 Brooks had a very comfortable lead of 1' 15" over Peter and 2' 04" over Mike.

Fangio had no luck with the surviving 450S, however, and after just two laps was back in the pits. It appeared that the rear suspension was suffering badly on the Ring, and this had caused the oil cooler which ran across the rear of the car to spring a

42

ASTON MARTIN'S GREATEST TRIUMPH

The Fangio/Moss Maserati lies abandoned at Schwalbenschwanz, having lost a rear wheel just after Moss had taken the lead. The Salvadori/Leston Aston Martin passes by, followed by the Sanderson/Steed D-type Jaguar and Noel Cunningham-Reid in the other Aston, which is now leading once more.

1957

Above: Tony Brooks (dark helmet) tells Noel Cunningham-Reid the state of the circuit as he hands over the Aston with a handsome lead. John Wyer and David Brown can be seen on the pit counter behind the rear of the car.

Below: Noel proved more than a match for the No 2 drivers of Ferrari and Maserati, later handing the Aston back to Brooks with an increased lead. Opposite: Michael Turner's painting shows Brooks being chased through Pflanzgarten by Moss (450S Maserati) and Collins (Ferrari 335S).

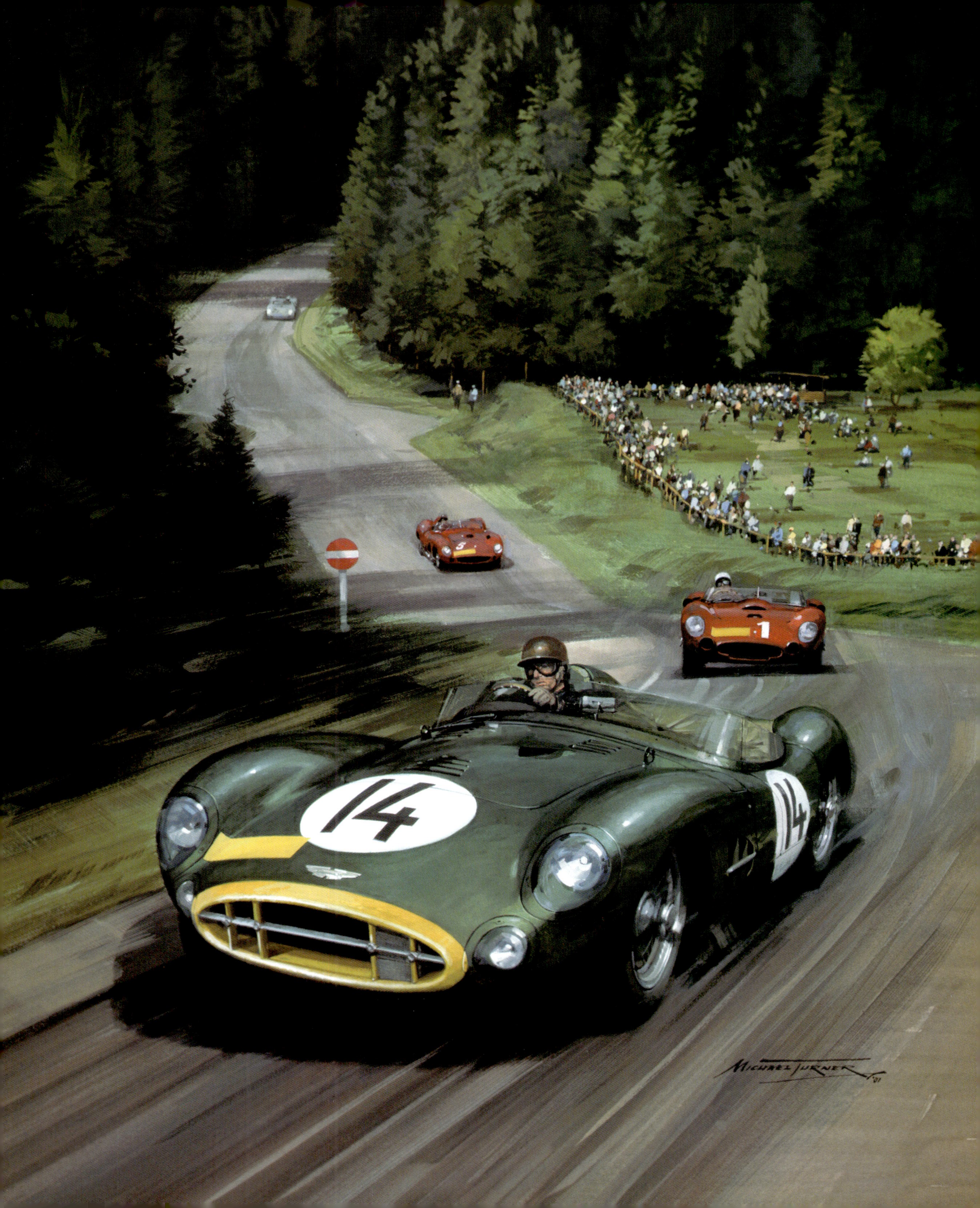
14

**Masten Gregory in the prototype Testa Rossa, which he drove for the first 22 laps,
co-driver Morolli having no experience of the car or circuit.**

leak. More than 17 minutes were lost while the Maserati mechanics tried to effect repairs, and Fangio walked away. Eventually Moss took it back into the race, but he only completed one lap before returning to the pits, the Maserati covered in oil. It was pushed to the dead-car park.

On lap 15 Peter Collins handed over his Ferrari to Olivier Gendebien, losing second place to Mike Hawthorn briefly, but Mike was in next time round to hand over to Trintignant. On that same lap Tony Brooks came in with the DBR1 and, in common with the Ferraris the Aston was refuelled and fitted with new rear wheels. After a relaxed stop of 1' 28" Noel Cunningham-Reid took DBR1/2 back into the race with the unenviable task of maintaining the Aston's lead – now some three and a half minutes – and keeping it on the island. As Denis Jenkinson noted in *Motor Sport*: 'Meanwhile Cunningham-Reid was setting about the difficult task of taking over the leading car with remarkable calm, and instead of Trintignant and Gendebien in the two Ferraris closing the gap, the reverse happened and the green Aston Martin increased its lead to nearly four minutes by lap 22, or half-distance. This was almost more than anyone could stand and the opposition became completely demoralised: first of all Brooks ran away from all the number-one drivers and now a real "new boy" was running away from all the number-two drivers.'

Despite the Aston's complete domination of the race Stirling Moss refused to accept defeat, and at his request the Maserati Team Manager, Nello Ugolini, called in the Godia/Gould 300S on lap 21 and he set off in that – his third car of the day. If Stirling's first love in racing was leading from start to finish his second was the challenge of driving through the field to victory from way back, a feat that became a hallmark of his glorious career. This was just such an opportunity, for with half the race still to run he was in 12th place and driving one of his favourite sports racing cars and he set about carving into Cunningham-Reid's long lead with a will, lapping regularly in under 10 minutes in the process.

Cunningham-Reid, however, was quite unaware of Stirling's meteoric progress and, even if he had been told of it, he would not have been bothered. Astons' new boy kept his head admirably and drove the DBR1 at his own, comfortable speed which was still fast enough to outpace the very experienced Ferrari hands, Olivier Gendebien and Maurice Trintignant and after 28 laps Noel was a remarkable 4' 32" ahead of Gendebien.

Masten Gregory was in a splendid sixth spot with the Testa Rossa prototype and valiantly drove it for the first 22 laps – half-distance – before handing over to Morolli. As he must have feared, the Italian was not up to the task, lapping as many as three minutes slower than his very frustrated co-driver. After just three laps, Morolli was called in, and Masten set off again.

Moss was now flying in the 300S and by lap 29 was up to seventh place. That same lap Cunningham-Reid came in to hand over the Aston to Brooks for the final 16 tours. Only fuel and oil were added and Tony was away after just 44 seconds. The two Ferraris also made their final stops, and after 33 laps the Aston was a massive 5' 16" ahead of Peter Collins, who was almost two minutes ahead of Mike Hawthorn.

Roy Salvadori and Les Leston had been driving the other DBR1 steadily if unspectacularly and by lap 19 were in fourth place, only to be passed three laps later by the indecently fast 1.5-litre Porsche of Umberto Maglioli and Edgar Barth. Les handed back to Roy on lap 26 without losing fifth place but 10 laps later the R1 became stuck in fourth gear. By now Fangio had taken over the 300S from Moss and, keeping the Maserati flying at under 10 minutes a lap he reeled in the stricken Aston, passing it on lap 41.

Gregory handed the prototype Ferrari back to Morolli for the final laps, but the car was now in trouble and losing ground in eighth place. On lap 41 it was 10th, and Morolli stopped at the pits with the car smoking badly. After a brief inspection he was sent on his way, still smoking.

And that was the final bit of excitement of a remarkable race. Tony Brooks eased up considerably in the last few laps, slowing from his early pace of almost 86mph to just under 83. He completed his 44th tour 4' 13.7" ahead of the Collins/Gendebien Ferrari to score the most resounding victory of Aston Martin's long history of competition. To put the icing on Feltham's cake, the Salvadori/Leston DBR1 finished sixth and the Whitehead/Whitehead DB3S was 10th, which secured the Team Prize for Aston Martin.

Les Leston swings DBR1/2 through the uphill swerves at Kesselschen. Towards the end of the race the Aston became stuck in fourth gear.

Among the first to congratulate the winners were Fangio and Moss, who must have wished that they had driven the 300S Maserati from the start, instead of the big V8s, which more or less pounded themselves to bits. Moss was generous in defeat, saying, "If anyone was going to beat us at the Ring, I wanted it to be Brooks."

The Aston was the first British car ever to win a major international race at the Ring, but it had been a close-run thing. Afterwards it was discovered that the off-side front trailing link carrier on the winner was broken as was the chassis frame, around the bearing mountings. No matter, the DBR1 had emerged victorious after seven and a half hours on the awesome Nürburgring gainst the toughest opposition in the world. As Denis Jenkinson summed up in *Motor Sport*: 'This victory by Aston Martin with a new car was as convincing and praiseworthy as one could wish for and it was not a hollow victory, nor was it handed to them on a plate. It had been achieved against full teams from all the big sports car factories, driven by the best drivers in the world, so that David Brown could feel justifiably proud of the Aston Martin team he has backed all these years. Any victory on the Nürburgring can be considered a victory well deserved, but one fought against the opposition that was running in the 1,000 Kms must rank as outstanding.'

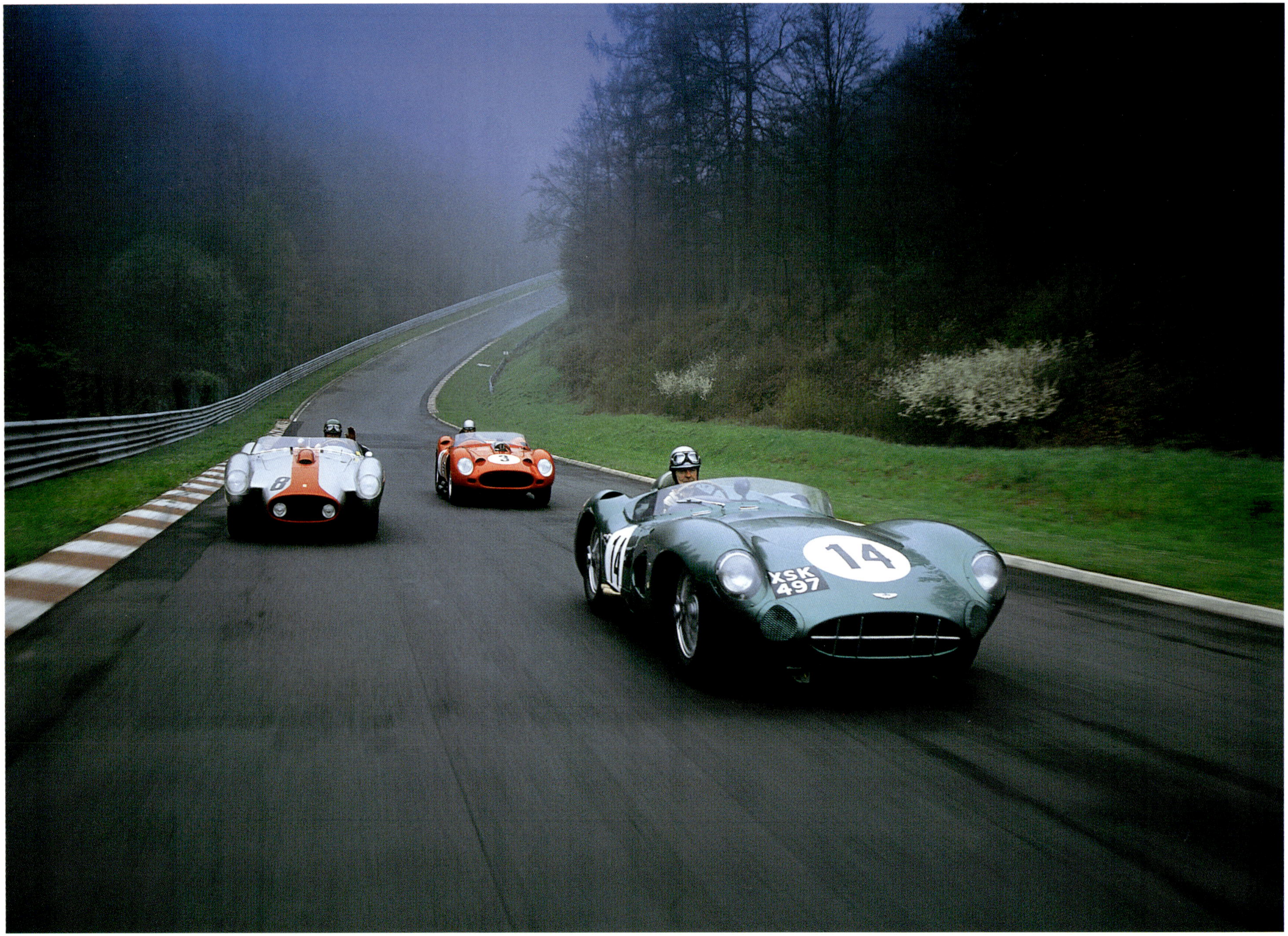
8
3
14
XSK
497

CHAPTER SIX

Reunion at the Ring

Brooks, Cunningham-Reid and the DBR1 38 years on

At the end of April 1995, I was able to reunite Tony Brooks, Noel Cunningham-Reid and their race-winning DBR1/2 at the Nürburgring. Tony had not been there since the German GP of 1961, and Noel had not seen the place since he and Tony had won the 1,000 Kms in 1957.

We were at the Ring as guests of Gerry Moroney, who invited us to join his Wheeltorque Nürburgring Festival. We arrived at the Dorint Hotel in bright sunshine and – as is typical at the Nürburgring – awoke next morning to find the countryside swathed in thick fog. So much for our 8am start on the circuit. Tony and Noel found each other at breakfast and talked animatedly, although they had hardly met since their great victory 38 years before.

After a very lengthy breakfast and endless cups of coffee, Gerry Moroney told us that the fog had lifted at Adenau Bridge and that it would be a good idea if we were to drive our cars round there and take some photographs before the fog really cleared and the circuit was opened to everyone. In no time at all we were on our way, Brooks in the Aston leading Cunningham-Reid in Brandon Wang's 1958 pontoon Testa Rossa (0718) and Tim Samways in a replica TR59, the type which Brooks and Jean Behra had driven to third place in the 1959 1,000 Kms race.

Noel Cunningham-Reid was quite happy to drive the Aston and the Ferraris for photographs, but declined to do any laps. Before he arrived at the Ring he had decided that his racing days were far too long ago, and besides, he found that his shoes were now too wide to work the pedals of the Aston properly. The driving therefore, was all down to Tony Brooks.

When I first approached Tony about going back to the Ring with the DBR1, he had agreed but was adamant that any fast driving was out of the question. Since his retirement in 1961 he had steadfastly refused to to be drawn back to racing cars or circuits in any way, despite numerous offers to drive Astons, Vanwalls, Ferraris and such in historic events over the years. "I'm an ex-racing driver," he told me firmly, "with the emphasis on the ex, so don't expect me to do any fast stuff."

It was on that understanding that we went to Germany, but I had agreed to Tony's demand because I knew that he loved the Nürburgring and thought the DBR1 was the best sports-racer he had ever driven, so I was pretty certain that once he was at the wheel of the latter driving on the former he would almost certainly be tempted to put on some speed. I was right.

Naturally, I wasn't going to let him go without me beside him, and we duly set off together once he had done a couple of laps to remind himself which way the road went, thirty-four years after his last visit. This is where the motoring writer has it over most of his colleagues who write about other skilful endeavours – a balletomane might wish to dance with Darcey Bussell; a tennis writer might long for a match with Pete Sampras; an opera buff might kill for the opportunity to sing with Luciano Pavarotti, but they would all be wasting their time, for they possess none of the skills required. However, given the opportunity, a motoring hack with the co-ordination of a drunk and the eyesight of Mr Magoo can still experience the skills of his or her hero by riding with him on a circuit.

And so it was with me and Mr Brooks in the Aston at the Nürburgring, a day that provided me with one of the most memorable experiences of my life. The noise was deafening, the ride bumpy as hell, and the sensation of speed tremendous. For the first mile or so Tony's legendary skills seemed disappointingly absent, until I woke up to the fact that, like all great artists, he was making the nigh impossible look ridiculously easy.

Later, with the aid of the gear changes he had marked on a map for John Wyer in 1957 and Ted Cutting's gear/speed chart, he described a flying lap of the 14.2-mile circuit which he had mastered so brilliantly that year: "For the race the Aston has been fitted with a 3.38:1 final drive in fifth gear which, with the 6.5 x 16 inch Avon rear tyres, gives a maximum speed of 152mph at 6,000rpm, and I hold that speed past the pits, heading into South Turn. The brakes on the DBR1 are pretty good so I go very deep into the corner, changing down through the gears to second. Although

'The Nürburgring is the best circuit in the world. It provides such variety and contrast that it resembles a true road circuit. You don't come up to the same stupid corner every minute and a half. The idea, which was the basis of motor racing, was to drive as fast as possible on public roads which, for safety, were closed to the public. Anything else is circus stuff. It's not motor racing.' Tony Brooks, seen here at Aremberg.

it looks fairly quick on the map, the South Turn is actually quite a tight semicircle, so I power through it, balancing the car on the point of breakaway with the accelerator, moving up into third and snatching fourth at about 105mph on the straight behind the pits which leads to the North Turn, which I also take in second. This is a double left-hander which I power through, taking third at 75mph for a quite tricky series of corners known as Hatzenbach. The Aston drifts beautifully through here, and we rush downhill and over the bridge at Quiddelbacher-Höhe, which is the first of the Ring's big-dipper effects where I really feel the force of gravity pushing me down in the seat as we go over the bridge.

"Then it's into fourth gear at around 105mph, still being pushed into the seat, soaring upwards and taking off just before a very tricky right-hander, drifting through that and over Flugplatz, taking fifth with the road still rising slightly. At the top of the rise the Aston is doing 5,000 in fifth (124mph) as we plunge downhill, reaching 136mph before I drop down to fourth for a tricky left-hander and then into third for the tight right-hander which is Aremberg. We power through here and as the Aston drifts through the corner I feel it moving sideways and feed in the slightest opposite lock, straightening the steering at the same time as I ease off the accelerator to correct the slide. If I keep the power on I just spin the rear wheels and lose time, so I'm always trying to keep the rear wheels on the point of spinning, because that's the quickest way round.

"We then rush down to Fuchsröhre and the second big-dipper effect. This is very sharp indeed and puts a tremendous gravitational force on me as we hit the bottom, by which time the Aston is doing around 135mph, before I change down to third and then second for the left-hander at Adenauer-Forst. That can catch you out, because the gravitational effect of the Fuchsröhre can leave you highly stimulated, if not quite stunned, so it is very easy to take the left-hander a little too fast. If I don't brake heavily here I am going to be on the wrong line for the sharp right which follows within 30 or 40 yards.

"Then it's maximum acceleration as the road curves gently to the left before tightening into a tricky second-gear corner, then turning sharp right at Kallenhard. Still in second gear I apply the power just enough to keep drifting, but not spinning the wheels and losing time. Then it's up into third for a longish right-hander before dropping to second again and drifting round Wehrseifen, which leads to a very tricky section going down to Adenau Bridge. Again, there is a tremendous gravitational effect as we rush down to it in third and then, having been forced into my seat over the bridge at around 85mph, there is a very tricky climbing right-hander, Ex-Mühle. It is very important to get through this corner quickly. because it leads on to quite a good straight where I take fourth at about 105mph before dropping down to third again and then second for the right-hander at Bergwerk.

"This, too, is very important because it leads into the long climb to the Karussell and your speed out of a corner is even more important if you are then going uphill. The climb is a series of swerves through Kesselchen, which I take accelerating hard through third and into fourth, reaching 5,800rpm which is 130mph. The last left-hander before the sharp right which leads to the Karussell is a tricky one which isn't quite flat in fourth and I have to feather the throttle lightly, but it is a corner where I can save a lot of time by getting it just right.

"So it is down to third and then second for the right-hander, accelerating hard up to the Karussell, snatching third very briefly and then back into second for the banking itself. I accelerate out of it and into third for the steep climb up to Höhe Acht, drifting round that right-hander and on through Wippermann before changing down to second for Brünnchen. I am drifting through most of these corners, balancing the car between the steering and the accelerator all the time and this is where I get a tremendous sensual feeling of poetry in motion, as the car moves from one drift into another.

"We continue rushing downhill through a series of corners of rather similar radius which makes it difficult to differentiate clearly one from the other. In many ways this section is the most difficult (after the rush down to Adenau) in that there is no visibility, the corners are blind and yet not so dissimilar that they are clearly marked in my mind as how best to take them. It is a tricky section of road where I am drifting to the right one minute and to the left the next, a marvellous sequence of drifts through corners of varying radius to the right-hander after Pflanzgarten. This I take in third gear before changing up to fourth at 105mph and accelerating towards Schwalbenschwanz, the Little Karussell.

"I drop down to third for a right-hander over a bridge and then turn left into the corner that leads to the Little Karussell. This is quite difficult because although it has a small concrete banking, it is only wide enough to take the inside wheels, so I have to assess just how much additional grip this small amount of banking gives me. It is hard to satisfy myself that I have gone through that corner at the best possible speed, it would be much easier with a flat piece of road.

"We then go through a very wooded section to a double right-hander which is crucial in that it governs both the speed at which I enter the three-kilometre straight and just how soon I achieve maximum speed on it. This corner is completely blind and I must take the two apices in one broad drift, clipping the first apex and allowing the car to drift wide, but not so wide that I miss the second apex, then allowing the curve of my drift to take me out to the full width of the straight.

"Once on the straight I change into fourth at 105mph before the bridge at Döttering-Höhe and into fifth at 136mph just before the second bridge. Accelerating hard, I reach 6,000rpm in fifth (the Aston's maximum of 152mph) just before the Antoniusbuche Bridge. Then there is a flat-out left-hander, slightly downhill, followed by a flat-out right-hander which is the trickier of the two. It is important to take these flat as immediately after the latter the road climbs quite steeply before it plateaus in front of the pits. And that is a flying lap of the Nürburgring in the DBR1, 1957-style."

Tony Brooks may not have seen the Ring for almost 40 years, but I would never have guessed it, for he was driving the Aston as if it were his everyday car and obviously enjoying himself hugely, his self-imposed ban on fast driving long forgotten. It was absolutely fascinating to watch one of the all-time greats at work in his favourite sports-racer on one of his two best-loved circuits. Despite the fact that the DBR1 is a relic of the 1950s, with substantial kickback through the steering, it still handles everything the Ring can throw at it with aplomb and is a great credit to its designer, Ted Cutting.

So what did Tony and his co-driver, Noel Cunningham-Reid think of the circuit 38 years after their magnificent victory?

BROOKS:

"It's still great, but it has lost something, because they have widened it and put curbs where there used to be vertical grass banks which were almost as tall as the

Brooks at the South Turn.

wheels. They've smoothed it out, cut back the bushes and created grass verges and once you do that, then so many of the corners which used to be blind are no longer so. When you can see through a corner you can judge correctly both its radius and how far you can afford to drift it, but when it's blind you have to rely on recall and total sensitivity as to how fast you can go into the corner.

"Today, particularly from Fuchsröhre on the run down to Adenau Bridge – where it is very fast downhill – it is quite different. In the 1950s the road was lined with a tall, solid hedge either side and there was no margin for error, you couldn't see the exact curvature of the bends that were coming up so you had to memorise them. The hedges were so high it was almost like the Hampton Court maze going down there and you could gain a lot of time on that section if you had learned it very well because it was completely blind. People tend to go more slowly downhill because they feel less confident than going uphill or on the flat. If you're going too quickly downhill, it's more difficult to slow if you've overcooked it. Psychologically I always felt that I could make up a lot of time on competitors by going for it downhill, because they would be that much more tentative.

"The widening of the circuit – opening up the corners and putting curbs there so that you can make a mistake without it being crucial, plus the smoothness of the surface – has made it a lot easier. It was originally much narrower and rougher, with vertical grass banks so there was no room for error whatsoever, whereas today there is."

CUNNINGHAM-REID:
"In 1957 I came here as an innocent, because no-one had told me what a daunting circuit the Ring was. It was something of a nightmare to begin with, as it was just impossible in the time allowed to memorise its 172 bends. All I could do was to try and think of it in sections and, if my memory failed, go over the brows of the hills at a speed at which I could get round the next bend.

"I think my first laps were probably in the DB3S we had as a practice car because originally I was going to drive DBR1/1 with Roy Salvadori, and he would have had first call on that. The Aston Martin Race Reports tell me that I did five laps in the 3S, with a best time of 10 mins 44 secs (much faster than both the Whiteheads in the other 3S) and two in the R1, with a best time of 11 mins 3.3 secs. The next day I only had two laps in each car, but my times came down to 10 mins 33 secs in the 3S and 10 mins 23 secs in the R1. A total of 11 laps in fits and starts was hardly the ideal preparation for the Ring, and in the race I was really driving by instinct.

"It was John Wyer's idea to put me in DBR1/2 with Tony. When I took over from him after 16 laps there was considerable pressure on me because the Aston was in the lead, but the beautiful thing was that Tony had wiped out the opposition from the very start and gave me a lead of three minutes plus, so I was under no pressure to go fast. Of course, if he had been neck and neck with someone when he handed over to me it would have been a different thing altogether.

"I had no 'moments' at all during my stint, although inevitably my driving was a bit ragged to begin with. The DBR1 handled superbly and I followed my golden rule of going slowly when I wasn't sure which way the road went. In spite of this every time I passed the pits, Astons gave me a signal telling me that I was getting further and further ahead of the Ferraris of Trintignant and Gendebien. When I saw that my lead was over four minutes I thought, 'This is lovely. All I have to do is stay on the road.' And my early raggedness began to disappear. If you can relax in any sport you do it better and I found myself going faster and faster."

Then and Now: Brooks and Cunningham-Reid look suitably chuffed after their superb victory (left), for which each won the handsome sum of £389 8s 1d. Thirty-eight years later they met again at the Ring to reminisce about that truly great day.

BROOKS:

"Although I was third fastest in practice I didn't think we were going to win, because Maserati were there with two 4.5-litre cars and Fangio and Moss and Ferrari had a couple of four-litre cars and Hawthorn and Collins.

"They were all very quick in a straight line and were making up considerable time on the Aston down the long, three-kilometre straight, so I didn't wake up on the Sunday morning thinking, "We're going to win this race." I had no doubts about Noel, who had done very well in practice, but I wasn't at all sure that the Aston was fast enough to beat the Italian cars. In the circumstances I was just determined to go out and drive as fast as I possibly could.

"Noel and I had to work very hard because the surface was so rough there was a lot of kickback through the steering and you were bouncing about in the cockpit with no time to relax – even on the straight the car was going from side to side and you were having to correct all the time. There was a very difficult kink in the straight which we took flat out and because the road was so rough you had to correct the steering constantly to keep on the right line.

"I'd driven a DB3S at the Ring in 1956, and it wasn't a bad car for its day, but it wasn't in the same class as the DBR1, the difference between the two was chalk and cheese really. The DBR1 was without doubt the best handling car of its time and it might have been made for the Ring because so many of the corners could be drifted and the Aston was so driftable. The sensation of drifting is so sensual it really is quite addictive, which is why I enjoyed the Ring and the Aston so much. You balance the car on a knife-edge with the accelerator and steering wheel, judging it so that while staying on the right line you're going to drift just wide enough to make full use of the road and not clout the bank on the exit. Drivers don't have that sensation today. What can be the pleasure in going round corners geometrically, at three or three and a half g?

"The Aston was a fun car to drive here, and you could really throw it about, because this circuit showed off its tremendous road-holding qualities, which enabled us to take on the much more powerful Ferraris and Maseratis. If only the R1 had had more power nothing would ever have got near it!"

Noel in 'the best-handling, the most fun motor car I ever drove in my life.'

CUNNINGHAM-REID:

"Since we won the 1,000 Kms in 1957, I've always felt that I would rather have won that particular race in that particular year than anything else in history, so I am eternally grateful to John Wyer and Reg Parnell for giving me the opportunity. John was extraordinarily pleased at the end as it had been his decision to put me in with Tony. Roy Salvadori was the known driver, very fast and with experience of the Ring and he and Brooks would seem to have been the ideal combination, but John made this extraordinary decision and it came off. Did we celebrate that evening? I have a complete memory lapse, so the answer is almost certainly yes!

"The Ring today has definitely been emasculated. It has been widened and thereby straightened; the surface is totally different; cambers have been put in all over the place, and I find it hard to recognise as such. On the other hand I found the Aston to be exactly as I remembered it: the best-handling, the most fun motor car I ever drove in my life – just sensational!"

BROOKS:

"The Ring was a giant switchback, a great challenge from start to finish, but with no one corner that I could pick as my favourite; they just piled one on top of another and none gave me a substantially greater kick than the others. The last one onto the straight was quite interesting, you could get quite a broad drift on there. The old North Turn was good too; you could set up a nice steady drift and hold it all the way round on the throttle. Then there was the Flugplatz, where you took off and had to set the car up for the next corner, a very fast right-hander – that was exhilarating. And going down Fuchsröhre was quite exciting too.

"When I retired at the end of 1961 I decided to leave racing completely alone because it's like heroin, or any other drug: you either quit completely or remain hooked. I'm very pleased I did give up because I haven't driven at speed on a circuit since then, yet when I drove the Aston at the Ring again for several laps it all seemed to be still there – quite honestly it didn't seem any different to 38 years ago, which is frightening really.

"I definitely got the taste back again, and it didn't feel strange at all. I was having to relearn the circuit, of course, particularly the last mile or so down to Adenau and all the way from the Karussell to the straight, but otherwise it was a flashback to 1957. I felt completely comfortable in the Aston, which is still a beautifully balanced car, and it didn't seem as though that interval of time had passed. There may be an element of kidology here but, with the right gearing I felt that I could still have had a go!"

Brooks with the Aston Martin DB3S in 1956 (above). His fastest lap was 10 mins 26 secs, whereas Fangio (below left) set fastest lap of the race with 10' 05.3" in his 3.5-litre Ferrari. The next year in the DBR1 (below) Brooks recorded 9' 48.2" in practice. This was 38 seconds faster than his DB3S time and a remarkable tribute to Ted Cutting's design.

CHAPTER SEVEN

Luckless at Le Mans

Failure for Ferrari and Aston Martin

As the teams assembled for scrutineering at Le Mans, one month after the Nürburgring 1,000 Kms, there was much of interest to be seen. Ferrari, Maserati and Aston Martin all produced new racers for this event, but it was canny old Enzo who was looking to the future, whereas Maserati and Astons presented cars that would soon be rendered obsolete by the FIA.

Anticipating a capacity limit, Ferrari had been developing two new versions of his V12 250GT unit. Both were now of 3117cc but, as Joel Finn revealed in his book *Ferrari Testa Rossa*, they differed in cylinder-head configuration as one had a twin-camshaft layout (one per bank) as on the 250GT, while the other featured four-camshafts (two per bank) as used on the 290MM and 315/335S cars. The latter was fitted into the first prototype chassis which had raced at the Ring.

The former used 250GT-based cylinder heads which had been modified to allow the 12 spark-plugs to be repositioned outside the Vee, between the exhaust ports. This meant that six twin-choke 38mm downdraught Weber carburettors could be used, each choke feeding a cylinder. Also fitted with larger valves, special conrods and lightweight aluminium pistons, this engine produced a reported 270bhp and was installed in a brand-new car, 0704.

This was a lengthened (by 10cms/4ins) two-litre Testa Rossa chassis with standard suspension and employing a reinforced, 250GT four-speed transmission. In contrast to the blunt and brutal-looking 315 and 335S Ferraris, the new prototype was sleek and streamlined, with eye-catching bodywork styled and built by Sergio Scaglietti. He had separated the front wings from the radiator air intake – the better to cool the front drum brakes – and had also cut away the front wings behind the wheels, in a similar fashion to those on the DB3S Aston Martins, but without Frank Feeley's curvaceous elegance.

The first prototype (0666) was fitted with the four-camshaft engine and was also present at Le Mans but did not even practice owing to suspected piston failure while it was being warmed-up – a foretaste of things to come for Ferrari. The Scuderia's entry for the race therefore comprised two 4.1-litre models, one 3.8 and the new

The new prototype 250 TR awaits Scrutineering. This was Sergio Scaglietti's first cutaway wing body and the separation between air intake and headlamps can be clearly seen.

prototype Testa Rossa.

Aston Martin's newcomer was the DBR2 and was hard to spot, as it appeared identical to the DBR1s until you saw them together. Then it became obvious that it was a somewhat bigger car, with its exhaust exiting on the passenger side rather than under the driver's door, as on the R1.

Hamming it up for the camera at the Hotel de France are (l-r) Tony Brooks, Roy Salvadori, Reg Parnell and Noel Cunningham-Reid.

The Astons in the paddock behind the pits. To the right of the DBR2 (5) is DB3S/10, which was used for practice only.

Astons' main weapons for the race were, of course, the DBR1s. These were the same two which had raced at the Ring, unchanged apart from being fitted with new bearings and a different final drive ratio. The driver pairings were the same too, with the Whitehead brothers handling the DBR2.

The other newcomer at the Sarthe was Maserati's 450S Berlinetta. To be strictly accurate, it was Stirling Moss' idea to have Frank Costin design an aerodynamic enclosed 450S especially for Le Mans. It was built in a last-minute rush by Zagato, who ignored many of Costin's design features, including the full-length undertray. As a result, the car was cramped (even for Moss) with appalling visibility and numerous other problems. And despite its supposed aerodynamic superiority it was slower than the open 450S. The French quickly dubbed the car Le Monstre and, as well as this beast, Maserati entered an open 450S (fitted with even larger drum brakes than before) and a 300S.

Juan Manuel Fangio was on hand but, as he hated Le Mans, he insisted on being Maserati's reserve driver and refused point-blank to drive the Berlinetta. Moss was lumbered with it, of course, and he was joined by a somewhat reluctant Harry Schell.

Jean Behra and André Simon had the open 450S and Giorgio Scarlatti and Jo Bonnier drove the 300S.

Somewhat surprisingly, perhaps, after his sterling efforts with the prototype at the Ring, Masten Gregory was not in the Ferrari team. It could be that he was not invited, but more likely that he fancied his chances better in a D-type – after all, Jaguar had already won this race four times. Whatever the reason, Masten joined Le Mans hero Duncan Hamilton in his works-prepared, 3.8-litre car. The Scuderia was officially represented by Peter Collins and that other talented young American Phil Hill and Mike Hawthorn/Luigi Musso in 4.1-litre cars; two newcomers – British 500cc champion Stuart Lewis-Evans and Ferrari's test driver, Martino Severi – were paired in the 3.8; and Olivier Gendebien/Maurice Trintignant were entrusted with the 3.1-litre prototype.

Despite Jaguar's remarkable record, none of the five D-types was really regarded as a potential winner. Jaguar had officially retired from racing, so all were allegedly private entries, but the two Ecurie Ecosse cars of Ron Flockhart/Ivor Bueb and Ninian Sanderson/Jock Lawrence were works prepared, as was that of Duncan

1957

**Ferrari out in force - No 9 is the brand new Testa Rossa 0704, with 3.1-litre engine.
Nos 6 & 7 are the 4.1-litre 335S models and No 8 is the 3.8-litre 315S.**

Hamilton/Masten Gregory – and Jaguar's Team Manager, Lofty England, was managing the pits.

In practice on the Thursday evening reserve driver Juan Fangio in the open 450S and Mike Hawthorn in the 4.1-litre Ferrari took it in turns to shatter the lap record and broke the 200kph barrier for the first time. Mike did 3 mins 59.0 secs, and then Fangio put everyone in his place with 3' 58.1" (203.53kph). And that was the last time he ever drove at Le Mans.

Brooks was impressive, recording 4' 6.5" in the DBR1 with Salvadori on 4' 11". Duncan Hamilton was fastest of the Jaguars, with 4' 08", and Flockhart managed 4' 10.8" with the 3.8-litre Ecosse car. The prototype Ferrari sounded some warning bells for those who would listen, when Olivier Gendebien recorded 4' 7.4".

Bells were ringing for Ferrari, too, for after the first prototype had been sidelined with suspected piston failure the Collins/Hill car suffered a severe engine blow-up. A new V12 was fitted overnight, and Phil Hill did a little running in on the road to Tours in the wee small hours, but Peter Collins was to render that a complete waste of time.

After the DBR1's brilliant showing at the Ring, many people fancied Aston Martin to win at Le Mans too, but Tony Brooks was not among them.

"The DBR1 was superb at the Ring but, being a realist, I never regarded it as a Le Mans-winning car. First of all, Astons had always been a little fragile (not least in the gearbox) and second, if there's one thing you need at Le Mans its power, which the DBR1 just did not have. I thought we would do well, but I wouldn't have put my money on an outright win."

The first few hours of Le Mans were always a nightmare for the Team Managers

LUCKLESS AT LE MANS

Left: the Astons in the pits before evening practice. Car 5 is the new 3.7-litre DBR2. Beside car 19 Roy Parnell talks with mechanic Jack Sopp while Graham Whitehead gives the car a once-over. Behind him are Noel Cunningham-Reid, Tony Brooks, Roy Salvadori, John Wyer and Reg Parnell.

Below: Tony Brooks leaps into DBR1/2 at the start.

This year it was Peter Collins who set the ball rolling, rocketing into the lead at the very start with his 4.1-litre Ferrari. Graham Whitehead's DBR2 was right behind him, but Graham's moment of glory was just that – a moment. "I was second under the Dunlop Bridge, but by the time I got to Mulsanne I was eleventh!".

Collins completed his standing lap in 4 mins 20 secs, which equalled the previous year's fastest! It was no way to treat his brand-new engine and, sure enough, at the end of the second tour he was down in 10th spot. One lap later he was in the pits, and the car was retired with a seized piston before Phil Hill had a chance to drive it.

Mike Hawthorn now took over from his team-mate, leading Moss, Brooks, Gendebien, Salvadori and Bueb. Meanwhile Jean Behra was really motoring in the open 450S and in no time at all was up to third place and menacing Moss, passing him at the very end of the first hour, now only 30 seconds behind Hawthorn. Advised of this, Mike put on speed and became the first man to do a race lap at more than 200kph, recording 3' 59.6" (202.52kph), but then he had to stop for a wheel change, which let Behra into the lead. Moments later Moss was in the pits for more than two minutes and a short time later went by with smoke pouring from the big Maser.

of the most powerful cars because, despite forceful instructions to take it easy and even dire threats of retribution if they didn't, their lead drivers invariably set about the 24-hour race as though it were a three-hour Grand Prix. There were two reasons for this, the first being that most of them were Grand Prix drivers who wanted to race, rather than cruise around and wait for the opposition to break and the second was that they hated Le Mans and were none too upset if their car expired early on, allowing them to pack up and go home.

Left: Roy Salvadori heaves himself out of DBR1/1 as Les Leston (on pit counter, with seat support) prepares to take over. Reg Parnell (in waistcoat) directs operations, watched by John and Tottie Wyer (above the right hand Aston sign).
Above: Olivier Gendebien drifts through the Esses in the new Testa Rossa 0704, closely followed by Tony Brooks in DBR1/2.

Shortly after 6pm Behra handed over the leading Maserati to Simon, but he retired after only a few laps with a broken rear axle. Moss was only too happy to give Le Monstre to Harry Schell, but then that, too, was out and for the same reason.

So, after four hours the Ecurie Ecosse Jaguar of Flockhart and Bueb was in the lead, ahead of the Gendebien/Trintignant prototype Ferrari, the Brooks/Cunningham-Reid Aston Martin; the Hawthorn/Musso Ferrari; the Hamilton/Gregory Jaguar and the Salvadori/Leston Aston. The Hawthorn/Musso Ferrari was soon to retire with piston trouble, but the prototype was still going strong – apparently recording 177mph on the Mulsanne straight just before dark.

Aston Martin were now in trouble, as first Les Leston brought DBR1/1 into the pits for more than six minutes with the gearbox stuck in fourth – the Ring revisited. It could not be freed, so Salvadori went back into the race with no real prospect of finishing.

At midnight, after eight hours Flockhart and Bueb (Jaguar) led Brooks and Cunningham-Reid (Aston Martin), both cars having completed 112 laps. Then came the Sanderson/Lawrence Jaguar (109 laps); the Gendebien/Trintignant Ferrari (108 laps); and the Ecurie Francorchamps D-type of Frère and Rousselle (107 laps).

Tony Brooks was going really well in the DBR1 and by the time he handed over to Cunningham-Reid he had reduced the Ecurie Ecosse car's lead from four minutes to two and a half. This overhauling of the Jaguar was not to last much longer.

Roy Salvadori soldiered on for his next stint before handing the Aston back to Leston after a stop of almost six minutes, while the mechanics once again tried vainly to disengage fourth gear. At half-past midnight the car ground to a halt at Mulsanne. At about the same time the Gendebien/Trintignant Ferrari retired with a broken piston, and by 1am the race order was Jaguar, Aston Martin, Jaguar, Jaguar, Jaguar, Ferrari.

No sooner had Leston retired DBR1/1 than Cunningham-Reid's lap times in DBR1/2 increased by some 30 seconds; he too was stuck in fourth gear. He made a scheduled stop on lap 140 and reported the problem to Brooks as he took over.

60

"It was now something like 3am," recalls Tony, "and the idea of another nine hours slowly slipping down the field to finish nowhere didn't grab me so, having got the car out of gear at Spa I decided to try and do the same again, while we were still in second place.

"On my first lap, without bothering to settle down, instead of looking where I was going I was looking at the damn gear lever and trying to knock it out of fourth. Suddenly I looked up and I was too far into Tertre Rouge. If I'd just gone straight off the road there'd have been no real problem, but I almost got round the corner with a broad drift and the car ran up the loose sandbank at the exit and flipped over, throwing me out and landing on top of me."

Moments later Maglioli's Porsche arrived and was unable to avoid the Aston. The ensuing crash pushed the car off Brooks, who was able to scramble to safety, but both cars were out of the race. Brooks sustained a nasty wound to his thigh and cuts and bruises, but was allowed to fly home on the Monday morning.

And that left the race to the magnificent Jaguars which, by half-distance were in first, second, third and fifth places, with only the remaining Ferrari of Lewis-Evans/Severi spoiling their fun. Twelve hours later the Ferrari had dropped a place, so the D-types cleaned up, the Ecurie Ecosse cars of Flockhart/Bueb and Sanderson/Lawrence leading home the French entry of Lucas/'Mary' and the Belgian one of Frère/Rousselle. The Hamilton/Gregory car was sixth.

The race was a second successive triumph for Ecurie Ecosse and a bitter disappointment for Ferrari, Maserati and Aston Martin. The Ferraris had clearly experienced a batch of bad pistons, but that does not excuse the flat-out antics of Hawthorn and Collins, for the problem had made itself known in practice. However, the prototype had shown a real turn of speed and had been driven very sensibly while it lasted. This, clearly, was where Ferrari's future lay.

In common with the big Ferraris, the Maseratis had been seriously overdriven (and, in the case of the Berlinetta, badly prepared). Aston Martin, however, clearly had a superb car in the DBR1 but it was severely handicapped by a lack of real power and that terrible five-speed gearbox.

Aston Martin's season, which had begun so well, was now virtually at an end with the Le Mans débâcle, and it can have been no consolation for Reg Parnell that the average lap time which he had planned for the Brooks/Cunningham-Reid Aston was spot on. He had decided that 4 mins 25 secs would be good enough to win the race and the winning Flockhart/Bueb Jaguar proved him right by covering 326 laps at 183.2kph/113.8mph – an average time of 4' 24.5".

**Above: Noel Cunningham-Reid drives DBR1/2 into the evening sun.
Centre: the prototype Testa Rossa's run comes to an end with a broken piston, whereas the Aston finished upside down in the sand (bottom)**

Two Ferrari mechanics push the second prototype Testa Rossa forward for Scrutineering prior to the Swedish GP.
0704 was now fitted with a more powerful version of the 3-litre, 250GT engine.
On the left is new Team Manager Romolo Tavoni (with briefcase).

CHAPTER EIGHT

Ferrari – Champions Again

The Swedish GP; the GP de Belge
and the GP of Venezuela

Aston Martin had missed the first three rounds of the Sportscar Championship, won the fourth and failed dismally at the fifth, so despite their magnificent Nürburgring victory they had blown any chance they might have had of winning the title. The Venezuelan GP still had not been confirmed, which meant that there was now just one round left – the Swedish GP at Kristianstad in August.

Previewing the event, *Autosport* stated that among the entries were two, possibly three, Aston Martins. Come the day, though, and they were conspicuous by their absence and quite why is hard to fathom. Three-quarters of the circuit was on public roads and the DBR1s should have acquitted themselves very well there and – properly prepared – the R2 should have done even better. In the hands of Brooks and Salvadori it could well have given the big Ferraris and Maseratis a severe fright, if not a beating.

Ferrari and Maserati were out in force in Sweden for the six-hour sportscar GP, with the Championship still unresolved. The best four results – in brackets – from the six races were to count and after five events the Championship table looked like this:

Ferrari 27 (23)
Maserati 16 (16)
Jaguar 15 (15)
Aston Martin 8 (8)
Porsche 3 (3)
OSCA 1 (1)

Clearly Ferrari were odds-on to win the title but if Maserati were to win with no Ferraris finishing in the points, then they would be the champions – an unlikely scenario but not an impossible one.

Ferrari came to the four-mile Rabelovsbana circuit with the two 4.1-litre cars which had been assigned to Collins/Hill and Hawthorn/Musso at Le Mans and both Testa Rossa prototypes, although the Nürburgring car – 0666 – was apparently entered by American entrepreneur Temple Buell for Masten Gregory and Wolfgang Seidel to drive. It was now fitted with the 3.1-litre engine from the Le Mans machine – 0704 – and the latter was equipped with a new three-litre unit. This had the identical dimensions (73.0 x 58.8mm) of the 250GT Europa engine, but revised camshaft timing and bigger carburettor chokes had raised the power output to Enzo's sought-after 300bhp. The 'cutaway wing' car was to be driven by its Le Mans pilots, Olivier Gendebien and Maurice Trintignant.

Maserati brought two 4.5-litre cars to the circuit where the 450S V8 had made its racing début the previous year. They had cheerfully abandoned the Costin/Zagato coupé body that had caused so much grief at Le Mans and had equipped that chassis with normal, open bodywork. One of the big cars was fitted with the extra two-speed transmission which had first been seen on the Moss Mille Miglia car. There was also a 300S with 450S front brakes.

The regulations allowed teams to use any driver in any car, so practice was a long game of musical chairs for Ferrari and Maserati. The two 4.1-litre Ferraris behaved themselves, and Tavoni decided that they would have the same drivers as at Le Mans: Collins/Hill and Hawthorn/Musso. The prototypes, however, were in trouble as the

Phil Hill's hands are a blur as he makes a point to co-driver Peter Collins before a practice session. Their 4.1-litre 335S is undergoing a plug check.

3.1-litre engine in 0666 was down on revs and the three-litre in 0704 suffered a cracked mainshaft in the gearbox. This could not be repaired in time for the race, so the Le Mans car was given to Masten Gregory/Wolfgang Seidel. The Nürburgring car – now regarded as the better bet – went to Gendebien/Trintignant.

The race started at midday, and both Ferrari prototypes were out within the first two hours, Gregory being the first to go – unsurprisingly – with gearbox failure on the Le Mans car. Gendebien lasted a bit longer before retiring with a serious engine failure. Neither Seidel nor Trintignant got to drive.

Moss and Behra started with the big Maseratis and were soon running one-two, with the Ferraris of Hawthorn and Hill third and fourth. After two hours Moss handed his 4.5 to Schell and not long after took over the other big banger from Behra. Just before half-distance Harry was forced out with the same rear axle trouble that had done for the Maseratis at Le Mans. His day was far from over, however, for Team Manager Ugolini now put him into the three-litre car which he later handed to Moss after he had finished his stint in Behra's 4.5.

Hill and Collins had a fairly uneventful drive to second place in the 4.1-litre Ferrari and this secured the Sportscar World Championship for the Scuderia by three points. Hawthorn and Musso suffered several misfortunes, including a puncture and a split brake fluid pipe. Still, they managed to finish fourth, behind the three-litre Maserati driven by Bonnier/Scarlatti/Schell and Moss.

The starting-money problems which caused the cancellation of the Belgian GP did not prevent the AC de Belge from having a race. If they couldn't have F1 cars on their magnificent Spa-Francorchamps circuit, they would hold a sportscar GP instead. Unfortunately both Ferrari and Maserati decided to stay away from this three-hour event and concentrate on the Grandes Epreuves at Pescara (the week before Spa) and Monza (two weeks after). However, Enzo Ferrari did send a works 4.1-litre 335S which was painted yellow and entered by Ecurie Francorchamps for local hero Olivier Gendebien to drive.

After their splendid one-two in May Aston Martin were only too happy to go back to Spa. DBR1/2 (which Brooks had crashed at Le Mans) was repaired just in time and fitted with the new 95° twin-plug cylinder head, which pushed the power output of the RB6 engine up to 252bhp. They also took along the 3.7-litre DBR2, now fitted with three twin-choke 50mm Weber carburettors.

This was to be Tony Brooks' first drive for Aston Martin since his crash at Le Mans in June. In the meantime, although not fully recovered from his injuries, he had gallantly kept his Vanwall in contention during the British GP at Aintree, handing it over to Moss when his car failed. In one of his epic drives, Stirling had sliced through the field from ninth place to win the race. Brooks then finished ninth in the German GP and retired after just one lap at Pescara.

Reg Parnell was planning to let him loose in the R2 at Spa, as it was now giving close to 280bhp and should have been very fast there. However the first practice began with Salvadori and Brooks in the R1s and Noel Cunningham-Reid in the DBR2. Despite being new to both car and circuit Noel managed an impressive time of 4 mins 28.3 secs (over one second faster than Salvadori's best in the R1) in just six laps. Unfortunately, he then went off the road, damaging the R2 severely.

"I had been signalled to come in," he recalls, "and as I went up the hill after Eau Rouge I saw what I thought was an Aston – it was green with a yellow nose – upside down in the ditch. I was distracted by this and arrived at the left-hander at the top

Olivier Gendebien rounds La Source with a flat rear tyre on the Ferrari, which undoubtedly cost him the race.

of the hill way beyond my braking point and there was nothing to do but go off the road. There was a big enough drop for the car to turn over in the air twice and throw me out. I landed on soft ground, got to my feet and saw the Aston wrap itself round a tree. I was very relieved to find myself unhurt, but then I had to go back to the pits and tell DB and Reg all about it!"

The car that Noel had seen in the ditch was not an Aston, but the two-litre Ferrari Testa Rossa of the Belgian driver, Milhoux. He too was unhurt, but his car and the R2 were in no fit state to go racing.

Tony Brooks was thus denied his chance of driving the big Aston but he had troubles of his own, for after 12 laps of practice he brought DBR1/2 to a halt at Stavelot, as the engine was sounding rough. Later it was found that number 2 bearing had failed.

Olivier Gendebien's car did not arrive on the Friday, so he did some quickish laps in Ecurie Francorchamps' other Ferrari, a 3.5-litre model which was to be raced by Alain de Changy. In this he recorded a fastest lap of 4' 27.9", which was a long way off Brooks' best of 4' 15.8". On the Saturday, however, the works 4.1-litre car was very much present and with it Gendebien demolished Tony's time with a lap in 4' 11.7". This was sensational – almost three seconds faster than the Grand Prix lap record set the previous year by Stirling Moss in his 250F Maserati. However, the circuit had been made considerably faster by improvements that had taken place in the intervening 12 months. Nonetheless, it was a superb performance by Gendebien.

Astons had a spare crankshaft and conrod for Brooks' car flown out that morning from England, and meanwhile all three drivers practised in DBR1/1, Tony being fastest with 4' 17.0", followed by Salvadori on 4' 28.8" and a chastened Cunningham-Reid on 4' 37.0". The latter two were somewhat put in the shade by Ivor Bueb, who got his Ecurie Ecosse D-type round in a remarkable 4' 27.9". After Salvadori on the timesheet came Brian Naylor (D-type) with 4' 31.5"; Jock Lawrence (D-type) with

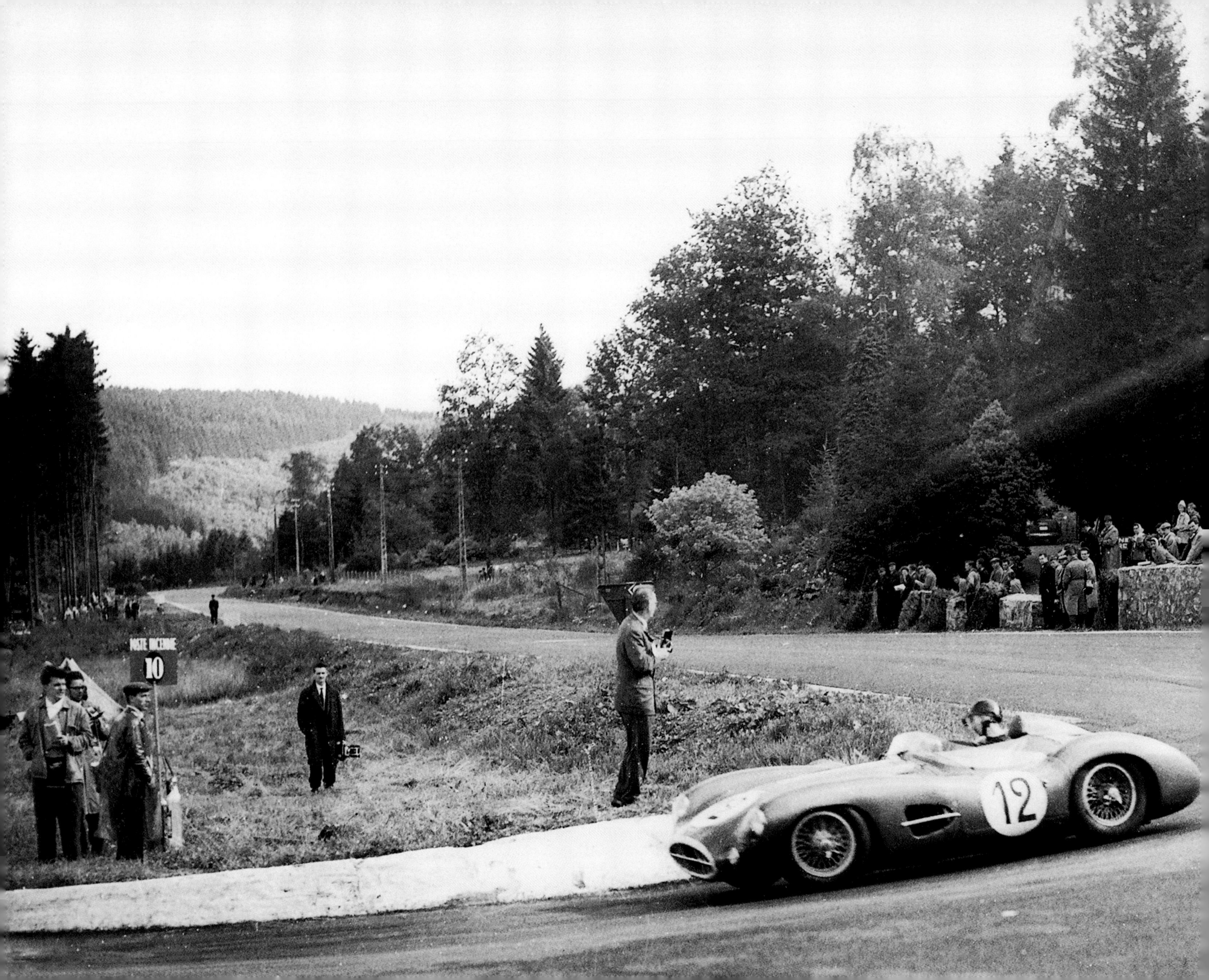
10
12

4'32.9"; and Masten Gregory (3.5-litre Ferrari) on 4' 33.5".

In the first practice session Brooks had been getting 6,300 in fifth with the 3.38 axle ratio, so it was decided to change it to 3.27:1 for the race on his car, in order to limit the rpm to 6,000 in top. The rebuild of Brooks' engine was completed at 8pm that evening and Roy Parnell then had the pleasure of running it in by driving the car around the circuit – now open to the public – for one-and-a-half hours in the dark.

Better weather conditions meant that Brooks had been able to improve his fastest lap by almost seven seconds over his best time in May, although Salvadori didn't quite match his previous best, which had been 4' 27.8". Tony was now almost 15 seconds a lap faster than Roy and his fuel consumption was correspondingly greater, so Reg Parnell decided that he would start with 30 gallons of fuel on board and make one stop, whereas Roy would carry 40 gallons and go right through the race.

The tremendous speed of the big Ferrari made Gendebien the great favourite to win, but the intransigence of Enzo Ferrari was to deny him victory in front of his home crowd, as Olivier recalled.

"We were using Englebert tyres, of course, and old man Englebert himself was there during practice, taking the temperatures. He found that they were getting too hot, so he told Tavoni, 'I would like you to put bigger tyres on the Ferrari, otherwise you will have trouble in the race.'

"Tavoni phoned Maranello for permission, but Ferrari said, 'No, you will race on the tyres fitted.' It was a three-hour race with a Le Mans start and the Ferrari was reluctant to fire, so Brooks got away in the lead and I was about the last to leave the pits. At the end of the lap I was up to sixth, but 28 seconds behind Brooks. After six laps I was in second place, but when I got to the top of the hill before the descent to Burnenville I suddenly smelt rubber and then the left rear tyre blew out. I went slowly back to the pits – a long way at Spa – where they changed the wheel.

"I then went flat out after Brooks and set a new lap record at 4' 16.5", but at the top of the hill I smelt rubber again and crack! – the same tyre blew out once more. I changed the wheel and went faster than ever – 4' 15.3"; then 13.1"; 13.0" and then 4' 10.4". As I arrived at La Source hairpin I could see Brooks going up the hill from Eau Rouge. On lap 29 I did 4' 9.8" – a speed of over 203kph – but it was too much and a third tyre blew. I stopped to change it and had to settle for third place."

On his way to his second win of the year at Spa, Tony Brooks sweeps DBR1/2 round La Source hairpin with not another car in sight.

By contrast, Tony Brooks had a most uneventful afternoon, leading from start to finish. On lap 26 he made his scheduled pit stop for 13 gallons of fuel and was back in the race, still in the lead, 29 seconds later. He won, averaging 118.56mph for the three hours. Masten Gregory was a fine second in his 3.5-litre Ferrari; Gendebien was a unhappy third; and Roy Salvadori fourth after an excellent drive which was, once again, dogged by gearbox trouble.

For much of the race he had been unable to select first and second gears and back at Feltham it was found that the selector shaft for these gears was sheared and badly bent. This meant that the oil feed to third, fourth and fifth gears was restricted, causing them to overheat.

In his Race Report, Reg Parnell admitted that but for his tyre trouble, Gendebien and the Ferrari would almost certainly have won the race, and noted that Brooks' victory was 'all the more satisfying to us since he started with a virtually new engine which had only been run in at road speeds for a short time. The reliability of the 95° cylinder head was confirmed, for when we inspected the engine after it had been dismantled, it was found to be in perfect condition. Further development is to take place of this cylinder head to obtain more power in the middle range.'

Early in September it was announced that the Venezuelan GP was now definitely on and would take place in Caracas in November. This meant that the Manufacturers' Championship was still wide open, as Ferrari were only three points ahead of Maserati. Now both teams would have to make the long and expensive journey to South America for the showdown.

Three weeks later the FIA announced that for 1958 there would be a three-litre limit imposed on the Sportscar World Championship. Despite the fact that this eliminated the very promising DBR2 Astons were happy, for in the R1 they now had the fastest three-litre car in the world. If they could just find a bit more power and improve the reliability of that five-speed gearbox, the Championship should be theirs.

In Maranello Enzo Ferrari was also a happy man. His foresight (or informants) had paid off and he could now set about finalising the specification of his three-litre Testa Rossa, which would not only be his front-line sports-racing car for the coming season, but would also bring in thousands of dollars from his American customers, who were longing for a successor to his two-litre Testa Rossa.

In Modena, however, Maserati were distinctly unchuffed. The company was severely strapped for cash despite its success in Grand Prix racing (Fangio had become World Champion – for the fifth time – driving a 250F) and had poured a great deal of money into the 450S. Now, just when they had developed it into a winner which would have brought much-needed dollars and possibly the 1958 Championship their way, the FIA had rendered the car obsolete. The Orsi family – which had owned Maserati since before the war – requested another year of racing for unlimited-capacity sportscars, but was turned down.

Nonetheless, with Ferrari only three points ahead there was still a chance that they could win the 1957 Championhsip, so four Maseratis were dispatched to Venezuela – three 450S models and a 300S. Just to prove that the Trident concern had not been ignoring their 3-litre cars, the latter was powered by a new V12, a 305 bhp, 3-litre version of the 3.5-litre unit which Hans Herrmann had used in the Mille Miglia. The 450S cars were to be driven by the very fast quartet of Stirling Moss, Jean Behra, Harry Schell and Tony Brooks – the latter on loan from Aston Martin just for this race. The third 450S actually had a 4.7-litre V8 fitted and was entered by Temple Buell for Masten Gregory/Dale Duncan. The 3-litre V12 was given to Jo Bonnier and Giorgio Scarlatti.

Ferrari also sent four cars: two 4.1-litre, 335S models and the two three-litre Testa Rossa prototypes. Both the larger cars had been to Scaglietti for his distinctive front end treatment – the wings separated from the main air intake – but not the cutaway wings, due to the large oil tank carried behind the near-side front wheel.

The first prototype – 0666 – had also been back to Scaglietti since the Swedish GP and fitted with pontoon-style bodywork, identical to that on the Le Mans car (0704) apart from the door hinges , which were mounted inside. They were equipped with the 250GT-based 3-litre engines.

As he had in Sweden, Enzo Ferrari entrusted his big cars to Peter Collins/Phil Hill and Mike Hawthorn/Luigi Musso. Of the Testa Rossa prototypes, 0666 was given to the German pair, Wolfgang von Trips and Wolfgang Seidel, while 0704 went to Olivier Gendebien and Maurice Trintignant.

The race was a triumph for Ferrari, as the Scuderia wrapped up the Championship with a comprehensive one-two-three-four victory. Collins and Hill won by over a lap from Hawthorn and Musso, who were two laps ahead of von Trips and Seidel. In fourth place was the other prototype of Gendebien/Trintignant. Both Testa Rossas ran faultlessly for the six hours (although 0704 was lacking in speed, for some mysterious reason) and left Enzo Ferrari secure in the knowledge that he had a real contender for Championship honours again in 1958.

In marked contrast the event was an utter disaster for Maserati as the team was virtually wiped out during the race. Masten Gregory crashed and overturned the Temple Buell car on the second lap and survived thanks only to a roll-over bar, which had been fitted the night before. In the early laps Moss and Behra on the works 450S cars did furious battle with Collins and Hawthorn on the big Ferraris until Moss – in the lead – collided with an AC Ace, which pulled across his path when he was doing a good 160mph. Both cars were written off and the AC driver was taken to hospital. Stirling returned to the pits and waited to take over the sole surviving 450S from Jean Behra.

When the Frenchman stopped to refuel the Maserati went up in flames, but they were rapidly extinguished, so Stirling hopped aboard and set off. Unfortunately, the efficient Venezuelan fire brigade had put out the blaze everywhere but on the driver's seat and two laps later Moss was back, to retire with a painfully burnt bottom! The seat was doused with water and Harry Schell took over, setting off after Collins and Hawthorn, who were leading the race in their Ferraris.

Harry began to catch them hand over fist, but then came the crash which wiped out the rest of the Maserati team. Schell was in the process of overtaking Jo Bonnier's 300S when it suffered a burst rear tyre and collided with the 450S. Both cars shot off the road at high speed and Bonnier was thrown out just before the 300S crashed into a concrete lamppost which snapped at its base and fell across the front of the Maserati. The car was a write-off.

The 450S slammed into a wall and bounced off it, throwing Schell out onto the road, which was just as well, for the big Maser then burst into flames and was soon reduced to ashes, which meant that all three works cars were written off. Harry Schell was dazed and burnt about the arms and face; Jo Bonnier suffered only minor cuts and bruises and Stirling Moss had to stand rather than sit for a while, but miraculously, that was the extent of their injuries after two horrific accidents which, sadly, signalled the end of the Maserati racing team.

In Modena the shell-shocked house of the Trident faced a bleak future. The Competitions Department would go on building and preparing cars for private entrants, but there would be no more works entries in Grands Prix or sportscar events.

A few kilometres up the road in Maranello, a jubilant house of the Prancing Horse invited the world's motoring press to view its latest challenger for sportscar honours in the coming year – the 250 Testa Rossa.

Results

1957
SPORTSCAR WORLD CHAMPIONSHIP

	Buenos Aires	Sebring	Mille Miglia	Nürburgring	Le Mans	Sweden	Venezuela	
1. Ferrari	8	3	8	6	2	6	8	41/30
2. Maserati	6	8	3	2	0	8	2	29/25
3. Jaguar	3	4	0	0	8	2	0	17/17
4. Aston Martin	0	0	0	8	0	0	0	8/8
5. Porsche	0	0	2	3	0	0	1	6/6
6. OSCA	1	0	0	0	0	0	0	1/1

The Championship was decided by the best four results. Points: 1st – 8; 2nd – 6; 3rd – 4; 4th – 3; 5th – 2; 6th – 1.

BUENOS AIRES 1,000 Kms
January 20

1) M. Gregory/E. Castellotti/L. Musso (Ferrari 290MM) 98 laps, 6 hrs 10 mins 29.9 secs (100.76 mph)
2) J. Behra/C. Menditeguy/S. Moss (Maserati 300S) 6 hrs 11 mins 53.4 secs
3) A. de Portago/P. Collins/E. Castellotti (Ferrari 290MM) 6 hrs 12 mins 59.6 secs
4) N. Sanderson/R. Mières (Jaguar D-type) 95 laps
5) L. Piotti/R. Bonomi (350S Maserati) 91 laps
6) Miss I. Haskell/A. de Tomaso (OSCA) 88 laps

Fastest lap: S. Moss (Maserati 300S) 3 mins 36 secs.

MILLE MIGLIA
May 12

1) P. Taruffi (Ferrari 335S) 10 hrs 27 mins 47 secs, (95.4 mph)
2) W. von Trips (Ferrari 335S) 10 hrs 30 mins 48 secs
3) O. Gendebien (Ferrari 250GT) 10 hrs 35 mins 53 secs
4) G. Scarlatti (Maserati 300S) 11 hrs 00 mins 58 secs
5) U. Maglioli (Porsche 1.5) 11 hrs 14 mins 07 secs
6) R. Luglio (Ferrari) 11 hrs 26 mins 58 secs

SEBRING 12 HOURS
March 23

1) J. M. Fangio/J. Behra (Maserati 450S) 197 laps, 1,024 miles at 85.34 mph
2) S. Moss/H. Schell (Maserati 300S) 195 laps
3) J. M. Hawthorn/I. Bueb (Jaguar D-type) 193 laps
4) M. Gregory/L. Brero (Ferrari 290MM) 193 laps
5) W. Hansgen/R. Boss (Jaguar D-type) 188 laps
6) P. Collins/M. Trintignant (Ferrari 315S) 187 laps

Fastest lap: J. Behra (Maserati 450S) 3 mins 24.5 secs, 92.5 mph.

NÜRBURGRING 1,000 Kms
May 26

1) C.A.S. Brooks/N. Cunningham-Reid (Aston Martin DBR1/2) 44 laps in 7 hrs 33 mins 38.2 secs (82.39 mph)
2) P. Collins/O. Gendebien (Ferrari 335S) 7 hrs 37 mins 51.9 secs
3) M. Hawthorn/M. Trintignant (Ferrari 315S) 7 hrs 39 mins 27.2 secs
4) U. Maglioli/E. Barth (Porsche 1.5) 7 hrs 47 mins 17.2 secs
5) J. M. Fangio/S. Moss (Maserati 300S) 43 laps
6) R. Salvadori/L. Leston (Aston Martin DBR1/1) 43 laps
10) M. Gregory/O. Morolli (Ferrari TR prototype 0666) 42 laps

Fastest lap: S. Moss (Maserati 450S) 9 mins 49.9 secs, 86.43 mph.

LE MANS 24 HOURS
June 22/23

1) R. Flockhart/I. Bueb (Jaguar D-type) 2732.36 miles at 113.85mph
2) N. Sanderson/J. Lawrence (Jaguar D-type)
3) J. Lucas/J. Marie (Jaguar D-type)
4) P. Frère/F. Rousselle (Jaguar D-type)
5) S. Lewis-Evans/M. Severi (Ferrari 315S)
6) D. Hamilton/M. Gregory (Jaguar D-type)

Fastest lap: J. M. Hawthorn (Ferrari 335S), 3 mins 58.7 secs (126.147 mph).
Aston Martins DBR1/1 and /2 failed to finish, as did Ferrari TR prototype 0704.

SWEDISH GP
August 11

1) J. Behra/S. Moss (Maserati 450S) 145 laps at 98.4 mph
2) P. Hill/P. Collins (Ferrari 335S) 144 laps
3) J. Bonnier/G. Scarlatti/H. Schell/S. Moss (Maserati 300S) 138 laps
4) M. Hawthorn/L. Musso (Ferrari 315S) 134 laps
5) A. de Changy/Dubois (Jaguar D-type) 132 laps
6) Bremer/Pinoari (Ferrari) 132 laps

Fastest lap: J. Behra 2 mins 20.9 secs, 104.4 mph
The Testa Rossa prototypes 0704 (M. Gregory/M. Seidel) and 0666 (O. Gendebien/M. Trintignant) failed to finish.

VENEZUELA GP
November 1

1) P. Collins/P. Hill (Ferrari 335S) 101 laps in 6 hrs 31 mins 55.6 secs at 95.4 mph
2) L. Musso/M. Hawthorn (Ferrari 335S) 100 laps
3) W. von Trips/W. Seidel (Ferrari TR prototype 0666) 99 laps
4) O. Gendebien/M. Trintignant (Ferrari TR prototype 0704) 97 laps
5) Marcotulli/Chimeri (Maserati 300S) 91 laps
6) W. Crawford.E. Hugus (Porsche 1.5) 90 laps

Fastest lap: S. Moss (Maserati 450S) 3 mins 38 secs

CHAPTER NINE

Spa Spectacular

Tony Brooks reminisces

It is a great boon to all racing enthusiasts that the two greatest road circuits in the world – Spa and the Nürburgring – are within a couple of hours' drive of each other. It is still possible to enjoy both, but whereas the Ring is a closed circuit with one-way traffic and can be driven as fast as you like, Spa is made up of public roads and normal rules apply.

Thanks to the enthusiastic help of Monsieur François, Chief of the Stavelot Police Department (who cheerfully held up the traffic for us) Richard Newton was able to photograph the Aston and the Ferraris at various points around the magnificent old 8.77-mile Spa-Francorchamps circuit. On this occasion Tony Brooks was joined by his 1959 Ferrari team-mate, Phil Hill, who drove the 1958 Testa Rossa.

Phil did not compete in any of the sportscar races at Spa in the late 1950s but, like Tony, he regards the circuit as one of the greatest of all and shares with him the distinction of having won the Belgian Grand Prix there. Tony won in 1958 with the Vanwall, and Phil was victorious in 1961 with the 'shark-nose' Ferrari 156.

Brooks won first time out at Spa, driving the DBR1 to its maiden victory in three-litre form in May 1957. How did he go about learning the circuit?

"First of all, I found a good road map and memorised the shape of the corners so I would have an idea of what was coming next. Then I drove round in an ordinary saloon car and confirmed that my impression of the curvature of the corners was correct. Obviously I couldn't get a real idea of the speeds involved as the roads were open; I had to memorise the shape and radius of the corners so that come official practice I didn't waste time learning the circuit.

"It was wet for that first race which made it very interesting going through those fast corners. It also probably explains why I didn't use first gear at La Source hairpin. There would be too much wheelspin, and you'd be quicker feathering the accelerator in second. And we'd have been that much slower through Malmédy in the rain, which would have affected the speed on the straight.

Above: Phil Hill (Testa Rossa) and Tony Brooks (DBR1) in close company on the run up to Blanchimont. Opposite: DBR1/2 lifts a front wheel off the ground as Tony powers out of Eau Rouge and up the hill towards Les Combes, on his way to victory number two at Spa in 1957.

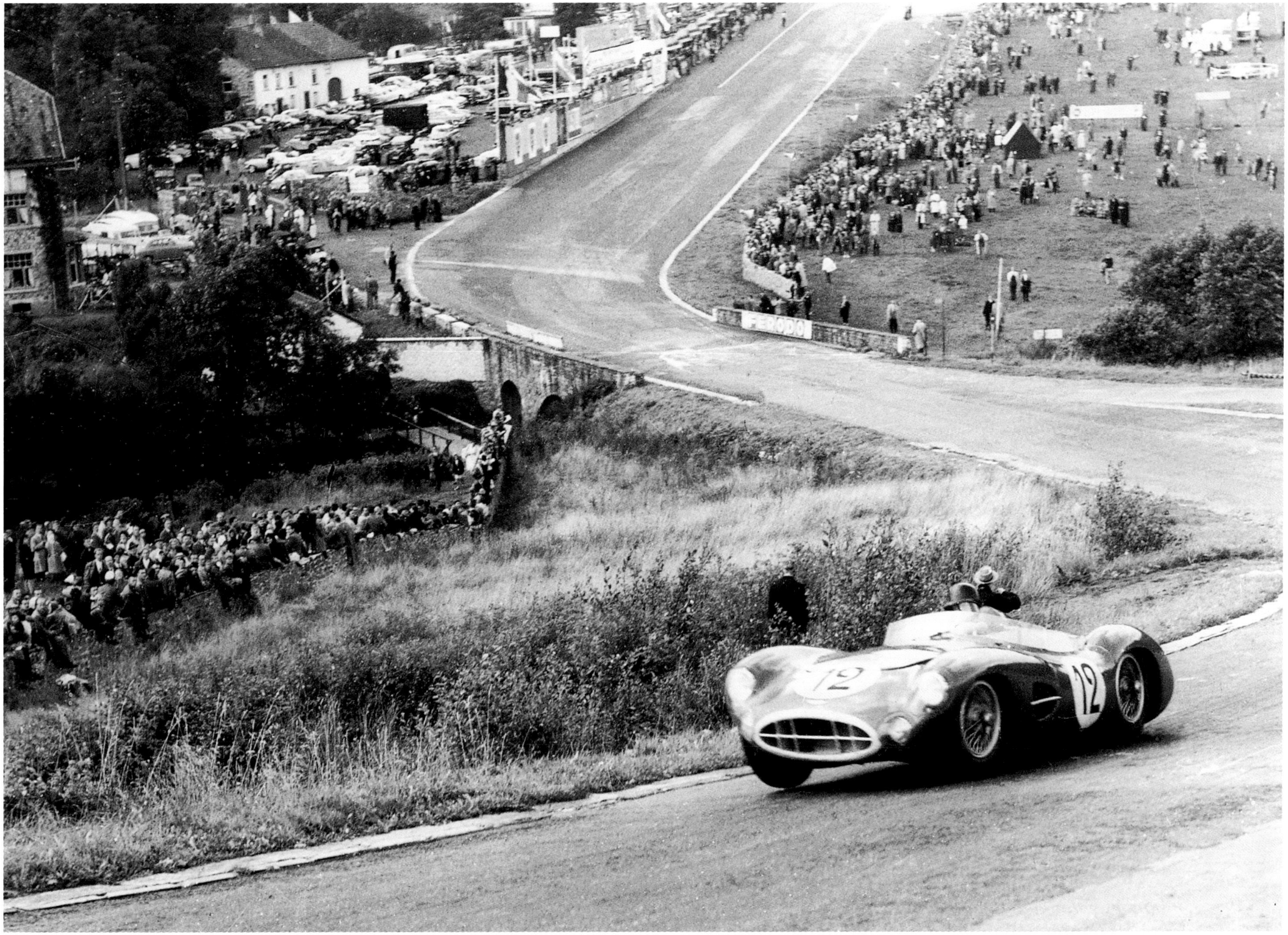
FERODO
12
12

"By the time of the second race in August I knew the circuit well and the weather was dry, so the race average was much higher, 118mph as opposed to 104. That was my first race for Astons after my shunt at Le Mans, and Spa was not too difficult physically, unlike the Nürburgring. The physical effect was minimal, as you were just balancing the car on a knife edge in a drift, most of the time. It was an absolutely fabulous circuit."

As at the Nürburgring, the Aston was fitted with the 3.38:1 final drive for practice at Spa, after which Tony marked his gear changes on a map for Reg Parnell. This is his account of a flying lap in the DBR1.

"Leaving La Source hairpin in first, I am in fourth gear by the time I pass the pits on the downhill run to Eau Rouge. I sweep over to the right, brake, change down to third and, at around 100mph, aim for the solid brick wall which is on the left-hand side of the road and which marks the apex of the first part of this great corner, putting the car within a few inches of it.

"There is a big-dipper effect here because as I am level with the wall the road suddenly leaps upwards and to the right, so I swing the Aston over into the climbing turn, drifting up it in third, clipping the apex on the right-hand side of the road and heading for the left-hand side on the exit. The big-dipper effect combines with the drift to give a truly wonderful sensation.

"Shortly after the exit from Eau Rouge I change into fourth gear and we now rush up the steep hill, reaching 5600rpm (about 125mph) before I drop down to third for Les Combes. This left-hander is virtually a right-angle turn and very tricky because it is blind. It is very difficult to be absolutely certain how fast you can go through it because you don't see how much road you've got until you're already committed to a) your speed and b) your line.

"Balancing the Aston between the steering and the throttle I drift through Les Combes, clipping the apex and slipping over to the right-hand side of the road before taking fourth gear at about 105mph and beginning the rush downhill, taking fifth at 135mph as I pass the three-kilometre stone. I then shape up for Burnenville, which is just about the most exciting corner I know.

"Eau Rouge is great, but Burnenville is truly fantastic, a long right-hand corner through which I balance the Aston on a knife-edge with the accelerator and virtually no movement of the steering wheel at all, drifting at about 150mph for many, many seconds. Burnenville just goes on and on and gives me the most sensual satisfaction of any corner on any circuit in the world.

"By the time I reach the Malmédy kink the Aston has been drifting for more than half a kilometre and I'm in Seventh Heaven! The revs have dropped from 5,900 to 5,100 in fifth, about 125mph, and this reduction is due entirely and deliberately to the slowing effect of the angle of drift and means that I don't touch the brakes for Malmédy, which I also take in a drift.

"I now accelerate down the Masta straight, reaching 6,300 pm (162mph) shortly before the left-right Masta kink, where I just ease off the throttle, but don't touch the brakes. I lose about 800 revs through here, but I'm soon back up to 6,100 (155mph) just before the eight-kilometre stone, where I barely brake for Stavelot, dropping down to fourth and scrubbing off speed by putting the Aston into a drift, having been in top for the best part of five kilometres.

"Stavelot is a minor Burnenville, another corner where you set the car up in a drift using a curvature which is going to take in the maximum width of the road upon entry and exit, but at the same time taking you to the optimum apex point. We leave the corner at 5,300 in fourth, moving quickly into fifth at 136mph and from here we are pulling uphill all the way to La Source.

"A couple of flat-out left-handers are followed by a flat-out right which leads to quite a tricky, sharpish right-hander at La Carrière, where I lift off and drop down to 5,100rpm before accelerating strongly through 900 revs to the 12-kilometre stone. Then I take fourth gear for Blanchimont, the blind, double left-hander which I drift through as one before accelerating towards my braking point for La Source, changing directly from fourth to first for the hairpin, as the less I have to use the David Brown five-speed gearbox the better! I go in wide, make an apex a fraction after the halfway point and come out wide, moving the back of the car out early. This allows me to get on the throttle sooner and gently power-slide the Aston out of the corner, accelerating up through the gears as I plunge downhill towards Eau Rouge again.

"Spa was exhilarating, absolutely superb in a fast car with appropriate power and roadholding. It was just fantastic in the Aston as so many corners could be taken in a broad drift. I loved it."

Opposite: Brooks rounds Les Combes and (below) begins the rush downhill to his favourite corner of all - Burnenville

1958

The Contenders 2
FERRARI 250 TESTA ROSSA

SPECIFICATION

DESIGN ENGINEER: Andrea Fraschetti
ENGINE: 60-degree V12, 73 x 58.8 mm,
2953cc, 2 valves per cylinder, single ohc, comp ratio: 9:1,
Max bhp: 300@7200 rpm,
Max bmep: 187 lb/sq in @ 4000 rpm,
Carburettors: 6 twin-choke Weber 38 DCN,
Plugs: 24 Marchal 34 HF,
Lubrication: wet sump.
TRANSMISSION:
Clutch: Fichel & Sachs single-plate,
Gearbox: front-mounted ZF with Porsche synchromesh, 4-speed & reverse.
CHASSIS:
Multi-tube,
Suspension (front): wishbones & coilsprings, (rear): coil springs & torque arms,
Shock absorbers: Houdaille,

Brakes: drum,
Tyres: Englebert (front) 5.50 x 16; (rear) 6.00 x 16,
Wheels: Borrani.
BODY:
Stylist: Sergio Scaglietti,
Builder: Carrozzeria Scaglietti.
DIMENSIONS:
Length: 13 ft,
Width: 5 ft,
Height: 3 ft 2 ins,
Ground clearance: 5.5 ins,
Wheelbase: 7 ft 9 ins,
Track (front) 4 ft 3.5 ins; (rear) 4 ft 3 ins,
Weight (dry) 1760 lbs.

The bodywork of the original Testa Rossa was dramatic in appearance, but none too efficient aerodynamically.

Halfway through the season Scaglietti produced a more conventional design which, in some cases (below), had the carburettor air intake at the base of the windscreen.

THE CONTENDERS 2

Ferrari 250 TR
1958

Design Engineer:
Andrea Fraschetti

Stylist:
Sergio Scaglietti.

1958

CHAPTER TEN

The Maranello Marvel

The new Testa Rossa; the Buenos Aires 1000 kms

Enzo Ferrari introduced his 250TR to the press at Maranello on Friday, November 22, 1957. On display was the very first customer model – chassis 1710 – a left-hand drive car which had been painted silver on the instructions of its American purchaser, John von Neumann. Its red-painted cylinder heads ensured that the name Testa Rossa was carried over from its two-litre predecessor. The TR's price in the United States was $11,800 at port of entry.

The new car had been the responsibility of the Scuderia's Technical Director, 29-year-old Andrea Fraschetti, with Franco Rocchi and Walter Salvarini in charge of the development of the V12 engine. Sadly the gifted and popular Fraschetti did not live to see his car presented to the press, as he had been killed at the end of August while testing Ferrari's new Formula 2 Dino at Modena Autodrome. Just a few months earlier a position had become vacant in the Racing Department, and he had introduced Enzo Ferrari to 34-year-old Carlo Chiti, then working as a chassis engineer at Alfa Romeo. Shortly after the tragedy Ferrari invited Chiti to take over Fraschetti's position at Maranello.

The Testa Rossa's very distinctive styling was by Scaglietti, of course, who had improved his 1957 Le Mans design by straightening out the curves, raising the height of the bodywork at the cockpit and reducing it over the rear wheels. His rear-end treatment of 0704 had been very similar to that of Ted Cutting's DBR1, but he now abandoned the falling curve of the rear wings and straightened them out, squaring them off at the back. Viewed side-on, the new Testa Rossa bore a certain likeness to the DB3S Frank Feeley had styled for Aston Martin late in 1954.

The front bodywork remained the same, with its gaps between the radiator air intake and the headlamps and the cutaway wings behind the wheels. Here Scaglietti's styling was the cause of some controversy, many observers believing that such work ought to be left to a qualified aerodynamicist rather than to a man who was not even an acknowledged stylist but a body-builder.

At the time the reason given for the front treatment and cutaway wings was that they allowed better cooling of the front brake drums, but there was a bit more to it than that, as Sergio Scaglietti told me more than thirty years later.

"We separated the air intake from the wings to get cooling air to the brakes; and originally the bodywork behind the front wheels was normal, not cut back," he recalled. "However, when we tested the car in wet weather, we found that a lot of water went through the gaps between the air intake and the wings and became trapped in the bodywork behind the wheels. The turbulence of the air then threw it forward on to the brake drums and this affected their performance, so I cut away the wings and the water went straight out. It seems a simple solution now, but if you

Opposite: eventual winner Phil Hill in TR 0704 leads Juan Fangio in his battered Maserati 300S out of the hairpin early in the Buenos Aires 1000 Kms. They are followed by the Porsche of Stirling Moss. Right: the first customer Testa Rossa (0710) on view for the Press at Maranello.

knew how long it took to work out! The result was very beautiful – a Formula 1 car with mudguards."

Enzo Ferrari made it clear that although journalists were looking at a customer car – to be flown to America in a few days' time – the Testa Rossa was also to be his works racer for 1958, but whereas all customer cars would have a solid rear axle and left-hand drive, the works cars might have a de Dion axle and right-hand drive. He made no mention of the five-speed gearbox, dry sump lubrication system or the four-cam cylinder heads that were under development for the team cars.

Later, when the journalists had had time to digest what they had seen, some criticised Ferrari for producing such an old-fashioned design. Instead of going for a modern, spaceframe chassis – as Aston Martin had done – he had opted for the relatively crude, ladder-type frame which was basically that of the two-litre Testa Rossa; the V12 engine was essentially a scaled-up version of Gioachino Colombo's 1.5-litre unit of 1947 and there was no sign of fuel-injection, disc brakes or a rear-mounted gearbox and final drive unit. How, they asked, could such an unadventurous motor car defend Ferrari's World Championship title?

Unadventurous maybe, but you underestimated Enzo Ferrari at your peril. Unlike David Brown – whose Aston Martins would be his main rivals for sportscar Championship honours in the coming season – Ferrari had to sell motor cars in order to go motor racing. He knew very well that his customers wanted to be able to buy a car that bore a close resemblance to those raced by the factory, even if they didn't plan on racing themselves. David Brown, on the other hand, had bought Aston Martin as a hobby and went racing in order to publicise the whole of his David Brown organisation. The cars that emanated from Feltham were gentle, well-bred ponies in comparison with the unbroken and bellowing stallions from Maranello.

Ferrari built GT cars that were virtually road-going racers – you could buy one and straightaway enter it for the Mille Miglia, Tour de France or any one of the many GT races that took place in Europe, with some chance of success. True, you could also enter an Aston Martin DB2/4, but you'd be wasting your time.

Ferrari was aiming his Testa Rossas mainly at customers in the USA, far from factory help, so they had to be simple and easy to maintain, which precluded such things as spaceframe chassis, fuel injection and rear-mounted transaxles. And, as always, his cars were built to last, which would not, alas, prove true of Aston Martin.

In the first week in December, Officine Maserati announced its withdrawal from International racing. This was not unexpected, following the loss of three cars in the recent Venezuelan GP and the FIA's announcement of a new three-litre limit for the sportscar Championship.

The week before the Testa Rossa had been shown to the press, the FIA published its racing calendar which showed that there were eight events scheduled to count for the 1958 sportscar Championship: the Buenos Aires 1,000 Kms; the Sebring 12 Hours; the Mille Miglia; the Nürburgring 1,000 Kms; the Le Mans 24 Hours; the GP of Sweden; the Tourist Trophy; and the GP of Caracas. Within weeks the Mille Miglia would be withdrawn, and the GPs of Sweden and Caracas would also fall by the wayside before the year was out.

The points system was as follows: 1st – 8pts; 2nd – 6pts; 3rd – 4pts; 4th – 3pts; 5th – 2pts; 6th – 1pt.

The opening races in South and North America were but two months apart and, mindful of their painful attempt to compete in both four years earlier, Aston Martin elected to give Buenos Aires a miss, preferring to concentrate on preparing two cars for Sebring, with an eye on American sales of the DB2/4.

As no works specification Ferraris had yet been constructed a brand-new customer car, 0716, was sent to Buenos Aires with the revamped 0666 and 0704 to complete the team.

Two other Testa Rossas were entered for the race – 0714, which had been purchased by a Venezuelan, Piero Drogo, who would have Sergio González as his co-driver – and John von Neumann had his car, 1710, flown down from Los Angeles for him to drive with Wolfgang Seidel.

The sad demise of the Maserati works team meant that several very fine drivers were looking for work. Fangio – now 47 years old – was talking of retirement, but could not resist racing in front of his home crowd once more. Twice more, as it turned out, for he drove a 250F Maserati in the Argentine GP a week before the 1,000 Kms and finished fourth. For the sportscar race he teamed up with Francesco Godia, who had just taken delivery of a brand-new Maserati 300S.

Stirling Moss and Jean Behra were recruited to drive a similar car belonging to Scuderia Sudamericana, but it broke its crankshaft in practice and Porsche Team Manager Huschke von Hanstein was very happy to lend them one of the latest 1.6-litre cars. A 1.5-litre works Porsche was in the hands of Edgar Barth and local man Roberto Mières.

The works Ferraris were to be driven by Peter Collins/Phil Hill (0704), Mike Hawthorn/Luigi Musso (0666) and Taffy von Trips/Olivier Gendebien (0716). Team Manager Tavoni had problems with Hawthorn and Musso in practice. Mike was suffering from severe sunburn on his legs (the result of a day trip to Punta del Este beach in Uruguay with Peter and Louise Collins) and did not want to drive at all. When Tavoni insisted he turn up for practice, he found he could barely get his

but next time round he tried to take Collins in what was an impossible manoeuvre – even for Fangio – and the Maserati went flying off the road and struck a fence. The front bodywork was badly damaged and the Old Man made for the pits for a five-minute stop. When Godia saw the damage to his brand-new racer he is reported to have told Fangio that he could have done that himself, without being World Champion! Juan Manuel rejoined the race, but was forced to retire after 26 laps.

Collins and von Trips now led handily, but Stirling Moss was doing incredible things with the 1.6-litre Porsche, and when von Trips suffered a blown tyre, suddenly Moss was in second place. Taffy eventually made up the difference, however, and at half-distance Collins and Phil Hill were in a very secure lead and Gendebien – now

Left: Peter Collins makes a fast getaway in TR 0704 at the start of the Buenos Aires 1000 Kms. Fangio is in Godia's Maserati 300S (12); Musso is in TR 0716 (6); John von Neumann in TR 0710 (8) von Trips in TR 0666 and Drogo in TR 0714 (26). Below: Collins leads von Trips and Drogo into the hairpin on the opening lap.

large frame in the car, so small was the cockpit.

Musso was throwing his weight around somewhat, well aware that he was the only Italian driver in a Ferrari team full of foreigners. When the de Dion rear axle of the original prototype gave trouble Luigi insisted on driving 0704, but Collins and Hill were already assigned to this and refused to give it up. Eventually von Trips was paired with Hawthorn in 0666, and Musso grudgingly agreed to drive the new, solid rear axle car with Olivier Gendebien.

Peter Collins was the current holder of the lap record for the 5.8-mile circuit, having set a time of 3 mins 26.7 secs (102.5mph) with the 4.9-litre 410S Ferrari in 1956. This came under threat in practice as Phil Hill set the fastest time, with 3' 27.5", followed by Fangio – 3' 28.2" and Musso 3'28.3". Sixth fastest was the amazing Moss, who recorded 3' 34.0" with the little Porsche.

At the Le Mans start Collins made a splendid getaway, followed by von Trips, but there was drama on the very first corner, when Musso collided with the GT Ferrari of Maurice Trintignant (who was busy avoiding a spinning car) and bounced onto a curb, which broke the Testa Rossa's left steering arm. A furious Musso stomped back to the pits, where his co-driver, Olivier Gendebien, was now without a drive. As Mike Hawthorn recalled in *Champion Year*: 'Like a flash the Boy Scout instinct always latent in Hawthorn sprang to the fore. "Why not let Gendebien take my place," I said to Tavoni, "and he can drive with Taffy."'

Meanwhile Fangio was going like the clappers, passing von Trips and chasing after Collins. On his first flying lap he set a new, three-litre record with a time of 3' 29.1",

in von Trips' car instead of Hawthorn – was second and getting away from Moss.

However, when Olivier finished his stint it was Musso who took over the wheel, but before he could get back in the race the Porsche – now with Jean Behra driving – had passed the Ferrari. Luigi soon put this right and was back in second spot when Behra stopped to return the Porsche to Moss. But later, while Musso was handing the Ferrari back – to von Trips this time – Moss regained second place.

The crowd was loving this, but Taffy was not having any of it and clawed his way back to be right behind Moss as Phil Hill – one lap ahead – rejoined the race after taking over from Collins for the final stint. Von Trips and Hill both got by Stirling, and Phil rode shotgun for Taffy, setting a new absolute lap record for sportscars on lap 94 with a time of 3' 25.9" and preventing Moss from getting at his team-mate before they finally took the chequered flag. It was a superb one-two for the new works Ferraris, and the Drogo/González Testa Rossa was fourth (the von Neumann car had retired after only nine laps with a broken rear axle), but the spectators reserved their loudest cheers for Stirling Moss, who had taken the fight to the bigger cars throughout the race.

For Phil Hill the victory was sweet, of course, but he looks back on those early Testa Rossas with a grumpy lack of affection.

"I was very fond of the big, 335S Ferraris of 1957 and I didn't like little-engined cars at all. I remembered the little Testa Rossas of 1956 – the two-litre cars we were stuck with at Monza and the 2.5-litre ones at Le Mans – and I deplored them , so I wasn't at all happy about the new three-litre limit for sportscars in 1958. I didn't like the cutaway fenders on the early TRs at all – I thought it looked unfinished and gimmicky."

Above: Peter Collins drives the TR 250 to its first victory.
Left: smile, darn yer, smile! In marked contrast to Tony Brooks and Noel Cunningham-Reid after their Nürburgring victory (p 51), Phil Hill and Peter Collins don't seem at all happy with their Buenos Aires win.

CHAPTER ELEVEN

First Blood to Ferrari

The 12 Hours of Sebring

In February 1958 Aston Martin's chances of success in the Championship were given an enormous boost when Stirling Moss joined the team. Unquestionably the finest sportscar racer in the world, Stirling had first brought his remarkable skills to Astons in 1956, when he had persuaded the ageing DB3S to perform the odd miracle or two. The following year he had been deeply impressed by the winning performance of the DBR1 at the Nürburgring and so, when Maserati were forced to withdraw from racing, Stirling called John Wyer. His first race for the team was to be at Sebring where he had put up one of his great 3S drives in 1956.

Roy Salvadori and Tony Brooks had signed with Astons again, and Carroll Shelby was welcomed back into the team after an absence of three years (apart from Sebring in 1956). Les Leston had decided to quite big-time racing and concentrate on his burgeoning accessory business, and Noel Cunningham-Reid had also decided to call it a day.

"After my success at the Ring with Tony (and a few other drives) several teams wanted to sign me for 1958." he recalls, "I had a long think about it and decided that – at the age of 27 – there were many things I wanted to do outside racing. It was not

Moss is impatient to rejoin the race, but Reg Parnell holds him back while mechanic Bill James removes the jack.

Left: Gendebien's Ferrari rides up the back of Scott-Brown's Lister-Jaguar, fortunately without injury to the very popular Archie.

Opposite: Roy Salvadori (DBR1/1) enjoying his great dice with Mike Hawthorn (TR 0728).

a great passion for me (I had got into it by accident) and I didn't honestly believe that I could become World Champion, I wasn't prepared to push myself to the 10 tenths and 11 tenths that Champions have to do.

"Also, I had been racing since 1955 and I counted up the number of people I had known who had been killed, and there were 16. I decided it was time to get out."

Astons prepared two cars for Sebring, both fitted with the new 95° cylinder head, and Reg Parnell put Salvadori and Shelby in DBR1/1 and Moss and Brooks in DBR1/2. A third car was now under construction.

As usual Scuderia Ferrari sent a three-car team, made up of 'old faithful' 0704 for Collins and Hill again and two brand-new left-hand-drive cars (0726 and 0728), all three fitted with four-speed transaxles and de Dion rear ends. The new machines were to be driven by Luigi Musso/Olivier Gendebien and Mike Hawthorn/Taffy von Trips. The car Musso had crashed in Buenos Aires (0716) was sold to an Italian amateur driver in May and the first prototype (0666) was retained at the factory. There were three customer 250TRs for von Neumann/Ginther (1710); Martin/Flynn (0730) and Hugus/Fitch (0732).

Ecurie Ecosse were present with two three-litre D-types for Ivor Bueb/Ninian Sanderson and Ron Flockhart/Masten Gregory, and Briggs Cunningham had bought two Lister-Jaguars which were in the hands of Archie Scott-Brown/Walt Hansgen and Ed Crawford/Pat O'Connor.

Practice marked the first time that the new Testa Rossas and the DBR1 Astons had been on a track together and both teams were keen to see who could do what. Even with the 95° heads, the Astons were still some 50bhp shy of the Ferraris, but were expected to make up for that in braking and road-holding.

It soon became very clear that the FIA's three-litre limit was having none of its desired effect of keeping speeds down. The Sebring lap record stood to Jean Behra who, the previous year had taken his 450S Maserati round in 3 mins 24.5 secs, yet in the first day's practice session Moss and DBR1/2 reduced this to 3' 23.6". Next day Mike Hawthorn and Testa Rossa 0728 recorded 3' 21.0" and Peter Collins did 3' 23.4" with 0704. A tremendous race was in prospect.

For once Stirling Moss was not the first away from the Le Mans start, as Phil Hill got the jump on him, but at the end of the first lap Stirling came by five seconds ahead of Mike Hawthorn, and after five laps his lead was an impressive 16 secs. On the previous tour Archie Scott-Brown's Lister-Jaguar had an unfortunate coming-together with Olivier Gendebien's Testa Rossa, as Olivier recalled : "Archie's engine seized when I was right behind him and the Ferrari rode up on the back of the Lister. I got out and found that my left front wheel had hit his helmet, but he was not hurt so I got back in the car and reversed it off the Lister. I drove back to the pits and after losing only a lap I was able to rejoin the race."

After one hour Moss was over a minute and a half ahead of Roy Salvadori and Mike Hawthorn, who were having a great battle. Phil Hill was fourth and followed by two more Ferraris: those of John Fitch and Olivier Gendebien. Half an hour later Moss had increased his lead to two minutes, and Hill had joined battle with Salvadori and Hawthorn, the three cars passing and repassing frequently.

"It was a truly great dice," remembers Roy. "The Aston was vastly superior to the Testa Rossas through the twisty sections and on braking. I was thoroughly enjoying myself – it was so lovely to nail them in the corners, for that's where the Aston made you king. But when we came to a straight, they were off!"

Stirling covered his 31st lap in 3' 20.8", a remarkable new record. Four laps later, just as he was due to hand over to Tony Brooks, a rear tyre burst and he drove in

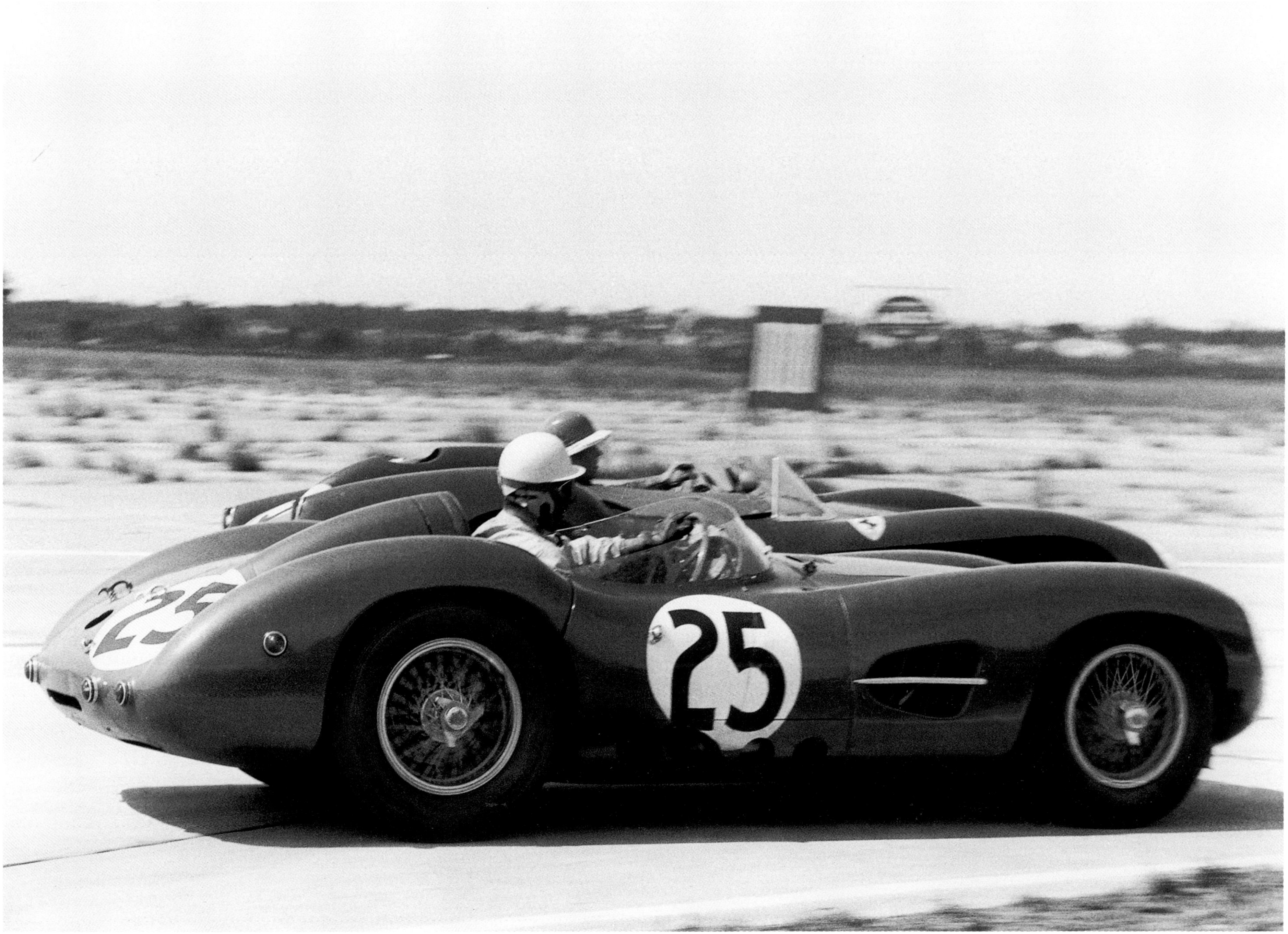
25
25

on the flat, but Brooks was able to rejoin the race without losing the lead. Meanwhile Carroll Shelby had taken over DBR1/1 from Roy Salvadori and was in third place, but 20 laps later he was back in the pits complaining of problems with gear selection. The Aston was stationary for almost an hour while the mechanics struggled to effect repairs.

Carroll did go out again, but after just four hours and forty minutes of the race he pulled in to retire. For once the Aston's five-speed transaxle was not to blame. Shelby's gear selection problems were caused by a broken chassis where the rear cross tube was bolted to the frame – and this had displaced the gearbox. On DBR1/2 the cross tube had been welded, providing greater rigidity, and DBR1/1's chassis was later modified.

Tony Brooks was still in the lead and stayed there until handing back to Moss on lap 69. The Aston was now stationary for 3' 27", while the rear wheels and all brake pads were changed.

Brakes took a terrible beating at Sebring, and although the Astons with their Girling discs could always out-brake the drum-braked Ferraris, Enzo Ferrari could see no good reason for fitting discs to his cars. This was incomprehensible to most of his drivers, especially Collins and Hawthorn, who had experienced the efficacy of discs with Jaguar, Aston Martin and Vanwall. However, in racing disc brakes were barely five years old and had yet to be developed to the point where they could go through a race such as Sebring without a change of pads.

In 1956 Astons had changed the front pads on both their DB3S cars during the race, the first attempt taking 7 mins 17 secs and the second 5' 45". This was a lot of time to make up, a fact which had not gone unnoticed by Enzo Ferrari who clearly would rather take his chances with drums which had served him very well all these years. And besides, if he fitted discs to his racing cars, his customers would expect to find them on their Ferraris too. However, under pressure from Peter Collins and Mike Hawthorn disc brake technology was soon catch up with him.

Opposite: Phil Hill joins in the fun, forcing TR 0704 betwen Roy and Mike.

Right: Phil waits to take over from Peter Collins for his second stint in TR 0704 as mechanics change wheels.

When Stirling Moss rejoined the race, he was in second place, 1' 18" behind the Ferrari of Peter Collins, who had taken over from Phil Hill. During the next 20 laps Moss once again showed why he was so invaluable to any team, reducing the deficit to 14 seconds, despite the fact that the Aston's bonnet flew off on lap 83, damaging the windscreen and hitting him on the helmet. He continued at unabated speed until lap 90, when the gearbox gave up due to the failure of the transmission input gears.

He and Brooks had led the race with some ease for four hours and, with one proviso, he was pretty impressed with the Aston, as he recalls:

"Sebring was a pretty tough circuit and I found the Aston to be very good on those rough roads. It had excellent brakes, and you could throw it around very easily, which was useful on an aerodrome circuit. I'd done one lap in 3' 20.8", which showed that the car had tremendous potential, but it was let down by that bloody awful gearbox!"

The departure of the second Aston left Ferraris in the first four places: Collins/Hill; Hawthorn/von Trips; Musso/Gendebien; and von Neumann/Ginther. With no Astons left to fight, Collins and von Trips decided to battle among themselves, to the despair of Team Manager Tavoni, who was only too aware that the brakes on both cars were fading fast.

Not long after darkness had settled over Sebring, Mike Hawthorn arrived at his pit with no lights on the Ferrari. After a prolonged stop the car was retired and the reason given was 'transmission trouble'. Apparently it did, indeed, have only one gear left (top), but also the generator had burnt out. This moved the von Neumann/Ginther Testa Rossa up into third place, but not for long, as the rear axle broke, just as it had in Buenos Aires, and their fine drive was over.

So Peter Collins and Phil Hill scored their third successive victory, and Testa Rossa 0704 its second. Remarkably, the 3-litre car had completed two laps more than the Fangio/Behra 4.5-litre Maserati had the year before. Collins drove to the Ferrari pit to collect his co-driver.

"I jumped into the car as Peter drove into victory lane," recalls Hill, "and we were both shouting, 'No brakes! No brakes!' as we were driving up on to the winner's platform. The car had no brakes left at all, and we expected to go right over the other side!"

The Musso/Gendebien Testa Rossa was second (also brakeless), and third was the 1.6-litre Porsche of Harry Schell/Wolfgang Seidel – another superb performance by the little car from Stuttgart.

So Enzo Ferrari's 'old-fashioned' Testa Rossas won this first battle with Aston Martin and had now finished first and second in the opening two rounds of the Championship, whereas Astons hadn't a point to their name.

85

1958

CHAPTER TWELVE

Testa Rossa Supreme

The Targa Florio

As expected, the Mille Miglia had been struck off the list of 1958 Championship events, which left Italy without one for the first time. This was unthinkable, of course, and Count Vincenzo Florio, founder of the great race in Sicily which bore his name, made strenuous efforts to get the event reinstated in the Championship. He succeeded, and in the first week in April it was announced that the 52nd Targa Florio would be run on May 11.

Stirling Moss had been so impressed by the handling of the DBR1 Aston at Sebring that he thought it could do really well in Sicily, so he asked John Wyer and Reg Parnell to let him have a car for the event.

Aston Martin had absolutely no experience of the Targa and were none too keen initially, as the FIA had announced it as a Championship race at only a month's notice and the Competitions Department at Feltham was busy preparing three cars for the Nürburgring 1,000 Kms. However, Moss could be very persuasive and so the brand-new DBR1/3 was prepared for him to race with Tony Brooks.

A month's notice was no problem for Ferrari, and the Scuderia sent four Testa Rossas. Once again 0704 was given to Peter Collins/Phil Hill; 0726 was assigned to Luigi Musso/Olivier Gendebien; 0728 went to Mike Hawthorn/Taffy von Trips, and the first prototype, 0666, was given to Wolfgang Seidel and Gino Munaron. This car was equipped with six twin-choke Solex carburettors which reportedly helped to increase the V12's power output to 330bhp.

Although the damage to 0726 caused by Gendebien's coming-together with Scott-Brown's Lister-Jaguar at Sebring had been minimal, this car was rebodied in time for the Targa, Scaglietti replacing his distinctive cutaway styling with a normal, envelope body.

Porsche had already shown that they were a force to be reckoned with this season and were likely to be in their element on the rough and twisty roads of the Targa's so-called Little Madonie circuit, which comprised more than 700 corners in its 72km lap. The Stuttgart concern brought along its latest spaceframe RSK model and a Spyder RS, the two cars to be shared between three drivers, Jean Behra, Edgar Barth and Giorgio Scarlatti. A third car was a Carrera coupé with Spyder engine, to be driven by Huschke von Hanstein and a local man named Pucci. Also present were the very fast works 1.5-litre OSCAs of Colin Davis/de Tomaso and Mantovani/Scarfiotti.

The Targa had last been a Championship event in 1955, when Stirling Moss and Peter Collins won in a Mercedes-Benz 300SLR. Then the race had been run over 13 laps, but for 1958 Count Vincenzo Florio made his great race even longer, announcing that it would be of just over 1,000kms, which meant 14 laps – more than 10 hours racing, even for the fastest cars.

There was no official practice, as such, for it was impossible to close the roads except on race day. As Bernard Cahier explained in *Road & Track*: 'The competitors have to learn this difficult circuit on the open roads with hundreds of scooters, cars, trucks and the gaily painted Sicilian chariots, cows, sheep, mules and goats, not to mention chickens, cats and dogs ... As usual, the training was done in the very relaxed Targa manner, the drivers interrupting it with pleasant luncheons and siestas on the beach.'

Ferrari sent a 290MM over for the week before the race and by the time all the drivers had had a go the poor thing had completed some 40 laps and was looking very second-hand indeed. Remarkably it suffered no mechanical problems at all.

Leaving the DBR1 under the eye of a local cop, Reg Parnell and mechanics John King and Eric Hind take a look at TR 0704 while Phil Hill talks to journalist Tommy Wisdom: Peter and Louise Collins (extreme left) wander over to see what they are up to.

spend a lot of time cornering on their door handles all round Sicily over the next few days.

In order to save their lone DBR1 for the race Aston Martin took DBR2/1 along for practice, chartering a York freighter to fly the two cars, spares and 12 personnel from Stansted Airport to Trapani in Sicily on May 6.

Tony Brooks got his first look at the circuit when Peter Collins offered to drive him round in the Fiat. "At least, Peter said it was the circuit," recalls Tony, "but by now I was wide awake to legpulls from my ex-Aston team-mate and I wasn't going to be taken in this time. When he'd finished I said, 'Thanks Pete, very funny. Now you've taken me round the goat-tracks will you please show me the circuit?' But it *was* the circuit! Once I realised that Peter wasn't having me on I got down to learning my way around in earnest and flogged the little Fiat to death."

Above: street racers! The Ferrari team lined up on a Sicilian street: 98 is 0704 for Peter Collins/Phil Hill; 106 is the winning 0726 of Luigi Musso/Olivier Gendebien; 104 is 0666 for Wolfgang Seidel/Gino Munaron and 102 is 0728, for Mike Hawthorn/Taffy von Trips.

Right: Aston Martin mechanics Eric Hind (left) and John King find something amusing as Reg Parnell brings DBR1/3 up to the start.

However, Cahier noted that after practice 'it had the best score of all the practice cars, having eliminated one Fiat 600 (Gendebien), one scooter (Hill) and one dog (von Trips). Moss had really been beaten in this department, scoring only a chicken.'

Of course the drivers did not just use the racers for practice. The staff at Hertz car rental in Palermo could only smile politely as they handed over their humble Fiat 1100s to 'tourists' with such illustrious names as Moss, Brooks, Musso, Collins and Hawthorn, surely knowing full well that their innocent little saloons were going to

Brooks did 15 or 16 laps in it and learned the 72km circuit sufficiently well to record a time of just over 47 minutes in the DBR1, he and Moss being allowed just a lap apiece in that. Stirling recorded 46' 14" (which included two stops for traffic) and then complained that the carburation was too rich. This was due to the altitude and poor-quality fuel, so the 70 pump jets were replaced by the 45 pump jets from the R2 and this improved the R1's acceleration out of corners.

The R2 was used sparingly too, but Stirling (with his wife, Katie, aboard) did two laps in among the daily traffic in 47 mins 34 secs and 46' 26" – pretty damn quick when you consider that he held the lap record in the 300SLR with a time of 43' 07."

Stirling and Tony were both very keen to do well in the race and practised hard, in contrast to Mike Hawthorn and Peter Collins, who did not take things quite so seriously. As Denis Jenkinson wrote in *Motor Sport*, 'The Anglo-Saxon speaking element in the Ferrari team seemed to take a very childish view of the race, which was obviously more difficult and harder work than they have been used to.'

This rebuke, it seems, was largely aimed at Mike Hawthorn, who had never raced in the Targa before and was more concerned with his challenge for the Drivers' World Championship than sportscar racing. He had also decided to retire at the end of the year and, as far as he was concerned, the Targa was just another race to be done with as quickly as possible.

As he explained in *Champion Year*, 'much as I admire Count Florio, I do not care for his circuit; I can muster no enthusiasm for rushing up and down mountains with hairpins all over the place and sheer drops on one side . . . The more I went round the circuit the less I liked it.'

"He thought the whole thing was futile," recalls Phil Hill. "He did his share of practice, but he clearly wanted to be somewhere else, like on the beach with Peter, Louise, Taffy and me."

The start numbers were drawn by lot and Astons drew 100 for the DBR1, which set of with Moss at the wheel at 7.02am. The Testa Rossa of Collins/Hill (98) had started 40 seconds ahead of it and those of von Trips/Hawthorn (102) Seidel/Munaron (104) and Musso/Gendebien (106) followed right behind.

The first of the big cars to roar past the tribunes at the end of lap one was the Collins Ferrari, followed by those of Musso and von Trips. But where was Moss?

Mike Hawthorn in TR 0728, which has been battered (but not broken) by Taffy von Trips on the opening lap. Mike did not enjoy the Targa Florio at all.

He eventually appeared some three minutes overdue and in 10th place. He had made a rare mistake and hit a kilometre stone with the Aston's nearside rear wheel. He had stopped to change it at the auxiliary depot 23kms from the start and another 20kms further on had stopped again, this time to investigate a vibration at the rear of the car. He could find nothing wrong, however, so continued back to the pits, where it was discovered that the crankshaft vibration damper had sheared. This was removed and, almost 24 minutes later Moss re-entered the race.

Before the start, Mike Hawthorn had suggested to von Trips that if he was going to crash the Testa Rossa would he please make a good job of it so he – Mike – would not have to drive? Hawthorn was delighted to see his Ferrari complete the first lap with a very bent front wing, but not so happy when von Trips continued without stopping.

Meanwhile Luigi Musso led following an opening lap in 43 mins 56 secs, followed by Collins who had been 12 secs slower. In the next three places were, amazingly, three 1.5-litre cars, the OSCAs of Cabianca and Davis and the Porsche of Jean Behra. Sixth was von Trips, after his collision with a wall. Colin Davis then lapped in 45' 45" to move his OSCA into third place, only to clout a kilometre stone and retire.

1958

Stirling at speed in DBR1/3. He hit a kilometre stone on his first lap (note damage to the rear wing) and had to stop to change a wheel. The engine finally expired, but not before Stirling had shattered the lap record he had set in 1955 with the Mercedes 300SLR.

Making these times look distinctly pedestrian, however, was Stirling Moss who, from his pit stop, broke his own Mercedes lap record with a time of 43 minutes exactly. 'The Aston Martin was really going now,' wrote Denis Jenkinson, 'timed at 233kph/145mph along the brief straight, and Moss came through the curves by the pits right on the limit in a wonderful series of slides.

'Moss was still a long way behind on the road, of course,' continued Jenks, 'but he was driving with that inspired brilliance he can show when he is "up against the odds". Before he arrived at the end of lap three Scarlatti had handed the RS Porsche over to Barth and Collins had given over to Hill and then Moss appeared, taking the pit curve in one long seemingly uncontrollable slide and roaring off up into the mountains again on lap four with dust and gravel flying in all directions. A new lap record came as no surprise at all, but the time was staggering – 42 mins 19.6 secs – almost a minute faster than Musso and 47 seconds faster than the 300SLR record.'

Despite a spin, his next lap was even faster 42 mins 17.5 secs – but sadly, this remarkable performance was too much for the Aston's gearbox (surprise) and halfway round his fifth lap Stirling stopped at the auxiliary depot and retired. After all his hard work with the Fiat 1100 Tony Brooks never got to drive in the race. To add insult to injury, he had to stay in the pits for the rest of the day, because once you were there, you could not get out until the race was over.

On lap six there was consternation in the Ferrari pit when Phil Hill failed to appear on time. "I slid off into a ditch and bent a wheel." he recalls. "I never really had the right approach to the Targa, which was that you had to slow down a tiny bit from absolutely flat out, or the gravel and stuff on the road was going to get you."

In fact, Hill had bent both wheels on one side of the Testa Rossa and by the time he had changed the front, driven to the Ferrari depot and had a new rear fitted and then returned to the pits the Ferrari was down to sixth place. The order was now Musso/Gendebien, Hawthorn/von Trips, the Porsche of Behra/Scarlatti, the OSCA of Cabianca and the Ferrari of Seidel/Munaron.

On lap eight Gendebien, Hawthorn and Munaron handed their Ferraris back to Musso, von Trips and Seidel, and Behra took over the RS Porsche from Scarlatti. The Frenchman proceeded to go faster and faster and completed his eleventh lap in 44 mins 32 secs, but despite this he could make up no ground on von Trips.

It was then Musso's turn to frighten Ferrari, by being four minutes late at the end of lap 11. When he did arrive he was waving both hands in the air – no brakes! The

TESTA ROSSA SUPREME

Peter Collins and Phil Hill finished fourth in 0704 and that was the end of their three-race winning streak. Ferrari just failed to bring all four works cars home as 0666 expired with a broken sump when in fourth place after Wolfgang Seidel went off the road on the last lap.

So once again the Testa Rossas had emerged triumphant, and from a brutally tough event. With three wins in three events, the Scuderia now had 24 Championship points to Porsche's 14. Aston Martin still had zero.

And once again Stirling Moss had shown that the DBR1 was the fastest three-litre car in the world – and the most fragile. It was good to see Astons take on a race such as the Targa, but pitting just one car against the might of Ferrari and Porsche was really a wasted effort.

Testa Rossa was eventually brought to a halt by sheer weight of numbers and then pushed back to its pit, where it was discovered that the brake-fluid reservoir was empty. It was refilled and, as no leaks were found, Olivier Gendebien was sent back into the race, his lead reduced to a mere eight minutes over team-mate von Trips.

Meanwhile Jean Behra was still flying and covered lap 12 in 44 mins 25 secs, which brought him to within one and a half minutes of von Trips who then stopped to hand 0728 over to Hawthorn for the final stint, but Behra was driving through to the finish and did his next lap in 44' 29", whereas Hawthorn's time was 46' 34", so the Porsche was now in second place. Hawthorn put aside his dislike of the Targa for that final lap, which he completed in a creditable 44' 34", but Behra recorded an extraordinary 44' 17" in the little Porsche and secured second place for the Stuttgart concern. The French champion had driven 10 of the 14 laps and was convinced that, had he been partnered by Moss, as in Buenos Aires, they would have won.

Almost unnoticed in this excitement, Olivier Gendebien brought Testa Rossa 0726 home to victory. He and Luigi Musso – both road-racers par excellence – had driven superbly and had led from start to finish, the first time ever in the Targa.

Left: Taffy von Trips about to take 0728 back into the race. He and Hawthorn finished third. Below: Luigi Musso on his way to victory with 0726. The car's original cutaway bodywork had been replaced with this new TR58 envelope body following Olivier Gendebien's accident at Sebring.

91

Stirling Moss (DBR1/3) is about to lap team-mate Tony Brooks (DBR1/2) at Schwalbenschwanz after the latter had lost half a lap due to an unexplained spin on lap two. He was not helped, either, by co-driver Stuart Lewis-Evans, who was unwell and seriously off the pace.

CHAPTER THIRTEEN

Meister Moss

The Nürburgring 1000 kms

The red cars from Maranello were on a roll, having won all three Championship races to date. Enzo Ferrari could have packed his Testa Rossas away and forgotten about the remaining three races – the Nürburgring 1,000 Kms, Le Mans and the Tourist Trophy – for even if Aston Martin or Porsche were to win all three, Ferrari would lose the title only if they failed to score a single point. However, it was success in the Championship races – especially the 24 Hours of Le Mans – which sold the production Ferraris, so Enzo kept on racing.

Ferrari had won the inaugural Nürburgring 1,000 Kms race in 1953 but had failed ever since, so he was very keen to score another victory on this very demanding circuit. Four Testa Rossas were dispatched to Germany, where he was determined to lock up the World Championship with his fourth win of the season.

Aston Martin were equally determined to repeat their shock victory of the previous year and with Stirling Moss now on the team as well as Tony Brooks they had a very real chance of doing just that. Three DBR1s were prepared for the race.

Porsche had shown repeatedly that their 1.5-litre cars were very nearly a match for the three-litre machines from Maranello and Feltham and on the tortuous Nürburgring – their home ground – they were clearly in with a chance of outright victory. Three RSK cars were sent from Stuttgart.

1958

Sergio Scaglietti's cutaway bodywork was being phased out on the works TRs in favour of the normal 'envelope' style first used on 0726 in the Targa Florio. To differentiate them from the customer 250TRs, the new factory racers were given the designation TR58. Only one works car – the second prototype 0704 – retained the cutaway bodywork at the Ring. The other cars were 0726, 0728 and 0746, which had run as a V6, three-litre Dino at Silverstone in May. The V6 had been replaced with a V12 and the car was fitted with F1 drum brakes at the front. All four Testa Rossas had de Dion rear suspension and four-speed transaxle. The Solex carburettors fitted to 0726 for the Targa Florio had been replaced by twin-choke Webers, which were fed from an air intake at the front of the engine, whereas those on 0728 and 0746 had the intake at the rear.

The variations in body shape are explained by Mauro Forghieri, who joined the design staff at Scuderia Ferrari in 1959, aged 21.

Nose jobs: the Testa Rossas sported three types of bodywork at the Ring. Above left is Mike Hawthorn with 0704, in its original cutaway version and below left is Phil Hill in TR58 0726 with envelope body and the same, rectangular radiator intake and forward-mounted carburettor air intake as 0704. Below is Olivier Gendebien in TR58 0746, which also has a new, envelope body, but with an oval radiator intake and the carburettor air intake right up against the windscreen.

"Scaglietti's envelope body was much better than his cutaway version because it was a better shape. With the cutaway wings the airflow from inside was disturbing the air all down the side of the car.

"As far as the carburettor air intake was concerned, Ferrari had a continual problem with the Testa Rossa trying to get an equal amount of air to each pair of carburettors, which were very sensitive to ambient pressure. To begin with we had a very long intake with the entry at the front. We never got all the cylinders working in the same way, and we had severe carburation problems at the Ring, where driveability at low revs is so important. When you have an air intake that doesn't give you the same pressure on every carburettor, you are going to have an engine that doesn't run cleanly.

"For this reason we reversed the intake on some cars, putting the air entry very close to the windscreen to get the pressure from the base of the screen, but it only partially solved the problem. The front entry still gave us better torque at low revs, but lost out at high speed because of the ram effect."

Aston Martin missed the first day of practice (Thursday), their departure from Feltham delayed by work on the the three cars' transaxle units, following the problems which had sidelined Stirling Moss in the Targa Florio. DBR2/1 was also taken as a practice car and Carroll Shelby drove it to Germany.

Although Stuart Lewis-Evans' performance in the DBR1 at Silverstone the previous September had not impressed Reg Parnell, he was signed up for the remaining three races, which meant that Aston Martin now had the entire Vanwall Grand Prix team – Moss, Brooks and Lewis-Evans – on its books. Stuart was undoubtedly shaping up to be a fine Grand Prix driver, but his stamina over longer distances was to prove suspect.

In common with many others, Parnell was convinced that the Australian Jack Brabham was a 'coming man' and invited him to join the team and partner Moss at the Nürburgring – a daunting task for any driver, let alone one with Brabham's limited sportscar experience.

"The regulations wouldn't allow anyone to drive for more than three hours without a break," recalls Jack, "so Astons wanted someone to look after the car for a few laps without falling off while Stirling took a breather. I was threatened with big trouble if I over-revved the car or hurt it in any way, but I wouldn't have dared! I just had to drive the DBR1 around and keep it on the road so Moss could do the racing.

"I had never sat in the car until I got to the Ring and I was only allowed a total of six laps during the two practice sessions. The DBR1 was a fantastic car – the best

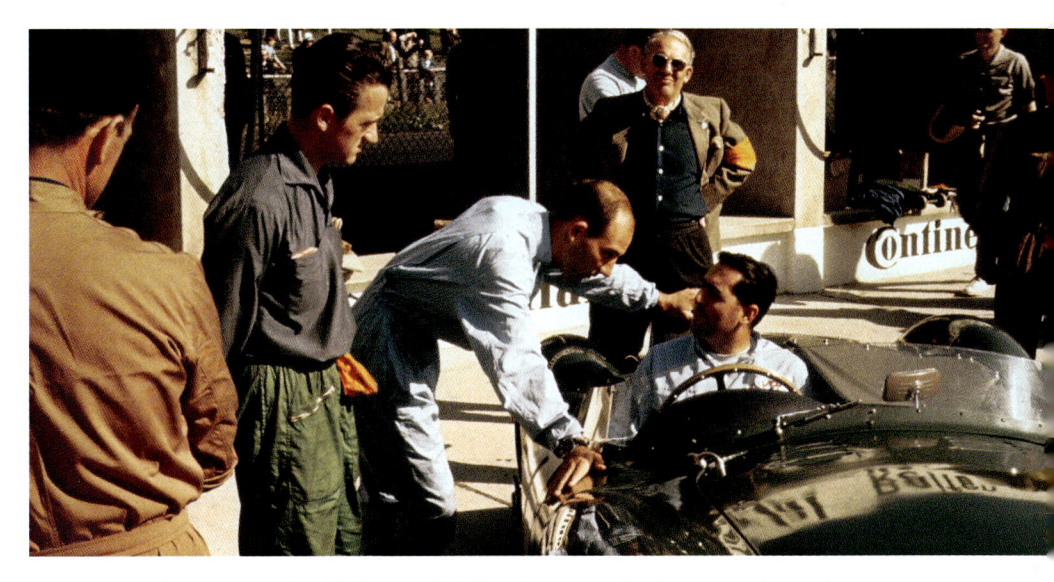

Watched by Patron David Brown, Stirling has a word with Astons' new boy Jack Brabham during practice.

sportscar there was in those days – and the team was good too. It was well run, and the cars were always well presented. I liked the Ring, which was a real challenge for a driver and quite dangerous. When I look back at the cars we drove and the things we used to do on that circuit, it's incredible that so many of us survived. The thing we had in our favour was that sex was safe in those days, which helped Moss no end!"

Brabham had raced a Formula 2 Cooper at the Ring in the previous year's German GP, when he had managed a lap of 10 mins 18.8 secs in practice. Now in DBR1/3 he got down to 10' 19.0" in just four laps on the Friday and reduced this by a creditable nine seconds on the Saturday, making him faster than both Shelby (who had not seen the Ring before) and Lewis-Evans (who had).

Roy Salvadori managed 10' 03" in DBR1/1 (a 14-second improvement on his best 1957 time) and Shelby 10' 12", but the Aston was already in trouble with that wretched gearbox, which was continually slipping out of third gear. A new unit was fitted using a 3.5:1 rear axle.

Tony Brooks was partnered with Lewis-Evans in DBR1/2 and recorded a best time of 9' 52.8" on the Friday and then 9' 50.0" the following day. Lewis-Evans did just four laps on the Friday, his best being in 10' 17.0".

Out of luck were Roy Salvadori (left) and Jean Behra (below). The Aston was forced to retire with gear selector problems on lap 2, whereas the Porsche was in a magnificent third place overall when it was halted by a fractured valvespring cap.

In common with R1/2, DBR1/3 was equipped with a 3.38:1 rear axle ratio, but when Moss could 'only' record 9' 45.4" in his first practice session he asked Reg Parnell to drop the ratio to 3.62. Next day Stirling was dismayed to find that Reg, always worried about the R1's critical rev range, had only dropped it to 3.5:1. They had another chat, and Stirling got the ratio he wanted for the race.

The RSK Porsches were in the hands of Jean Behra, Edgar Barth, Giorgio Scarlatti, Harry Schell and Paul Frère, but Scarlatti wrote off one of them on the Friday and broke his arm. The engine from his car was put into an RS which Porsche had brought along and this was given to Richard von Frankenberg/Count Carel de Beaufort. Not surprisingly, Behra was fastest of all with the remarkable time of 9 mins 57.0 secs.

Enzo Ferrari kept his drivers in the dark as to who would be driving with whom, and they all tried all the cars. When practice was finally over, Romolo Tavoni reported to his boss in Maranello. The Old Man decided that they would be paired according to their practice times, which meant that triple winners Collins and Hill were separated. Peter kept his winning mount, the cutaway 0704, but was joined by Mike Hawthorn. Wolfgang Seidel and Gino Munaron were given 0728; 0746 went to Olivier Gendebien and Wolfgang von Trips; and Phil Hill was paired with Luigi Musso in 0726.

"I was very upset about not driving with Peter," says Phil. "We had been very successful and I never understood why Ferrari was always doing that – waiting until a couple of drivers made a good team and then splitting 'em."

Actually, the reason is probably not hard to find. The cult of driver personality always bugged Enzo, who regarded drivers as necessary baggage to be carried to victory by his wonderful machines. But when his cars did win, it was the drivers who got the publicity, and so he was perverse enough to split a successful team in order to prove his point – anyone could win in a Ferrari.

Mike Hawthorn had been fastest of all in practice, with a time of 9' 43.1", which was a remarkable improvement on the fastest lap of the 1957 race – 9' 49.8", set by Moss in the 4.5-litre Maserati. So Mike had pole position on the Le Mans grid with Testa Rossa 0704, and Stirling was beside him in DBR1/3 on 9' 45.6". Alongside him, however, was the Testa Rossa 0728 of Seidel/Munaron, credited with 9' 45.0",

Phil Hill (second from right) looks ruefully at 'his' TR 0704 in the Nürburgring's garage square.
He was not happy to learn that Enzo Ferrari had decided that he should no longer race this car with Peter Collins.

1958

Above: having jumped the start, Hawthorn leaps into his Ferrari fractionally ahead of Moss, but Stirling has the last laugh and is first away (opposite top).

Below: Mike made up for his bad start and completed his first lap in second place, ahead of Tony Brooks (DBR1).

despite the fact that both these drivers had had trouble cracking 10' 30"! The faster time had actually been set by Musso, but he and Hill were back in seventh place in the line-up with 0726. Brooks and Lewis-Evans were fourth in DBR1/2; von Trips and Gendebien fifth in 0746; and Behra and Barth were sixth with the RSK Porsche.

Stirling Moss was known as the King of the Le Mans start and was invariably the first to his car and – provided it would start – the first to get away. As the 10-second countdown towards 9am began, Mike Hawthorn decided to play a joke on Stirling and, as the count reached 'one', he ran like hell.

"You bastard, Hawthorn!" yelled Moss, who waited until zero before sprinting towards his Aston. By the time he reached his Ferrari, Mike was helpless with laughter and had trouble starting the car, getting away behind Moss, Brooks, Behra and Schell.

In practice Peter Collins had lapped within a 10th of a second of Mike's best time, and Stirling was well aware that Jack Brabham could not be expected to stay with Pete. He therefore set out to put as much time between himself and the Ferrari as possible before his first pitstop, which Reg Parnell had scheduled for the end of lap 10. The result was yet another example of the genius of Stirling Moss.

At the end of lap one the Aston rocketed past the pits to record a time of 10 mins 02 secs, 11 secs ahead of Hawthorn, who had recovered well from his joke start. Brooks was just one second behind Mike and was closely followed by von Trips, Salvadori, Behra and Willy Mairesse in the Ecurie Francorchamps Testa Rossa.

To the delight of the Aston Martin team Moss now proceeded to leave everyone for dead, setting a new lap record of 9' 47" on his second lap and reducing that to 9' 43" on his third. In fact this *Ringmeister* supreme broke his 1957 Maserati record of 9' 49.9" every lap until he stopped, as scheduled, on lap 10. It was a simply stunning performance which put several other very fine drivers in the shade.

The excitement in the Aston Martin pits was tempered by the fact that their other two cars were in trouble. On the opening lap Roy Salvadori found difficulty in selecting second gear and on lap two he came to a halt at the Karussell with no gears at all. By rocking the Aston to and fro he managed to find third and then drove slowly back to the pits, where it was discovered that the pin in the bottom gear selector fork had sheared. Exit one DBR1.

Also on lap two Tony Brooks had an uncharacteristic spin just before the Karussell and stopped. As he did so, the engine blew back, and a large sheet of flame from the DBR1's exhaust set fire to the driver's door. As if on request, a spectator appeared out of the woods armed with a hand fire extinguisher, doused the very blistered paintwork, and Brooks rejoined the race, now down in 14th position.

On the same lap Willy Mairesse in 0736 suffered a blown tyre and stopped on the circuit to change it before coming in for a new spare wheel, which dropped him to 51st and last place. In the next dozen laps the Belgian driver drove like one possessed (which many thought he was) and dragged the Testa Rossa up to 29th position before handing over to de Changy.

Below: Brooks comes to a halt in a haze of tyre smoke on the run-up to the Karussell after spinning the Aston on lap 2. He could not explain the spin, but several Aston drivers reported excessive oversteer on the DBR1s in this race.

Jack Brabham prepares to leap into the still moving Aston (which almost knocks over a mechanic) as Moss leaps out during their first pit stop, although 'pit slow' would be a more apt term. Reg Parnell (with megaphone) watches closely from the pit counter.

'Black Jack' adopts his well-known crouch in the Aston's cockpit. Not surprisingly, he was no match for Hawthorn and the Testa Rossa on the Ring.

By dint of some very fast motoring Brooks was back in sixth place when Moss came in at the end of lap 10. In *Autosport*, Stuart Seager reported, 'He handed over to Brabham in what must be one of the slickest driver changes ever; the car did not actually stop rolling as Stirling leapt out one side and Jack jumped in the other. Including the stop, I made the lap take but 10 mins 7.8 secs.'

Jack's lack of familiarity with both car and circuit now played into Hawthorn's hands. His standing lap took 10' 20", and as he crossed the line Mike was right on his tail, passing the Aston as they headed into the North Turn behind the pits. Pressing on now, Mike recorded 9' 45" and in two laps put one minute 10 seconds on Brabham who, on schedule, stopped at the end of lap 13.

This time all four wheels were changed, and the Aston was refuelled, von Trips in the Testa Rossa moving into second place briefly as Moss rejoined the race after a stop of 1 min 21 secs. As in the Targa Florio, it was now one Aston against four Ferraris, with the odds in the latter's favour, thanks to the superiority of Peter Collins over Jack Brabham and the known frailty of the DBR1's gearbox.

Hawthorn now had a two-minute lead but, just as he was preparing for his pit stop, the Ferrari threw a rear tread on the approach to Pflanzgarten. Mike drove on to the pits, still in the lead, but the mechanics had trouble in getting the jack under the car. Eventually Collins got away but, as he did, Moss went by into first place. Hawthorn was convinced that the burst tyre cost him and Peter the race and he may well have been right.

Drivers were now changing thick and fast: Barth took over the Porsche from Behra, who was in sixth place; Lewis-Evans took over DBR1/2 from Brooks; Phil Hill replaced Musso in 0726, and von Trips gave 0746 to Gendebien.

Porsche were unfortunate enough to lose the Behra/Barth car to a broken valvespring cap after 19 laps, and then it was Ferrari's turn for consternation as Phil Hill went missing. He had suffered the same fate as Hawthorn, but his burst tyre happened as he left the Karussell, so instead of continuing slowly to the pits he stopped at Höhe Acht and changed the wheel. However, the burst tyre was at the rear and the spare was a smaller front wheel, so Phil had a fun time driving back on rear wheels of a different size. And he was none too happy to be criticised for not driving straight back, as Hawthorn had done, his critics failing to understand that Höhe Acht is a lot further from the pits than Pflanzgarten.

At half-distance Moss was 2 mins 14 secs ahead of Collins. Gendebien was third,

Mike at speed in TR 0704, the only works Ferrari with the original cutaway bodywork in this race. He was convinced that he and Collins would have won, but for a burst tyre....

....which is seen, shredded, on the concrete as Pete jumps into the Ferrari after Mike had driven in from Pflanzgarten on the flat. Team Manager Romolo Tavoni stands on the pit counter (left) beside Hawthorn.

Brooks fourth, the von Frankenberg/de Beaufort Porsche an indecent fifth and the Gregory/Flockhart Ecosse Jaguar sixth.

On lap 24 Moss had a lead of 2' 24" as he handed over to Brabham for five laps. There was trouble again in the Aston camp as Lewis-Evans was not feeling well and covered the 27th lap in a tardy 11' 20", signalling that he was coming in next time round, one lap early. Brooks took over, the R1 still in fourth place. Also on lap 27 the Mairesse/de Changy Testa Rossa was forced out with a broken rear axle.

Meanwhile Peter Collins had been gaining on Jack Brabham who stopped after his five laps to hand over to Moss for the last time. As the Aston was being refuelled and having two new rear wheels fitted, Collins drew into the Ferrari pit, right behind the Aston and after 29 laps of the Nürburgring the first and second cars were separated by just a few feet of concrete. Moss got away first, of course, Hawthorn following shortly afterwards, with a broad grin and a two-fingered salute for Reg Parnell as he accelerated past the Aston Martin pit!

Stirling's heroic efforts early in the race should not be allowed completely to overshadow those of Masten Gregory, who had driven the wheels off his D-type and, in the process, done the unimaginable by getting the Ecosse car round in under 10 minutes – 9' 58", to be exact. (Consider this: in 1956 Mike Hawthorn's best time with the works Jaguar had been 10' 16".)

Unfortunately, earlier in the race Masten had hit a bank when avoiding a very slow Porsche and although he had stopped for repairs the front brake cooling had been affected. On lap 30 the near-side front disc seized, and he spun into retirement at the North Turn. It was a poor reward for a very fine drive.

Hawthorn was now valiantly chasing Moss, but the Aston was almost one and a half minutes ahead and the race was put completely out of Mike's reach on lap 34 when, in his efforts to reduce the deficit, he spun at the Little Karussell, and the Ferrari went nose-first into a ditch. Mike managed to heave it out with a fence-post, but by the time he got going again Stirling's lead was more than four minutes and, barring an accident, the race was won. He lapped team-mate Brooks on lap 36 and went serenely on his way.

Taffy von Trips was now third, and Tony Brooks fourth and closing, but on lap 41 he was pushed off the road by the Belgian-entered Peugeot 403 saloon of Dubois/Georges. Just what such a car was doing in a World Championship sportscar race is a good question, but there it was, in company with a Volvo 444.

1958

Above: Mike Hawthorn seems to be looking at something on the roadside as he takes the Ferrari through Flugplatz. Below: Moss has just passed him at Schwalbenschwanz and Mike waves the Behra/Barth Porsche through, too, as he heads back to the pits with that burst rear tyre.

Opposite: the magnificent Nürburgring afforded photographers many wonderful vantage points. Here Tony Brooks drifts DBR1/2 through the Hatzenbach curves towards Hocheichen, about 3 km from the start.

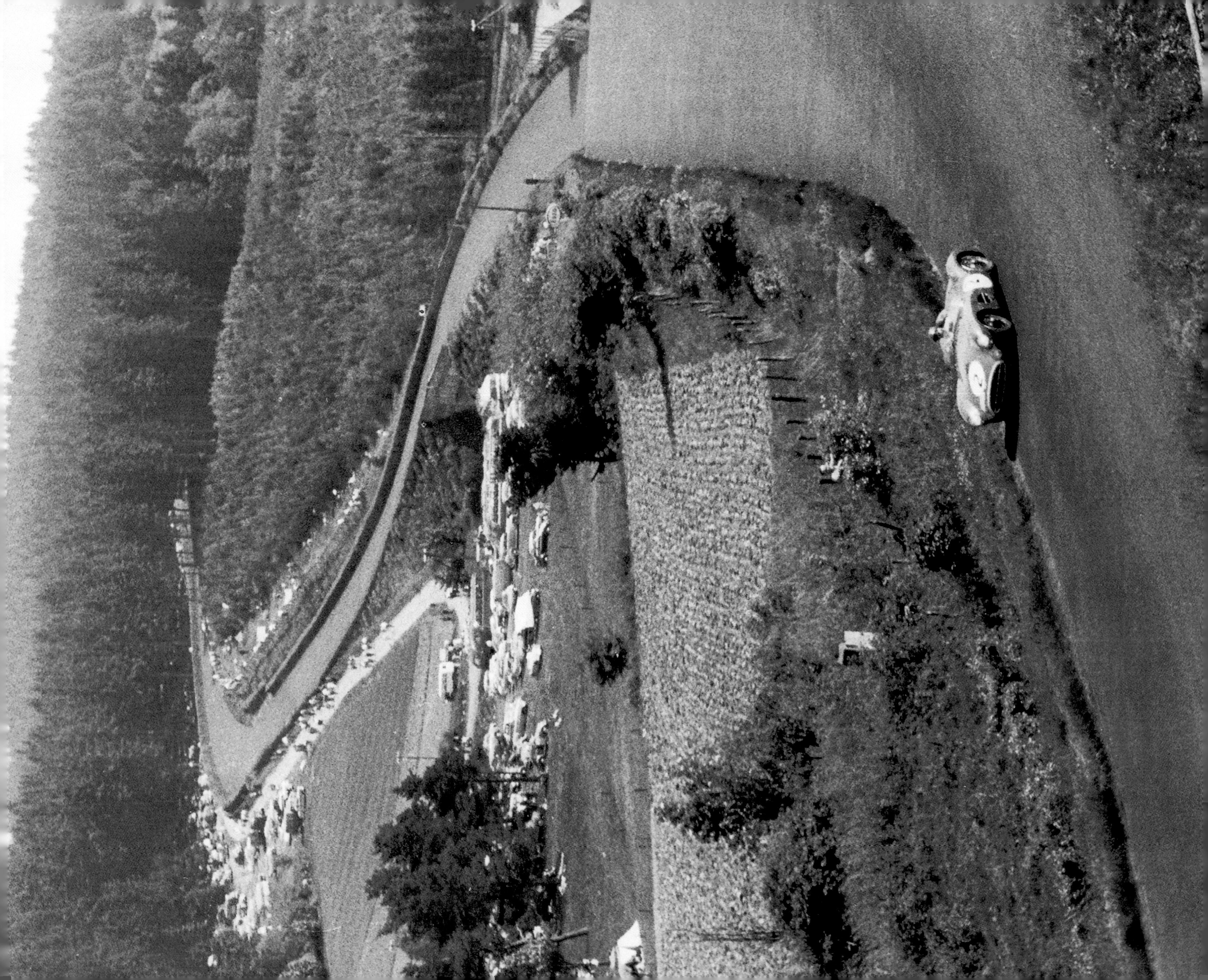

Peter Collins in the South Turn with TR 0704. He and Mike Hawthorn finished second.

"I was in the long left-hander after Flugplatz," Tony recalls, "leading to the sharp right-hander at Aremberg. There was a Peugeot saloon on the left, leaving me plenty of room to go by but, as I approached to overtake he started moving over. I was too committed to brake and drop back as I was doing about 5,000rpm in fifth – 130 or even 140mph – so I had no option but to brake and allow him to push me into the ditch. The Aston was undamaged, but the ditch was so deep I couldn't get it out."

It was later reported that the mild-mannered Mr Brooks was so angry with the Peugeot driver that he actually cursed him, but this was almost certainly a scurrilous rumour, probably put about by Hawthorn and Collins.

Astons' latest misfortune meant that the other works Testa Rossas of von Trips/Gendebien; Musso/Hill and Seidel/Munaron moved into third, fourth and fifth places and up into sixth came the Aston Martin DB3S of Graham and Peter Whitehead. The Kochert/Bauer Ferrari (0748) was battling for tenth place with the Schell/Frère Porsche and this was to end in tragedy. Instead of finishing the race as soon as the winner took the flag, the organisers insisted that all the classes covered the full distance, so when Moss completed his 44th lap, Erik Bauer's race was over, but Harry Schell (1.5-litre class) had to complete another lap and continued at racing speed. Caught up in his battle with Schell, Bauer did the same and went off the road just past Wippermann. He died of his injuries the next day.

Writing in *The Motor*, Rodney Walkerley praised Stirling Moss for 'a drive of superb virtuosity in which he personally was never led; in which he was slower than 10 minutes for a lap (85mph) only twice, and ran his 36th, 37th, 38th, 39th and 40th laps without a variation of a second at exactly that speed.'

The Aston Martin too deserved praise, for it had never missed a beat. Easing off, a very tired Moss completed the closing two laps with his goggles down to record yet another remarkable victory. Showing his complete mastery of the Nürburgring once again he had driven for 36 of the 44 laps, admitting afterwards that that the effort left him absolutely knackered!

"It took me longer to get over that race than any other I can remember," he says. "I'd driven terribly hard for much too long and it took me a week to get over it – even more than I'd needed after the Mille Miglia in 1955."

It may be said that his win at the Nürburgring three years later was just as great a victory, but amazingly the best of Moss was yet to come.

Above right: Stirling drifts the Aston through the first of the Hatzenbach curves on his way to a superb victory. Below: he brings the DBR1 in to receive the victor's laurels. Below right: knackered! Stirling was exhausted after his monumental drive.

1958

CHAPTER FOURTEEN

Triumph and Tragedy for Ferrari

The 24 Hours of Le Mans;
the deaths of Musso and Collins

Stirling's superb win at the Ring had at last put some points on the Championship board for Aston Martin, but it was too little, too late. By filling the next four places, the works Testa Rossas had sewn up the title which, at the beginning of the year, Astons really thought would be theirs.

There were still two races to be run, however, and while the Tourist Trophy was likely to suffer from lack of interest, Le Mans most certainly would not. This was the biggest race of the year, the one which even the non-motor racing public knew about, and none of the big teams could afford to give it a miss, despite the fact that it would now have no effect on the Manufacturers' Championship.

Scuderia Ferrari sent the same four cars they had run at the Ring, determined to cap their Championship with a win in the 24-hour race, which they hadn't managed since 1954. Unfortunately, they were short of two drivers, Luigi Musso and Gino Munaron. The latter had been the victim of an unspecified accident somewhere, and Musso had been very lucky to walk away from a huge shunt in the previous weekend's Belgian GP at Spa when his Ferrari had suffered a burst tyre. His only injury was a strained back, but it was enough to keep him away from Le Mans.

Opposite: Phil Hill was a superb wet-weather driver and his performance at Le Mans in appalling conditions was outstanding. Here he leads Duncan Hamilton in the D-type Jaguar, which was to crash later.

Both the prototype Testa Rossas were at Le Mans with new bodywork. Following Wolfgang Seidel's excursion off the road in the Targa Florio, 0666 had been sent back to Scaglietti for new cutaway metalwork and was then sold to the North American Racing Team (NART), which was owned by Ferrari's main US importer (and three-time Le Mans winner) Luigi Chinetti. He entered it for two promising American drivers: Bruce Kessler and Dan Gurney.

In the three weeks since the Nürburgring race the second prototype, 0704, had also been back to Scaglietti, emerging with the latest envelope bodywork, to bring it in line with the other two works TR58s, 0726 and 0728. Its carburettor air intake was at the rear. As at the Ring, this was to be driven by Mike Hawthorn and Peter Collins. In the absence of Musso and Munaron, Taffy von Trips was paired with Wolfgang Seidel in 0726, and Phil Hill with Olivier Gendebien in 0728.

Backing up these works cars were no fewer than six privately-entered 250TRs, including the NART car. Ecurie Francorchamps had 0736 for Alain de Changy and 'Beurlys', with Willy Mairesse and Lucien Bianchi as a reserve entry. Erik Bauer's tragic crash in 0748 at the Ring meant that Gottfried Kochert's entry became available and it was taken by Ecurie Francorchamps' second car 0724. From America came 0732 (E. Hugus/E. Erickson) and 0730 (E.D. Martin/F. Tavano); from Cuba came 0722 (A. Gomez-Mena/P. Drogo); and from France 0754 (F.Picard/J.Juhan). Should all the works cars expire during the race, chances were that at least one of these private entrants could pick up the pieces and keep Ferrari in the results.

Astons being fettled in the courtyard of the Hotel de France are DBR1/2 (Brooks/Trintignant - foreground) and DBR1/3 (Moss/Brabham).

The same could not be said of Aston Martin. Back in 1955 they too had produced a production version of their racing car, the DB3S. Unfortunately it was to 1953 specification and, unlike the Testa Rossas, had nothing like the performance of the works racers. There was never any question of Astons producing a run of 'production' DBR1s but, as at the Nürburgring, the factory was backed up by Graham and Peter Whitehead in their 1956 specification, ex-works DB3S.

Stuart Lewis-Evans had had a very unhappy time at the Nürburgring, and Reg Parnell was worried that he might not last the distance at Le Mans, although he had finished fifth in a works Ferrari the previous year. Reg therefore nominated him reserve driver and brought in Maurice Trintignant, who was very experienced on long-distance races – and successful. In 1954 he had won Le Mans with José Froilán González and the Tourist Trophy with Mike Hawthorn and in 1956 the Swedish GP with Phil Hill, all these victories being for Ferrari. Most recently, he had stunned the motor-racing world by winning the Monaco GP in Rob Walker's privately-entered Cooper-Climax. So the initial Aston Martin entry for Le Mans was Moss/Brabham (DBR1/3); Brooks/Trintignant (DBR1/2); and Salvadori/Shelby (DBR1/1).

At scrutineering all the works Astons weighed in at under 1,000kg, as did the customer Testa Rossas. The works Ferraris were all over the 1,000kg mark, as were the two Ecurie Ecosse D-type Jaguars, but not the Hamilton/Bueb car.

In the first practice session on the Wednesday evening the Astons were by far the fastest and looking good. Moss headed the time sheets with 4 mins 7.3 secs, and Brooks was just one second slower. Next up were Salvadori (4' 11.1") and Shelby (4' 13"); Jack Fairman and Duncan Hamilton did 4' 13.4" and 4' 14.3" in their D-types; then came Trintignant (4' 15") and Brabham (4' 16"). Reserve driver Lewis-Evans did four laps, with a best of 4' 20" Fastest of the Ferraris was that of Olivier Gendebien with 4' 21.6", and Jean Behra did 4' 30" with the 1.6-litre RSK Porsche.

Astons were well pleased with their performance and quietly confident that, at last, their day had come at Le Mans. The following evening Moss was the only Aston driver to practise, as once again he had asked for a lower axle ratio.

Overnight, that in DBR1/3 was changed from 3.09:1 to 3.19:1, and Stirling was much happier. With the original ratio he had been getting only 5,900rpm and with the lower one he was up to 6,100rpm, which made things much better all round the circuit, except on the straight. With the higher ratio Brooks was recording 163mph down Mulsanne at 6,000rpm, whereas Moss was only doing 156mph at the same engine speed. Nonetheless, he recorded the fastest time of the session, with 4 mins 10 secs.

The sensation of the evening, however, was provided by Cliff Allison, who took the two-litre Lotus he was to share with Graham Hill round in the staggering time of 4' 12.7", which was faster than everything except the three works Astons.

On the morning of the race, Carroll Shelby woke up suffering from food poisoning, so Lewis-Evans was delegated to drive R1/1 with Salvadori.

Moss made his usual superb getaway and was followed under the Dunlop Bridge by Brooks, Salvadori and Graham Whitehead in the DB3S. Hawthorn chased after them, slipping his clutch furiously and at the end of that opening lap was up to second place, but some four seconds behind Moss. Brooks was third, von Trips (Ferrari) fourth, Salvadori (Aston Martin) fifth and Gendebien (Ferrari) fifth.

Stirling's opening lap, including the run-and-jump start, had taken a remarkable 4 mins 29 secs. He proceeded to pull away from the rest of the field at a rate of knots and after 10 laps was 16 secs ahead of Hawthorn. By this time both Ecurie Ecosse Jaguars were out, sidelined by piston failure just as they had been at Sebring. The de-stroked Jaguar engine was not proving to be a success.

By lap 20 Moss was 49 seconds ahead of Hawthorn, and Brooks passed von Trips and went after Mike, only to be repassed by the German, who then overtook his team-mate into second place. Mike promptly put in a lap in 4 mins 08 secs, which was to be the fastest of the race, the fourth year in succession that he had achieved this feat.

Stirling's superb run came to an ignominious end on lap 30, when the Aston's engine threw a rod on Mulsanne and that was that. Moments later, as *The Autocar* reported: 'Suddenly a damp breeze stirred the flags over the tribunes and whisked little clouds of sand into the air; umbrellas went up, head lamps went on and a great darkness rolled up from the direction of White House. Then the heavens opened and a tremendous deluge swept along the course; the fastest cars were reduced to a common crawl, the drivers holding up their hands to shield their eyes, and sheets of spray flying up from tyres which sought in vain to grip the macadam.'

Above: Stirling Moss cuts in close through the Esses with DBR1/3.

Below: Hawthorn in the rebodied TR 0704 leads von Trips (0726) and Brooks (DBR1/2) through Mulsanne.

**Above: Mike Hawthorn drifts through the Esses early in the race.
Above right: Phil Hill in his element in 0728, on their way to a fine victory.
Right: Peter Collins shared 0704 with Mike Hawthorn again, but they failed to finish.**

Just at this point the first pit stops began; Hawthorn and Brooks being very happy to hand over their cars to Collins and Trintignant. Jack Brabham cheerfully admits that he was none too disappointed when Moss failed to come round.

"I'd raced a Cooper at Le Mans in 1957," he recalls. "We started at four; it was raining by six; then it got dark and by midnight we had fog. That wasn't my idea of motor racing. In 1958, that fantastic storm broke just as I was due to take over the Aston from Stirling, but he never made it round his last lap. I was able to go to the airport, get in my aeroplane and I was home before dark. That was the best Le Mans I've ever been to!"

Now the von Trips/Seidel Ferrari was in the lead, 13 seconds ahead of the Hill/Gendebien car. Some way back came the Brooks/Trintignant Aston followed by the Hawthorn/Collins Ferrari, the Salvadori/Lewis-Evans Aston and the NART Ferrari of Kessler/Gurney. Seventh was the Hamilton/Bueb Jaguar. At about 7.30pm, as the rains came down again, Peter Collins brought Ferrari 0704 into the pits, and the car was stationary for more than 20 minutes as mechanics struggled to restore some life to the clutch.

Pete was very glad to have this brief respite from the rain, but Duncan Hamilton simply revelled in it. In 1954 he and Tony Rolt in the works 3.4-litre D-type had waged a race-long battle against the 4.9-litre Ferrari of González/Trintignant, also

It is early on Sunday morning at as Olivier Gendebien climbs aboard the leading Ferrari, the rebodied 0728. He and Phil Hill drove superbly to win one of the wettest Le Mans on record, finishing 100 miles ahead of the second-placed Aston Martin DB3S of the Whitehead brothers.

in the rain. Now in his own D-type (rumoured to have a works, three-litre engine installed) Duncan once again went at the Ferraris and would eventually take the lead for a brief period. By 8pm he was in a remarkable third place, behind the Ferraris of Hill/Gendebien and von Trips/Seidel, after 'a splendid demonstration of courage and determination on a slippery surface.' as *The Autocar* noted, adding, 'Clearly the Jaguar was much more controllable under these conditions than the Aston Martins.'

This was all too true, as Stuart Lewis-Evans found out the hard way when completing his 48th lap. He spun lazily under the Dunlop Bridge, hitting the bank and damaging the bodywork. The offside headlamp was broken beyond repair and the radiator air intake was partly blocked, so the Aston had to be withdrawn.

Lewis-Evans complained that the car's handling in the rain was terrible, as did Trintignant later. Both felt that the pressure in the Avon tyres – 60psi front and rear – was far too much in the very wet conditions, and the Avon technicians were persuaded to reduce the pressure to 35psi all round on a set of slotted tyres. This was then fitted to the Brooks/Trintignant car and the handling showed a marked improvement.

However, the sole surviving DBR1 was now three laps behind the leaders, which were the Hill/Gendebien Ferrari and the Hamilton/Bueb Jaguar, both of which were being driven superbly in the appalling conditions. As Bernard Cahier reported in *Road & Track*:

'The two cars, the red and the green, were now travelling together, and the pair was soon joined by von Trips, splendidly driving the other Ferrari . . . A few minutes before midnight Hill took over Gendebien's Ferrari and it was not long before Hamilton did the same on the Jaguar and Seidel on the second Ferrari. This brings us to the most crucial moment of the race. It was at this moment, full of tension, that Hill chose to give us the best demonstration of his talents and to establish himself as one of the world's finest sports-car drivers on a wet surface. In roughly two hours and a half this California driver not only regained first place, but managed to put his car over a lap ahead of Hamilton's Jaguar. It is known in motor racing circles that Hamilton is one of the best you can find in the wet, and especially at Le Mans. Well, it was this man who was beaten there by Hill, and everyone could only cheer in praise of his performance.'

Shortly after midnight Wolfgang Seidel crashed the third-place Ferrari into a sand bank at Indianapolis Corner and returned to the pits on foot, where he was admonished for not digging the car out of the sand. At half-distance Hill and Gendebien led by a lap from Hamilton/Bueb, who were three laps ahead of the Brooks/Trintignant Aston. Four laps behind that was the Behra/Herrmann Porsche, a lap ahead of the Whitehead brothers' DB3S Aston Martin.

The Hawthorn/Collins Testa Rossa had been steadily losing ground as its clutch became less and less effective and it finally died at about 2.15am, leaving Peter with a long, wet walk back to the pits.

At 3am Tony Brooks was the fastest man on the course, hurrying the DBR1 round in 4 mins 20 secs, which was seven seconds faster than Gendebien (three laps ahead) and 13 seconds faster than Hamilton in the Jaguar. An hour and a half later Tony was still taking five seconds a lap off the Ferrari, but it was not enough, and it was not to last, either, for at 6am the Aston's gearbox gave up the ghost when the input gears failed and Maurice Trintignant parked it at Mulsanne.

For the second year running the works Astons had failed. The mechanics in particular were very fed up and as soon as they got back to the Hôtel de France they wandered across the road to drown their sorrows in a café, Le Cheval Blanc. Then the drivers began to arrive with their wives and girlfriends, followed by John Wyer and his wife, Tottie, and before long the most tremendous party was in progress, the best in Astons' history by all accounts.

Meanwhile the race went on. The Whitehead brothers' DB3S was now the sole surviving representative of the Feltham concern and Peter Whitehead found himself in a fine duel with Jean Behra in the Porsche, but the German car was having trouble with its brakes and eventually fell back.

Hill and Gendebien drove on through the intermittent rainstorms, ahead of the Hamilton/Bueb Jaguar and just before midday on the Sunday the D-type left its pit with Duncan aboard – just ahead of Phil in the Testa Rossa. With his one-lap lead, Hill was content to sit a hundred yards or so behind Hamilton. "He was still in second place," says Phil, "and I decided to stay right behind him so that I knew where he was. But without warning, as we came round Arnage, his car went off the road and end over end."

It was a very big accident which wrecked the D-type, and Duncan was lucky to get away with severe bruising.

The Jaguar's dramatic departure left the Ferrari 12 laps ahead of the Whiteheads' Aston Martin. Filling the next three places were the Porsches of Behra/Herrmann; Barth/Frère and de Beaufort/Linge – a tremendous performance by the Stuttgart cars. In sixth and seventh places came two customer Testa Rossas, the Ecurie Francorchamps car of 'Beurlys'/de Changy and the American entry of Hugus/Erickson.

The others had all fallen by the wayside. 0754 (Picard/Juhan) crashed into an abandoned Lotus; 0730 (Martin/Tavano) suffered clutch failure, as did 0722 (Gomez/Drogo) and 0724 (Bianchi/Mairesse) crashed at Mulsanne, injuring an official. The first prototype (0666) was involved in a tragic accident when the Jaguar of 'Mary' (M. Brousselet) crashed in the rain under the Dunlop Bridge and Kessler could not avoid it. 'Mary' was killed, Kessler was hospitalised, and the two cars were burnt out.

At 4pm Phil Hill and Olivier Gendebien came home in triumph to record Ferrari's fourth Championship victory of the year, Hill's third and Gendebien's second. They were just 100 miles ahead of the Whiteheads, who had driven their ex-works DB3S superbly to save face for Aston Martin. It had been just about the wettest Le Mans on record and only 20 of the 55 starters finished the race and of those, only 17 were classified as having covered the official distance.

The winners averaged 106.2mph, which was remarkable given the conditions, which both men had handled superbly, Hill in particular being awesomely fast in the rain. His earlier successes that year had been out of sight in South and North America but here, in the most famous race in the world, he had shown himself to be a driver of the very front rank.

He and Gendebien had first driven together in the 1956 Buenos Aires 1,000 Kms, finishing second for Ferrari, but it was at this Le Mans race that their partnership really gelled.

"That was one of my greatest wins and I particularly enjoyed it." says Phil. "The weather was appalling and it really felt like an accomplishment to overcome that situation. The car was outstanding – my favourite Testa Rossa of all – with the back end very sure behind the front, which made it very driveable.

"Olivier was a wonderful co-driver and tremendously predictable, which was so

Triumph and tragedy for Ferrari.
Above: Hill and Gendebien celebrate their fine win.
Right: Luigi Musso and Peter Collins, who were killed within a month of each other.

important when the emphasis was on regularity and not trying to go as fast as you could."

Gendebien was equally complimentary about Phil, saying, "He was my best co-driver ever. We could drive a car at the same speed and if we decided to stick to a limit of 7,500rpm I knew he would do just that. Every time I got in the car after he had been driving for a couple of hours it was just as I had left it."

The Ferrari victory meant that the Scuderia had scored a maximum 8 points for all its best four results in the Championship, giving an unbeatable total of 32 points. Porsche were lying second with 18 points and Aston Martin third with 14, but only thanks to the six won at Le Mans by the Whiteheads. The outcome of the remaining event, the Tourist Trophy at Goodwood, was now irrelevant, other than deciding who would finish second to Ferrari – Porsche or Aston Martin.

The Scuderia had every right to feel pleased with its success at Le Mans and in the Championship, but the rest of that summer of 1958 was to be a terrible one for Ferrari. First Luigi Musso, Italy's only surviving driver of the front rank, crashed to his death during the French GP at Reims. Then, after a brilliant start-to-finish victory in the British GP at Silverstone, Peter Collins was killed two weeks later at the

Roy Salvadori drifts DBR1/1 through Woodcote on his way to second place in the TT with Jack Brabham.

Nürburgring. In the German GP he and Mike Hawthorn were locked in a flat-out battle for the lead with Tony Brooks in the Vanwall when Peter inexplicably lost control of his car at Pflanzgarten. In the space of one month Ferrari and motor racing had been deprived of two of their finest.

As Ferrari had wrapped up the Manufacturers' Championship at Le Mans the Tourist Trophy was reduced to a running time of four hours and carried only half Championship points. When entries were announced it was seen that Aston Martin were sending three cars to Goodwood with their full line-up of drivers: Stirling Moss; Tony Brooks; Roy Salvadori; Carroll Shelby; Jack Brabham and Stuart Lewis-Evans. Ecurie Ecosse had abandoned their D-types and now were to be represented by a Lister-Jaguar and a Tojeiro-Jaguar; and Porsche were planning to send two cars for Jean Behra/Edgar Barth and Wolfgang von Trips/Huschke von Hanstein. Ecurie Francorchamps entered their Testa Rossa and nominated Olivier Gendebien as one of the drivers and, to everyone's surprise, Scuderia Ferrari promised one car, to be driven by 'the two best team drivers available'. To no-one's surprise, it never materialised.

There was no opposition worth a damn for the Astons in the race, which provided them with a very hollow victory. It also allowed the team to maintain its unbeaten record in long-distance events at Goodwood, where it had won all three Nine Hours races. The cars finished a couple of lengths apart in the order Moss/Brooks (DBR1/2); Salvadori/Brabham (DBR1/1); and Shelby/Lewis-Evans (DBR1/3).

Jean Behra and Edgar Barth were fourth in the Porsche, but Astons' clean sweep meant that, with only half points awarded, Feltham and Stuttgart shared second place in the Championship with a total of 18 points each from their best four results (or, in the case of Aston Martin, the best three).

Ferrari had won the Manufacturers' title by a country mile with a car whose design many had derided as old fashioned, but not for the first time Enzo Ferrari had shown that he knew a thing or two about motor racing. His Testa Rossa had proved itself to be a superb sports racing car – not the fastest, but undeniably the best.

Conversely, Aston Martin had shown themselves to have had the fastest car, but a frail one. Back at Feltham they must have been wondering just what they had to do to win the Championship which, at the beginning of the season, appeared to have been a gift for the DBR1.

David Brown had never had a better chance of winning the Championship and he was naturally disappointed at the result. He was not one to give in to adversity, however, and a month after the Tourist Trophy he issued a statement confirming that: 'Aston Martin have no intention of withdrawing from sports-car racing. The Aston Martin DBR1 which won the 1958 Nürburgring and Tourist Trophy races holds the sports-car lap record for Sebring, Targa Florio, Nürburgring and Goodwood. This car, developed to even higher performances (sic) will continue in 1959 with the principal effort upon Le Mans.'

Results

1958
SPORTSCAR WORLD CHAMPIONSHIP

	Buenos Aires	Sebring	Targa Florio	Nürburgring	Le Mans	Tourist Trophy	
1. Ferrari	8	8	8	6	8	0	38/32
2. Aston Martin	0	0	0	8	0	4	12/12
3. Porsche	4	0	0	0	0	0	4/4
4. Lotus	0	3	0	0	0	0	3/3
5. Maserati	2	0	0	0	0	0	2/2
6. OSCA	0	0	2	0	0	0	2/2

The Championship was decided by the best four results.
As Ferrari had won the title after Nürburgring, the Tourist Trophy was run for four hours and for half points.
Points: 1st – 8; 2nd – 6; 3rd – 4; 4th – 3; 5th – 2; 6th – 1

BUENOS AIRES 1,000 Kms
January 26

1) P. Collins/P. Hill (Ferrari 250TR/0704) 106 laps in 6 hrs 19 mins 55.4 secs (98.47 mph)
2) W. von Trips/O. Gendebien (Ferrari 250TR/0666) 106 laps
3) S. Moss/J. Behra (Porsche 1.6-litre) 106 laps
4) P. Drogo/S. González (Ferrari 250TR/0714) 102 laps
5) R. Mières/E. Barth (Porsche 1.5-litre) 99 laps
6) A. Peduzzi/G. Munaron (Ferrari 2-litre) 98 laps
Fastest lap: P. Collins (Ferrari 250TR), 3 mins 25.9 secs (102.96 mph).

SEBRING 12 HOURS
March 22

1) P. Collins/P. Hill (Ferrari 250TR/0704) 200 laps at 86.6 mph
2) L. Musso/O. Gendebien (Ferrari 250TR/0726) 199 laps
3) H. Schell/W. Seidel (Porsche 1.6-litre)
4) S. Weiss/D. Tallakson (Lotus 11)
5) B. Kessler/P. O'Shea/D. Cunningham (Ferrari 250GT)
6) C. Chapman/C. Allison (Lotus 11)
Fastest lap: S. Moss (Aston Martin DBR1/2), 3 mins 20.3 secs (93.6 mph)

TARGA FLORIO
May 11

1) L. Musso/O. Gendebien (Ferrari 250TR/1726) 14 laps in 10 hrs 37 mins 58.1 secs (58.78 mph)
2) J. Behra/L. Scarlatti (Porsche 1.6-litre) 10 hrs 43 mins 37.9 secs
3) M. Hawthorn/W. von Trips (Ferrari 250TR/0728) 10 hrs 44 mins 29.3 secs
4) P. Collins/P. Hill (Ferrari 250TR/0704) 11 hrs 10 mins 01.4 secs
5) G. Cabianca/Bordoni (OSCA) 11 hrs 25 mins 35.7 secs
6) H. von Hanstein/Pucci (Porsche Carrera) 11 hrs 34 mins 04.6 secs
Fastest lap: S.Moss (Aston Martin DBR1/3) 42 mins 17.5 secs (66.3 mph)

NÜRBURGRING 1,000 Kms
June 1

1) S. Moss/J. Brabham (Aston Martin DBR1/3) 44 laps in 7 hrs 23 mins 33 secs (84.26 mph)
2) M. Hawthorn/P. Collins (Ferrari 250TR/0704) 44 laps in 7 hrs 27 mins 17 secs
3) W. von Trips/O. Gendebien (Ferrari 250TR/0746) 44 laps in 7 hrs 33 mins 15 secs
4) L. Musso/P. Hill (Ferrari 250TR/0726) 43 laps
5) W. Seidel/G. Munaron (Ferrari 250TR/0728) 42 laps
6) G. Whitehead/P. Whitehead (Aston Martin DB3S/6) 42 laps
Fastest lap: S. Moss (Aston Martin DBR1) 9 mins 43secs, (87.55 mph)

LE MANS 24 HOURS
June 21/22

1) O. Gendebien/P. Hill (Ferrari 250TR/0728) 4101.9 kms at 106.2 mph
2) P. Whitehead/G. Whitehead (Aston Martin DB3S/6)
3) J. Behra/H. Herrmann (Porsche 1.6-litre)
4) E. Barth/P.Frère (Porsche 1.5-litre)
5) G. de Beaufort/H. Linge (Porsche 1.5-litre)
6) A. de Changy/'Beurlys' (Ferrari 250TR/0736)
Fastest lap: M. Hawthorn (Ferrari 250TR 0704) 4 mins 08 secs (121.46 mph)

TOURIST TROPHY
September 13

1) S. Moss/C.A.S. Brooks (Aston Martin DBR1/2) 148 laps in 4 hrs 01 mins 17.0 secs (88.33 mph)
2) R. Salvadori/J. Brabham (Aston Martin DBR1/1) 148 laps in 4 hrs 01 mins 17.4 secs
3) C. Shelby/S. Lewis-Evans (Aston Martin DBR1/3) 148 laps in 4 hrs 01 mins 17.8 secs
4) J. Behra/E. Barth (Porsche 1.5-litre) 144 laps
5) M. Gregory/I. Ireland (Jaguar D-type) 143 laps
6) D. Hamilton/P. Blond (Jaguar D-type) 142 laps
Fastest lap: S. Moss (Aston Martin DBR1) 1 min 32.6 secs (93.30 mph)

CHAPTER FIFTEEN

Winter Moves

Teams and drivers

With one World Championship in the bag, Scuderia Ferrari now set about trying to secure the other two: the Formula 1 Drivers' and the Constructors', the latter being contested for the very first time.

Mike Hawthorn's chances of becoming World Champion driver were looking good because, although his arch-rival, Stirling Moss, had won the Portuguese GP, he had finished second and set fastest lap (for which there was one point), and in the Italian GP Moss had retired, whereas Mike had finished second again, this time behind Tony Brooks.

Still trying to come to terms with the death of his great friend, 'Mon Ami Mate' Pete Collins, Mike was nonetheless determined to be World Champion, but was becoming increasingly frustrated at the inefficiency of the drum brakes on his Ferrari Dino. In Portugal they had faded completely by the end of the race, and he very nearly failed to finish. A few days later he flew to Maranello to see Enzo Ferrari and demanded that Dunlop discs be fitted to his car in time for the Italian GP.

This was done, but Mike very nearly ruined everything at the start of the race by almost destroying his clutch. It just lasted the distance and he was able to finish second, but had he won at Monza he would have been World Champion.

Now he had a agonising wait until the Morocco GP in October, when the fate of the title would be decided at Casablanca.

Immediately after the Italian GP a story sprang up regarding the disc brakes fitted to Mike's car that was completely erroneous. It remained uncorrected until 1991, when I was able to discover the truth of the matter and publish it in *Mon Ami Mate*, my biography of Mike and Peter Collins.

In *The Autocar*, Sports Editor Peter Garnier wrote, 'At Monza last weekend there were several people with sanctimonious expressions and raised eyebrows, shocked that the Dunlop company should apparently have been so unethical as to fit disc brakes to Mike Hawthorn's Dino 246 Ferrari. Incidentally the popular impression that Dunlops supplied the disc brake equipment is incorrect. They were standard Jaguar XK150 brakes that had been fitted by Dunlops to the Ferrari coupé owned by Peter Collins and which had been taken off by Ferrari – with Dunlop assistance – to fit to the Grand Prix car.'

A week later Gregor Grant raised the subject in *Autosport*, repeating the tale that the brakes had been taken from Peter Collins' personal Ferrari and asking, 'why not?'

'Surely,' he wrote, 'it is also in the interests of the British concern to convince Enzo Ferrari that disc brakes are the wear for modern racing and high-performance cars? Were Ferrari to produce the famous 250GT with Dunlop or Girling disc brakes, it would be a feather in the cap of British industry.'

It would indeed and soon it was to be, but the story that Mike's discs had come from Peter's car – almost certainly put about in good faith by Mike himself – was nonsense. Having persuaded Enzo Ferrari that he should have disc brakes for Monza, Mike flew home and telephoned his friend Harold Hodkinson at Dunlop. As a result Hodkinson and development fitter Maurice Rowe flew to Italy and went to Maranello, where they found Ferrari and his Chief Engineer, Carlo Chiti, toying with the brake callipers from Peter Collins' car. At Peter's request, Harold had fitted these brakes earlier in the year, and shortly before his death at the Nürburgring Collins had left the car at Maranello so that Ferrari and his engineers could study the brake

Mon Ami Mates. The friendship between Peter Collins and Mike Hawthorn did not produce results for Scuderia Ferrari.

layout. Peter Garnier had been correct in saying that these were standard Jaguar XK150 brakes, but they were no good for racing and were not fitted to Hawthorn's GP car, as Hodkinson confirms.

"We used nothing from Peter's car and I don't know how that story got started. Possibly Mike thought it was just a simple job of transferring the brakes from one car to the other and told people that was what had been done, but in fact the two brake installations were incompatible. Everything we fitted to Mike's Dino was brand new, but we didn't object to his version. The publicity we got for using production disc brakes on a leading Grand Prix contender didn't do Dunlop any harm at all."

Enzo Ferrari finally bowed to the inevitable and Dunlop disc brakes – and tyres – were tested rigorously on Testa Rossa 0726 over the next few months. The Scuderia had not had a happy time with Englebert in recent years, and soon Dunlop were poised for the breakthrough they were after, a contract to supply brakes and tyres to Ferrari.

Even before Peter Collins' death, Mike had decided to retire from racing, come what may with the Championship. He did not tell Ferrari, however, and the Old Man was very keen to sign him again for 1959. After the Italian GP he invited Hawthorn to write his own contract for the coming season saying, "I will sign it without reading it." Mike promised to discuss the matter with him after the race in Casablanca.

In order to become World Champion Stirling Moss had to win the Morocco GP and make fastest lap, with Mike finishing no higher than third. In the event Stirling did everything he had to but, with the help of Phil Hill, Mike finished second and so won the title by one point – the first British driver to become World Champion.

Hawthorn didn't formally announce his retirement until early in December, but Ferrari lost no time in filling his depleted ranks of drivers. He had also lost Collins and Musso in tragic circumstances, and von Trips and Seidel had decided to return home and drive for Porsche in 1959. Still on board, however, were Hill and Gendebien. Several Italian drivers were tested at Modena Autodrome, but none showed any real promise, so Enzo looked abroad again.

Cliff Allison had been making a name for himself as a very fast and reliable driver with the very fast and unreliable Lotus cars. He was on the Lotus stand at the Earl's Court Motor Show one day that October when two Italians invited him for a drink.

"At a nearby bar one of them lifted the lapel of his jacket to reveal a Ferrari badge." recalls Cliff. "He then asked me to fly to Italy and meet Mr Ferrari. Three days later I was driving various red cars around the Modena Autodrome. I then had an audience with Mr Ferrari and later flew back to England with a contract in my pocket. It was unsigned because I wanted to discuss it first with Mike Hawthorn. It was only when I talked with him that I learned that he personally had recommended me to Ferrari, as he regarded me and Phil Hill as the two most promising Grand Prix drivers around."

Boosted by Mike's vote of confidence, Allison signed with Ferrari for 1959.

In November there was another visitor to the Modena Autodrome, a young American named Dan Gurney. Since late in 1957 he had been making a name for himself in California driving – among other things – a 4.9-litre Ferrari for Frank Arciero. Phil Hill had been so impressed that he had taken Gurney to Sebring in March, 1958, driving from California to Florida in a vintage Packard. There he introduced him to Luigi Chinetti, who gave Dan a run in one of his cars in practice. Chinetti too was impressed and later signed him to drive with Bruce Kessler in the NART Testa Rossa at Le Mans. After five hours they were in a remarkable fourth place when Kessler was involved in a crash with a D-type Jaguar, and the Ferrari was

Cliff Allison, who became Mike Hawthorn's protégé at Scuderia Ferrari.

Ferrari put Dan Gurney (left) on the fast track to GP racing, but kept Phil Hill waiting for years.

burnt out.

Chinetti then found Gurney another drive, at Reims, where he shared a Ferrari Berlinetta with André Guelfi in the 12-hour GT race. Dan made second-fastest practice lap, but Guelfi crashed in the race when in second position. After a quick trip to England to watch the British GP Gurney went to the Nürburgring, where Mimo Dei of Scuderia Centro Sud offered him a drive in an OSCA in the six-lap, 1500cc sportscar race that preceded the German Grand Prix. He finished eighth in a field that included such luminaries as Jean Behra, Jo Bonnier, Edgar Barth and Hans Herrmann. "I managed to turn the fastest lap that an OSCA had ever done there," says Dan. "The Ring was a fantastic circuit and I just loved it."

Luigi Chinetti was convinced that Gurney was a special talent and lobbied hard on his behalf with Enzo Ferrari.

"Mr Chinetti wrote to say, 'I have found a very good driver and, if you like, he is ready for your sportscars and maybe Formula 1'." says Romolo Tavoni. "Ferrari replied 'I would like to see your driver in Modena for a test.' and sent a plane ticket. Dan arrived in November."

First, Gurney went to New York to discuss the matter with Phil Hill before flying to Italy where "I found that I was the only driver at the Modena Autodrome," he says, "and I drove two sportscars, a two-litre and a three-litre Testa Rossa, and Mike Hawthorn's Grand Prix car. Enzo was there himself, with all the other top Ferrari people. A day or so later I drove a Testa Rossa in the rain at Monza with test driver Severi. That TR was a bear in the rain!"

As a result of these tests, Gurney was offered a contract for 1959. "They didn't have to ask me twice," he says. "It was a fantastic break, the chance of any driver's lifetime, and I grabbed it."

On December 9 Ferrari showed his latest Testa Rossa at his annual press conference. The work of Carlo Chiti, this was not a 1959 car but an interim model based on a modified 296S, and fitted with Dunlop disc brakes. It also had a new front-entry carburettor air intake of clear plastic and its location on the engine cover showed that the V12 had been moved to the left of the centre line.

A week later Enzo Ferrari announced that Jean Behra was to succeed Mike Hawthorn as the Scuderia's number one driver for 1959 and 'Jeannot' was seen testing a Ferrari Dino GP car at Modena Autodrome. The French champion had had a miserable F1 season with BRM but had put up some sensational performances in sportscar races with Porsche. He was looking for better things in 1959 and so turned to Maranello. Ferrari made him welcome, but their relationship was to have an unpleasant and premature ending.

The first of the new Testa Rossas made its début at Modena Autodrome in January 1959 when, still unpainted, it was driven by Behra, who had now signed with the Scuderia. The TR59, as it was known, was chassis number 0766 and had new bodywork with small, horizontal air intakes for the front brakes, neat air vents behind the front and rear wheels and a clear plastic air scoop over the carburettors. Although Sergio Scaglietti had delivered his 19th (and last) customer Testa Rossa the previous July, he was now fully occupied building Ferrari's new GT cars, so the new Testa Rossa had been styled by Pinin Farina and built by Medardo Fantuzzi who, until recently, had been responsible for Maserati's metalwork.

The new car was right-hand drive (as were all subsequent works cars) with the engine four inches to the left of the centre line. This was to accommodate a new, five-speed gearbox of the step-down type, with the output on the layshaft, designed by Valerio Colotti. The de Dion rear suspension now incorporated coil springs and the Houdaille shock absorbers were replaced by Konis all round.

Mauro Forghieri remembers, "The Testa Rossa that I saw in 1959 had a good chassis, fully capable of taking the power of the engine, but the de Dion rear end was too heavy and they needed a better suspension. Also we used a five-speed gearbox after the drivers had asked for it.

"That season Ferrari went from the ladder-type chassis to a space frame, but it was only half a space frame because they didn't want to change the car completely. We tried to reduce the weight and increase the stiffness. We couldn't change the front suspension because it was the production suspension, so all we could change was the chassis."

One of the main reasons why Carlo Chiti could not give the new car a completely new chassis was a lack of money, as Romolo Tavoni recalls.

With this Press Release photo, Enzo Ferrari announced that Jean Behra had joined his Scuderia as Team Leader for 1959.

"In 1959 Ferrari spent very little money on the sports racing cars because he had spent a lot — maybe 15 or 20 million lire — on new machine tools, which were necessary to make the new 250GT car. He also enlarged the foundry and rebuilt much of the factory, so there was really nothing extra for the Racing Department. Franco Rocchi (in charge of engines) asked him to split it between the two, 50-50, but he refused."

Nonetheless Ferrari still expected his Racing Department to embark on a full season of competition with Grand Prix, Sports and GT cars, telling them, "We are

119

Tony Brooks – seen here at the Nürburgring in 1958 with his fiancée, Pina Resegotti – was Ferrari's last and most important signing for 1959.

entering three FIA World Championships – we must win one of them, at least!"

A lack of money was something they knew all about at Aston Martin, where the racing budget was much smaller than Ferrari's. Having failed to win the sportscar Championship in 1958, when it had been theirs for the taking, David Brown, John Wyer and Reg Parnell decided that they would ignore it in 1959 and concentrate all their efforts on winning Le Mans. Well, not quite all their efforts, because they also agreed to go Grand Prix racing with their DBR4, which had been gathering dust throughout 1958.

As far as the sportscars were concerned, Astons decided to do no development work on the DBR1s but to do everything they could to improve reliability. To this end, DBR1/1 was prepared for a 24-hour run at Monza, specifically to test the new wide input gears. These had caused no problems in their first outing in the TT, but Reg Parnell wanted to give them a stiffer trial than that four-hour race.

The run began on Thursday, December 11, with Roy Salvadori and Masten Gregory driving. However, this was not the ideal time of year to go testing at Monza and after only 15 laps heavy snow brought things to a halt. For the next two days the team was confined to its hotel, so Masten taught Roy to play gin rummy. This was not a good move, as by the time the tests were over, Roy was $75 ahead.

On the Sunday the two managed 105 laps in the snow; on the Monday 179 laps, also in snow; and on the Tuesday 160 laps, when conditions were merely wet and foggy. On the final day, Wednesday, it was wet and very misty, and they completed 62 laps. During this session, while changing from fourth to fifth, the drive remained in fourth while the gear lever was in fifth. This happened twice.

After four days in very bad weather Astons ran out of time, but the DBR1 had covered 1,863 miles in just under 18 hours at an average speed of 104.2mph. Both drivers were very impressed with the performance and handling of the car, and Gregory thought that the brakes were outstanding.

Early in January, British Grand Prix hopes received a body blow when Tony Vandervell announced that he was pulling out of racing. This meant that two of the finest drivers in the world – Stirling Moss and Tony Brooks – were available. Both had tested the GP Aston Martin, but were only too aware that it had missed a whole year's development.

Although Ferrari had already signed the gifted but moody Jean Behra to his team he wanted to strengthen it still more, as Phil Hill and Cliff Allison were very new to F1. However, Moss had made it clear long ago that he would never drive for the Scuderia, having had a promised works car snatched away from him at Bari back in 1951.

Brooks had no such hang-ups and by now had an Italian connection all his own, having married Pina Resegotti the previous October. For his part, Enzo Ferrari thought very highly of the Englishman, who had won three Grandes Epreuves for Vanwall. As Olivier Gendebien recalled:

"Early in 1958 Enzo Ferrari invited my wife and me, and Peter and Louise Collins to lunch in Modena and my wife, who knew very little about racing, asked Ferrari who was the best English driver. He said Tony Brooks."

This, of course, was typical Ferrari indulging in his dangerous game of playing one driver off against another, as he had done with Gendebien and de Portago before the 1957 Mille Miglia – and it is quite possible that, on this occasion, he was trying to needle his own English drivers, Collins and the absent Hawthorn.

Be that as it may, now that Brooks was available, Ferrari lost no time in making contact. "Very soon after Tony Vandervell announced his withdrawal from racing Tony received a phone call from Ferrari, asking him to go to Maranello." says Pina Brooks. "We went in January and met Ferrari, who entertained us royally with lunch and dinner at the Fini restaurant in Modena. He was a great charmer. Tony signed a contract for 1959."

He did indeed, but that contract was unique in that Brooks demanded and won a remarkable exemption – he would not have to drive at Le Mans.

"By this time I had driven there four times for Aston Martin and was thoroughly disenchanted with the whole thing." he says. "It is not a race, but a high-speed tour, and the the idea of driving for 24 hours at a pace so much below the potential of both the car and myself was not satisfying or challenging for me. Add to that the speed differential of the cars, and it was potentially very dangerous. Finally, the 1958 race had been extremely wet and I had found myself getting back into wet overalls for my next run, so I swore that if I ever went back to Le Mans I would present myself to the nearest mental home.

"I signed with Ferrari on the understanding that I would not race there – probably a unique achievement, as he still regarded it as a most important event in terms of sales. He didn't argue but he was amazed that I could give up the 'glory' that went with the 24 Hours!"

Romolo Tavoni remembers, "Tony especially did not want to do Le Mans – definitely! Mr Ferrari said, 'OK, but if some time I need you for other sportscar races, you must drive.' and Tony agreed to this. Mr Ferrari wanted Brooks very much for F1, so he agreed about Le Mans."

Despite Ferrari's proviso, Brooks began his association with the Scuderia by not taking part in the first Championship sportscar race of the season, the Sebring 12 Hours. Over the years, a myth has grown up to the effect that he at first refused to do any sportscar racing for Ferrari and that he was only persuaded to change his mind by being given Grand Prix cars that were inferior to those of his team-mates. He refutes this absolutely.

"I never disliked sportscar racing; just Le Mans. I enjoyed Grand Prix racing more, it's true, but I very much enjoyed driving a decent sportscar on a decent circuit. I did not go to Sebring in 1959 and I can't now remember why. Perhaps I was given the option, in which case I would have said, 'If you don't need me – count me out,' as I was never in a hurry to race there."

While Scuderia Ferrari were preparing three new TR59s for Sebring, Aston Martin were testing their GP car, having put the DBR1s aside to await Le Mans.

'We decided that we really must win Le Mans at what was to be out tenth attempt,' wrote John Wyer. 'Apart from Formula 1, it was to be our only race – we would not tolerate any diversions, like going to the Ring two weeks beforehand, but we would do a lot of testing and make sure things were absolutely right.'

In the event these good intentions were soon undermined, and Astons were to make no fewer than three diversions into Championship races. The first would prove to be a complete waste of time; the second would result in yet another miraculous performance by Stirling Moss and the third would provide a finale to the sportscar Championship of such breathtaking drama that to this day it is relished by all who saw it.

The Contenders 3
FERRARI TR59

Design Engineer:
Carlo Chiti

SPECIFICATION

DESIGN ENGINEER: Carlo Chiti
ENGINE: 60-degree V12, 73 x 58.8 mm, 2953cc, 2 valves per cylinder, single ohc, Comp. ratio: 9.8:1
Max bhp: 330@8000 rpm,
Max bmep: 187 lb/sq in @ 4000 rpm,
Carburettors: 6 twin-choke Weber 38 DCN,
Plugs: 24 Marchal 34 HF,
Lubrication: wet, then dry sump.
TRANSMISSION:
Clutch: Fichel & Sachs single-plate,
Gearbox: Colotti front-mounted non-synchro 5-speed and reverse.
CHASSIS:
Semi-spaceframe,
Suspension: (front) wishbone & coilsprings, (rear) de Dion & coilsprings,
Shock absorbers: Koni,
Brakes: Dunlop disc,
Tyres: Dunlop (front) 5.50 x 16, (rear) 6.00 x 16,
Wheels: Borrani,
Steering: ZF.
BODY:
Stylist: Sergio Pininfarina,
Builder: Medardo Fantuzzi.
DIMENSIONS:
Length: 13 ft 5 ins,
Width: 5 ft,
Height: 3 ft 3 ins,
Ground Clearance: 5.5 ins,
Weight (dry): 1653 lbs,
Wheelbase: 7 ft 8 ins,
Track: (front) 4 ft 3.5 ins, (rear) 4 ft 3.5 ins.

Ferrari TR59
1959

working drawing by Tony Matthews

1959

Mike – the motor racing world was rocked by the death of its new Champion (and one of its most charismatic personalities) in a road accident.

CHAPTER SIXTEEN

Ferrari's Flying Start

The 12 Hours of Sebring

The year began as the previous one had ended – in tragedy. The death of Stuart Lewis-Evans at Casablanca had cast a pall over the end of the 1958 season, and now 1959 was barely under way when Mike Hawthorn lost his life in a road accident on January 22.

The new World Champion was on his way to London for a lunch appointment when he saw ahead of him his friend Rob Walker, who was in his Mercedes-Benz 300SL. Mike liked Rob enormously, but he hated all things German and regarded his own car (a works-prepared 3.4-litre Jaguar saloon) as a 'Merc-eater'. Despite the appalling wintery weather conditions – wet roads and blustery rain squalls – Mike could not resist a dice with Rob. The two cars accelerated to over 100mph on the de-restricted Guildford by-pass until Rob realised that he was out of his depth and backed off. Mike did not, lost control of his Jaguar on the slippery surface and crashed to his death. It was a sad and foolish end to a glittering career.

The Manufacturers' Championship sportscar races were now getting very thin on the ground. In 1956 there had been six; in 1957 seven, and in 1958 six again. With the cancellation of the Buenos Aires 1,000 Kms only five were scheduled for 1959: the Sebring 12 Hours (March); the Targa Florio (May); the Nürburgring 1,000 Kms (June); Le Mans (June); and the Tourist Trophy (September).

Aston Martin were out of the running, so the Championship looked set to be a walkover for Scuderia Ferrari, with some opposition from Porsche. With this in mind, no doubt, the FIA decided that the TT should once again only run for half distance and score half points.

In February there occurred the first of the diversions that Aston Martin had decided expressly to avoid. Alec Ulmann was very keen to have some opposition for the works Ferraris at Sebring and decided that he had to have at least one Aston. When the Feltham concern stuck to its 'nothing but Le Mans' policy, Ulmann played his ace and offered $4,500 for one car. This was unheard of, as Sebring never paid starting money, only a limited amount of expenses. In the circumstances, Reg Parnell decided that Sebring wasn't such a bad idea, after all.

Ferrari sent three brand-new TR59s to Florida, to be driven by Jean Behra, Phil Hill, Olivier Gendebien, Dan Gurney, Cliff Allison and Chuck Daigh, the latter being another protégé of Luigi Chinetti.

It was initially stated that the lone Aston Martin would be driven by Roy Salvadori and Masten Gregory, who had worked well together at the Monza tests in December, but in the event Roy was partnered by his old friend Carroll Shelby. DBR1/1 was powered by a 2992cc engine with – for the first time – seven main bearings, as a try-out for Le Mans. (Curiously, a number of contemporary race reports claim that the seven-bearing unit first appeared at Sebring the previous year. It was certainly under development then, but Ted Cutting is adamant that it made its début in the 1959 event, a fact that is borne out by the Aston Martin Race Reports.)

The CG 537 gearbox was fitted with wide input gears and stub teeth, as tested at Monza, and had also been equipped with a selector locking device, to prevent the gearbox becoming jammed in one gear, as had happened on the last day of the tests.

After the previous year's 24-hour race, several of Astons' drivers had reported a slight falling off in oil pressure on the Mulsanne straight, so for Sebring a larger, one-inch diameter main feed pipe was fitted from the oil tank to the pressure pump.

Porsche had brought along two 1600cc RSK cars for Jo Bonnier/Wolfgang von Trips and Edgar Barth/John Fitch. Briggs Cunningham entered three Lister-Jaguars, a brand-new car for Stirling Moss/Ivor Bueb and two 1958 machines for American drivers. Instead of having the de-stroked, 3.4-litre engines of the previous year, all three were powered by works-prepared 2.4-litre units that had been bored and stroked to 2986cc, giving a reported 270bhp @ 6700rpm.

There were four customer Testa Rossas present. The North American Racing Team's original prototype 0666 had been rebuilt after its big shunt at Le Mans and painted Lincoln Continental blue with a white stripe down the middle. Luigi Chinetti invited Rod Carveth and Gil Geitner to drive it at Sebring with the promise of drives at Nürburgring and Le Mans if they did well. Jim Johnston had bought 0720 early in 1958 and was to drive it with Augie Pabst and Eb Lunken; the 1958 Le Mans-winner 0728 had been sold to Luigi Chinetti who sold it on to Don Pedro Rodriguez for his outrageously talented young sons, Pedro and Ricardo, to drive under the NART banner, but at Sebring the elder Pedro drove with Paul O'Shea. Finally, E.D. Martin entered his 0730 with Lance Reventlow as co-driver.

The Sebring race was sponsored by AMOCO, which had an agreement with the organisers that all competing cars should use their fuel. This caused problems for Ferrari as they were contracted to Shell.

"Mr Ferrari agreed to go to Sebring provided we could use Shell and he received a cable saying 'yes'," Romolo Tavoni recalls. "However, when we arrived at Sebring for registration Reg Smith, the Secretary of the United States Automobile Club, told me, 'You must use our fuel or we will not pay your expenses.'

"Our American distributor, Mr Luigi Chinetti – a very good friend of Mr Ferrari – flew a lawyer in from New York who told me that the cable would only stand up providing we had received a letter confirming the cable. We had the original cable but we had never received the confirming letter.

"Reg Smith then said, 'Tavoni – either you use AMOCO or you don't start.' I called Mr Ferrari, but he would not say 'Race' or 'Don't race'. He told me, 'You know our agreement, you make the decision.' So I decided we had to race with AMOCO."

The sunshine state of Florida proved to be anything but that week, and the first two days of practice were almost washed out by heavy rain.

On the first day Moss was still in Miami, but Ivor Bueb (Lister-Jaguar) and Lance Reventlow (Testa Rossa) were joint fastest with a time of 3 mins 53 secs. Roy

Opposite: Roy Salvadori splashes through the rain in DBR1/1 during practice and Phil Hill does the same in TR 0766 during the race (right) on his way to victory.

Salvadori did just eight laps with the Aston, returning a best time of 4' 19.2". On the Friday, with the course drying out, both he and Carroll Shelby got down to 3' 40.8". Olivier Gendebien did 3' 41" and Phil Hill 3' 50" before the gearbox of their Testa Rossa failed. Ominously Edgar Barth and John Fitch did 3' 42" and 3' 43" in the Porsches. Moss quickly got to grips with the Lister-Jaguar and eventually made fastest time of all with 3' 29" – still a long way off his 1958 lap record of 3' 20" in the Aston.

Ferrari kept his Le Mans-winning team of Hill/Gendebien together in Testa Rossa 0770, putting Behra and Allison in 0768 and Gurney and Daigh in 0766. Roy Salvadori's DBR1 had pole position for the 10am start by virtue of having the largest engine and he made a splendid getaway, leading for the first lap, with Pedro Rodriguez right behind him and followed by Gurney (Ferrari), Bueb (Lister) – Stirling Moss not starting a race for once – and Behra. Gendebien had spun but recovered quickly.

Salvadori's lead was short-lived, as Gurney and Behra roared past him, but he then had a fine old battle with Rodriguez for a few laps until the Aston slowed with clutch slip. At the end of lap 11 Roy stopped at the pits and it was found that oil was leaking from the engine on to the clutch. He went back into the race, but stopped again on the 18th, 21st and 25th laps as the problem worsened. As Salvadori slipped down the order, Olivier Gendebien was driving very fast indeed and moved up to third place behind the other two Ferraris. Ivor Bueb was fourth, and Taffy von Trips a remarkable fifth in the Porsche.

On lap 26 Carroll Shelby took over the Aston, only to stop out on the circuit two laps later when the gear lever broke off in his hand. He walked back to the pits and jokingly threatened to hit Reg Parnell over the head with it. Then he returned to the car with some tools and managed to get the Aston back to the pits. Twenty-five minutes later a new lever had been fitted and he rejoined the race. Four laps later he was back, stuck in second gear. The car was withdrawn.

After three hours the three works Ferraris were in the ascendant, only to suffer a setback when Jean Behra came in to hand over to Cliff Allison. The Testa Rossa refused to start for six long minutes, and Cliff eventually rejoined the race in fifth place. In his efforts to make up the time lost he set fastest lap of the race in 3 mins 21.6 secs. Gendebien's fine charge had enabled Phil Hill to move into the lead, with the Gurney/Daigh car now in second place.

The Americans knew all about Gurney, but to the European contingent he was very much an unknown quantity. During practice several old hands who could count their races in the hundreds had been astonished to learn from a bashful Dan that Sebring was only his 25th, since beginning his career with a second-hand Triumph TR2 in October 1955.

During his first turn at the wheel Dan's speed and consistency had been very impressive, but the man himself was only too glad to be out of the Ferrari. In common with the late Mike Hawthorn, he was 6ft 2ins tall and when he had tested the Testa Rossa at Modena he found it a very tight fit. Unlike Hawthorn, he didn't complain.

"I felt that my status at the time didn't include the privilege of complaining," he says, "but at Sebring I found out that I should have, because I was history after my first stint. My driving position amounted to being in a squatting position for an hour and 45 minutes and I could barely walk when I got out of the car."

Stirling Moss now made his move and began taking three or four seconds a lap off the Ferraris and stole third place when Allison handed his car back to Behra. When Phil Hill rolled into his pit with a seized gearbox, the other two Ferraris were immediately signalled to slow down, their times falling to around 3' 31". Moss soon caught them and as the race entered its fifth hour he moved into the lead with the Lister-Jaguar and when Gurney replaced Daigh Jo Bonnier moved the RSK Porsche into third place. Ferrari were in bother!

Jean Behra took an early lead in 0768 and set a new lap record, later broken by his co-driver, Cliff Allison. They finished second.

Now it began to rain, and Moss drew farther and farther away from the Testa Rossas. This year drivers were allowed to drive any and all their team cars, so Tavoni brought in Dan Gurney and Hill and Gendebien took over 0766, but not until an electrical fault had been put right, costing five minutes and dropping the Ferrari to third place, behind the Behra/Allison car and the Bonnier/von Trips Porsche. Phil Hill then set off and soon showed that Moss was not the only rainmaster present, driving superbly in the awful conditions and reeling in the Porsche by some seven seconds a lap.

Maddeningly for all British and Lister fans, Moss then ran out of fuel. He hitched a lift back to the pits on a marshal's Lambretta, returned to the car with a can of petrol and rejoined the race. Sixteen laps later he was disqualified, for the rules stated that he should have gone to the pits on foot . . .

With seven hours gone Hill was in second place, sixteen seconds behind Jean Behra, taking the lead shortly afterwards when the Frenchman stopped to hand over to Cliff Allison. It was during his next stint that Cliff had a very narrow escape.

"As I was coming out of the turn before the pits in the pouring rain I hit a big puddle," he recalls. "There was an AMOCO bridge over the track on the main straight, and the Ferrari acquaplaned on the water and headed straight for it. Just before it hit the supports the front wheels found a bit of tarmac and we whizzed past, otherwise Sebring would have been my first and last race for Ferrari. Next time round I stopped and asked the mechanics to check the steering, but that was just an excuse – I'd frightened myself silly and needed a breather!

"Later, I gave the car back to Behra, but he decided that the conditions were too dangerous and came straight back in, saying, 'I'm not driving in that!' So I had to go out again in the rain and finish the race."

A lap apart, the two Ferraris now held a commanding lead to the end, from the works Porsche of Bonnier/von Trips and the privately entered one of Don Sessler/Bob Holbert. Fifth was the other works car of John Fitch/Edgar Barth and in sixth and seventh places were the customer Testa Rossas of Martin/Reventlow and Johnston/Lunken/Pabst.

Rod Carveth and Gil Geitner were very unlucky, for after eight hours they were in sixth place, but then the car ran out of fuel on Warehouse straight, about a mile past the pits. Geitner walked in and announced that he had had enough, so Carveth went to 0666 and heroicly pushed it back to the pits in the rain. He refuelled and rejoined the race, only to hit one of Sebring's notorious marker barrels and damage a headlamp irreparably. He had to retire.

So once again Scuderia Ferrari had started the season with a victory, and once again Porsche had finished third, and Aston Martin were nowhere. Back at Feltham it was found that the gear lever on DBR1/1 had snapped off at the weld at its base and that the first and second speed selectors had broken because they had been weakened by the incorporation of the locking device. In solving one problem, Astons had made another.

And Development Engineer Bryan Clayton recalled that oil got into the clutch, "Because although we had increased the size of the pipe to the oil pump, we still had the same size pipe scavenging from the engine. We were putting in more oil than we could take out and the level in the sump slowly built up until it began to seep into the clutch. That car had done 18 hours at Monza with no trouble at all, yet in the first few minutes of Sebring it played up."

Despite the loss of one Testa Rossa with gearbox problems, Romolo Tavoni had a much happier tale to tell. Once again, Ferrari's new cars had won convincingly first time out and new recruits Behra, Allison and Gurney had driven superbly. As usual, on his return to Maranello Tavoni went to report to his boss. Typically, instead of congratulating his Team Manager on his success Enzo berated him for giving in to the Americans in the matter of fuel.

"You are not sufficiently strong with these people!" he shouted, banging his fist on his desk. A pause, as he fixed Tavoni with a steely glare from behind those tinted glasses. "Now tell me again – how did we finish?"

"First and second, Mr Ferrari."

The merest glimmer of a smile:

"That is sufficient."

CHAPTER SEVENTEEN

A setback for Astons, a shock for Ferrari

Le Mans Test Day; the Targa Florio

Towards the end of 1958 Aston Martin delivered their one and only 'customer car', DBR1/5. David Brown had never intended to make this model available, even to experienced racing drivers, as he had with the production DB3S, but he made an exception for Graham and Peter Whitehead. The half-brothers had kept the company's flag flying at Le Mans by finishing a splendid second in their ex-works DB3S when all the team DBR1s had failed and afterwards, a duly grateful DB had asked Graham how he could repay them for their bacon-saving performance.

"A DBR1 would be nice," said Graham.

Sadly Peter Whitehead never lived to see his new car for he was killed during the Tour de France in September, when the 3.4-litre Jaguar he was sharing with Graham plunged down a ravine. Graham was injured but made a full recovery and continued his racing career in 1959, planning a full season with the Aston.

In April Astons sent two DBR1s to Le Mans for the first official Test Day, organised by the AC de l'Ouest. Ferrari sent one Testa Rossa and a 2-litre V6 Dino.

Paul Frère had been invited to join Aston Martin for the 24-hour race, returning to the team for the first time since 1955, when he and Peter Collins had finished a fine second there in the DB3S. It very soon became clear to Paul and everyone else from Feltham that the policy of not developing the DBR1 but only seeking better reliability was a big mistake.

All were dismayed by the lack of speed of the Astons, which were slower than they had been the previous year, and alarmed by that of the Ferraris, which were indecently fast. Jack Fairman set the best Aston time with a dismal 4 mins 17 secs, and Carroll Shelby was 10 seconds slower, whereas he had managed 4' 13" in practice in 1958, when Brooks had recorded 4' 08".

By contrast Phil Hill came within a hair's breadth of Mike Hawthorn's outright lap record with a time of 3' 59.3", and Dan Gurney very nearly equalled that. They were driving a Testa Rossa (probably 0772) which had an engine fitted with large-choke 42mm Weber carburettors, the V12 allegedly producing 330bhp @ 7,700rpm. And this despite the fact that the car was seriously undergeared, Cliff Allison reporting that he was reaching 8,000rpm by the time he reached Les Hunaudières restaurant early on the Mulsanne straight.

Even worse was the news that Cabianca in the two-litre Ferrari was consistently faster than both Astons and recorded a best time of 4' 10.7". Somehow the DBR1s were going to have to find a lot more speed before June.

Tony Brooks (right) turns photographer as his co-driver Jean Behra sets off on the Targa Florio in 0768.

Astons made the second diversion from their 'Le Mans only' policy with the announcement that that Stirling Moss would be driving a works DBR1 in the Nürburgring 1,000 Kms race, partnered by Jack Fairman. This news must have made a few hearts sink in Maranello and Stuttgart.

Tony Brooks' first experience of a Testa Rossa came in the Targa Florio. He had enjoyed what little driving he had done there in the Aston Martin DBR1 and R2 the previous year and was keen to do some proper road racing on the remarkable Sicilian circuit. He was paired with Jean Behra in 0768 while Phil Hill and Olivier Gendebien were given 0766. Dan Gurney joined forces with Cliff Allison in 0770, powered by the 330bhp engine which had been fitted at Le Mans. Cabianca and Scarlatti had the two-litre, V6 Dino sportscar which had also appeared at the Le Mans Test Day.

Porsche also brought four cars: two RSK models for Taffy von Trips/Jo Bonnier and Umberto Magioli/Hans Herrmann; one 1.5-litre for Edgar Barth/Wolfgang Seidel, and a Carrera GT for von Hanstein/Pucci. Maglioli (who had won the 10-lap Targa single-handed in 1953 and 1956) was returning to racing after an 18-month layoff, following a bad accident in the 1957 Gaisberg Mountainclimb.

Wisely Aston Martin made no attempt to enter the race this year and surprisingly there was no car of any kind for Stirling Moss.

After his very uncomfortable ride at Sebring Dan Gurney had asked for some more room to be made in the Testa Rossa's cockpit, and this was done in time for the Targa. Dan just loved that circuit.

"When we arrived, Phil Hill took me around in the Ferrari muletta – a four-cylinder, two-litre car – and then I took Cliff round. I thought the circuit was absolutely fantastic, a tremendous trip back into the history of motor racing and quite overwhelming. It demanded staggering concentration to try and remember the track, but I just thought it was a fabulous experience, one of the best and most memorable of my whole career."

For the very first time the authorities decided to close the roads for one day of official practice, but they weren't closed for very long, as the locals didn't really care for the idea. Most drivers only managed one quick lap and at the end of the day the remarkable Maglioli was fastest of all with a time of 45 mins 51 secs in the RSK Porsche. He was followed by team-mates von Trips with 46' 00" and Bonnier in 46' 45". Best of the Ferrari drivers was Brooks with 48' 06"; then came Barth (48' 09"); Gendebien (48' 16"); and Phil Hill (48' 24"). Behra recorded 49' 49"; and Dan Gurney did 49' 52", which included a stop to see if Scarlatti (who had lost a wheel) was OK.

At 5am 50 cars stood nose to tail, waiting for the start of the 43rd Targa Florio. The first to leave was a streamlined, 750cc DB-Panhard, and the last was Dan Gurney in the Testa Rossa. And it was the American was who leading overall at the end of the first lap, which he covered in 45 mins 01 secs. Eight seconds behind him came Jean Behra, who was followed by no fewer than five Porsches. The German cars were on the march!

Not quite believing that he is about to take the battered Testa Rossa back into the race, Tony Brooks buckles up his helmet as Jean Behra assures him – with all the charm of a used-car dealer – that, despite having been overturned, the Ferrari is "a nice little runner, M'sieur."

Some five minutes behind Gurney came Olivier Gendebien, whose Testa Rossa had ominous noises coming from the rear axle. He pulled into the pits to retire with a broken crownwheel and pinion and announced that he had seen Cabianca's Dino on fire. By the end of lap three Jo Bonnier had forced his way into first place, and a lap later Barth in the other RSK Porsche was in second, with Gurney and Behra relegated to third and fourth and powerless to do anything about it.

Next Cabianca arrived with a scorched Dino and demanded a new spare tyre, as his had been burnt by the fire which had started on top of the fuel tank! The washer on the Dino's fuel filler was replaced with that from Gendebien's car, and Cabianca rejoined the race.

Tavoni now made plans to put Gendebien and then Hill in Gurney's 0770 when he finished his five-lap stint, but before Dan arrived, Cabianca stopped again, to announce that first, he had no gears on the Dino; and second, Jean Behra had overturned his Testa Rossa. As if this wasn't bad enough, Gurney now staggered in with all-too familiar noises coming from the Ferrari's rear end. Nonetheless, Gendebien asked to be allowed to use it to collect Behra, but no sooner had he made his leisurely departure from the pits than the Frenchman arrived in one very battered Ferrari. With the race folding around his ears, Romolo Tavoni had to listen to Behra excitedly try to explain what had happened.

On the run down to Campo Felice he had lost the Ferrari in a big way, and it had skidded for about 100 yards and then rolled over. Behra ducked down in the cockpit, and when the dust had settled, he found himself inverted over a hollow in the ground, so he wriggled out from under to survey his up-turned Testa Rossa. Seeing three locals in a field he persuaded them to help him right the car, which started on the button, so he drove it to the pits.

Denis Jenkinson noted that, 'All four humps over the wheels were flattened, the windscreen was smashed, the perspex cover over the carburettors was broken, the headrest was dented, the tail jagged and torn and the right-hand exhaust pipe was trailing, yet the car sounded very healthy, and Behra insisted that it handled all right!'

Tony Brooks recalls, "I could not believe that Tavoni expected me to get in and drive this heap, but he did, so off I went. Unfortunately, I didn't complete a lap as the car just went straight on somewhere and I hit a wall. I was very disappointed because the Targa was a great race and I never got a drive. In 1958 the Aston broke in Stirling's first session and then Behra presented me with a drastically modified Ferrari in 1959. It was very difficult to overtake there but while the road was clear it was great fun."

Actually Tony did complete one lap and it was on his second that he hit the wall. He drove the Ferrari to the team's mountain depot, but by now the steering was damaged and the noise from the rear end signalled that the crownwheel and pinion was failing. He drove slowly back to the pits and the third Testa Rossa was retired.

Meanwhile Olivier Gendebien, finding no upturned Jean Behra, toured gently round the 45-mile circuit, enjoying the odd chat with spectators here and there and – rumour has it – stopping for lunch with some locals in one of the villages. He eventually returned to the pits to retire after a three-hour lap. Meanwhile, Cliff Allison joined Dan Gurney and Phil Hill with nothing to do and nowhere to go, for they couldn't leave the pits until the race was over.

A SETBACK FOR ASTONS, A SHOCK FOR FERRARI

But the Stuttgart concern was to have its troubles too for on his first lap after taking over from Maglioli, Hans Herrmann suffered engine failure on their RSK, which expired some 17km from the start. He gallantly stayed with his car for the next 13 hours, to ensure that nothing was stolen from it. For the rest of the race the other Porsche drivers ran a 'meals on wheels' service to the stranded Hans to ensure he had plenty to eat and drink.

Taffy von Trips took over the leading car for the final two laps and was cruising to a sensational win when the experimental wishbone rear suspension failed on the Porsche, just 23km from the chequered flag. So victory went to 1500cc RSK of Edgar Barth and Wolfgang Seidel, with Porsches also filling second, third and fourth places.

This was a crushing defeat for Ferrari, whose cars had too much power for their own good on the wild and rough Sicilian circuit. By contrast the Porsches were agile and very quick, more than a match for the Testa Rossas on this occasion. Their superb performance put them in the lead for the Championship, with 12 points to Ferrari's eight. Could they pull off another shock victory at the Nürburgring?

Losers and winners: Brooks passes the pits in his battered Ferrari (above) shortly before retiring. Eventual winner Edgar Barth (right) sets off for a practice run in the Porsche.

Trapped, the Ferrari team had the galling experience of watching Porsches settle into the first six places. The 1600cc RSKs of von Trips/Bonnier now led from the similar car of Maglioli/Herrmann; Barth and Seidel were third in the 1500cc version; the Mahle/Linge RS was fourth and two Carreras were fifth and sixth.

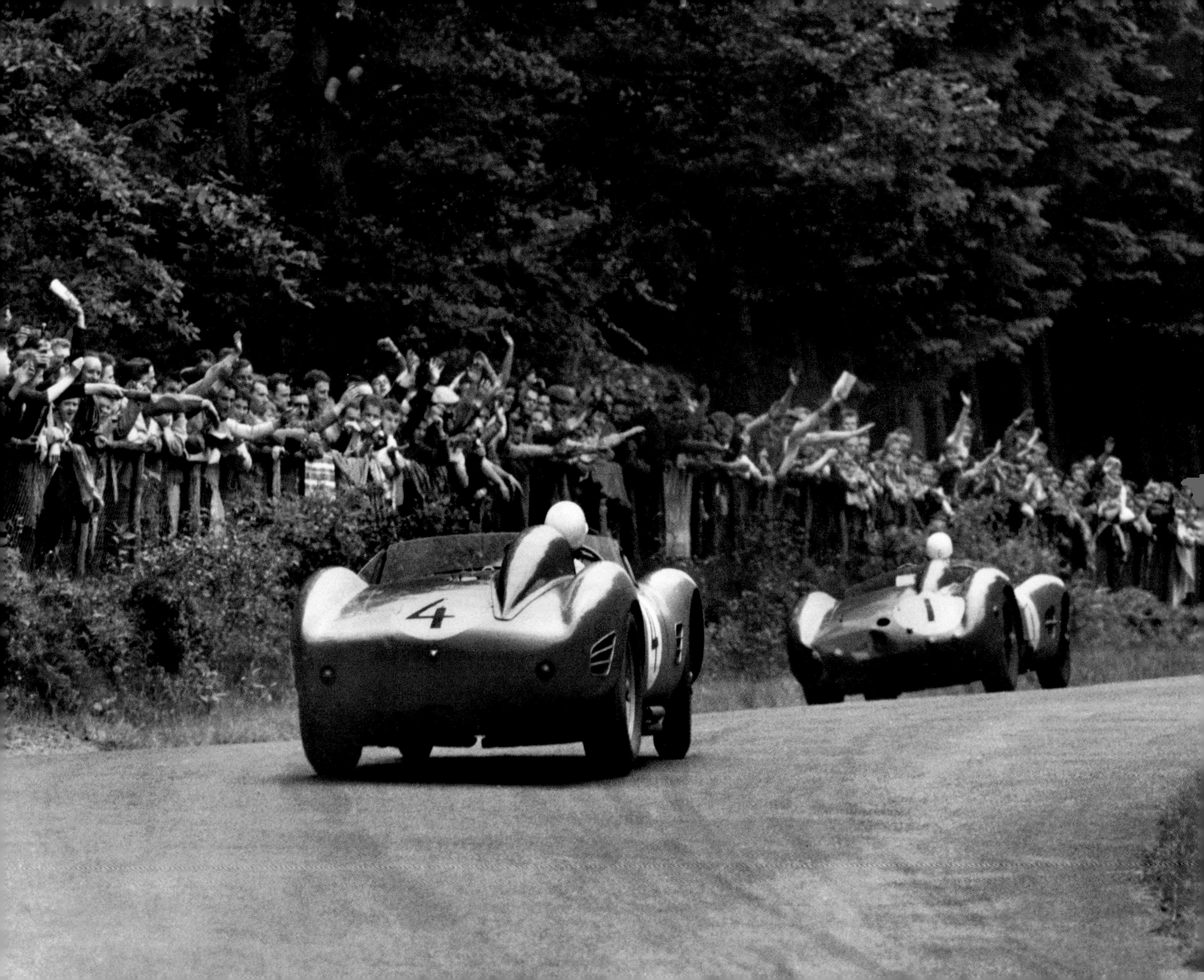

CHAPTER EIGHTEEN

Moss, the DBR1 and the Greatest Drive

The Nürburgring 1000 kms

"The DBR1 was so good at the Nürburgring that I asked John Wyer if I could have the spare car (which was not being prepared for Le Mans) for the 1,000 Kms race. I was so sure that I could win that I offered to pay all expenses, including transport, if they would let me have the car and, on these terms, John felt he could be generous about it! In fact they sent the car over with a couple of mechanics but all other expenses were mine, as was any prize money we might win."

With this request, Stirling Moss persuaded Aston Martin to make their second diversion from their 'Le Mans only' policy, and not only did they send mechanics, but Reg Parnell also went along as Team Manager. It was really a one-car works team, although on this occasion it was Stirling who was calling the shots. The ensuing victory was was to set Astons on the road to the Manufacturers' Championship and was the result of a drive of such sustained brilliance by Moss that it may be considered as the greatest in motor-racing history.

Stirling was well known (and often criticised) for his hard-nosed, professional attitude to racing, which upset many in what was still regarded as an age of amateurism in sport. However, although he made his living from motor racing and was always on the lookout for the best deal, his primary interest was in winning. In the circumstances, his offer to pay all expenses for the Nürburgring race was a remarkable vote of confidence in the Aston Martin DBR1 and the people who built

Opposite: cheered on by the spectators, Stirling Moss takes the lead from Phil Hill (busy correcting a slide) on his way to another sensational victory at the Ring. Note the Aston's dented tail - courtesy of Jack Fairman.

it. That confidence was to be repaid with a victory hailed by Martyn Watkins of *Autosport* as 'one of the most stupendous races of all time'.

The fabulous Nürburgring repeatedly brought out the best in the best and throughout the late 1950s a handful of great drivers used it as a canvas on which to paint a masterpiece or two and mark themselves as *Ringmeisters*. In 1956 Stirling Moss in a 300S Maserati defeated Juan Fangio in a Ferrari 860 Monza during the closing laps of the 1,000 Kms race. In the German GP a few months later Fangio stamped his authority on the race and the circuit with a masterly start-to-finish win in the Lancia-Ferrari. The following year Tony Brooks joined the exclusive band with his superb victory for Aston Martin in the 1,000 Kms, and then in the German GP Fangio produced what has long been acknowledged as the greatest Grand Prix drive of all time to catch and pass the seemingly uncatchable Ferraris of Mike Hawthorn and Peter Collins.

The great drives continued in 1958: first came Stirling's tremendous win with the DBR1 in the 1,000 Kms and then Tony Brooks' brilliant performance with the Vanwall to win the Grand Prix. Now, in June 1959, it was to be the turn of Moss once again.

After their complete débâcle in the Targa Florio, Ferrari had just a week in which to repair and prepare their cars before sending them to Germany, all three fitted with strengthened crownwheel and pinion units. The Testa Rossas were to be driven by the same pairings as in the Targa. The Behra/Brooks 0768 showed signs of extensive body repairs after its Sicilian rollover, and its engine had been modified to the same stage of tune (a claimed 340bhp) as the Gurney/Allison 0770, with the larger-choke

1959

Above: Phil Hill in TR 0766 on the run down to Flugplatz. The Ferraris were plagued with shock absorber problems during practice. Below: no such problems for Stirling Moss, seen here in DBR1/1, also approaching Flugplatz.

Opposite: with the three Testa Rossas in line astern, Cliff Allison settles into 0770 before setting off on a practice run.

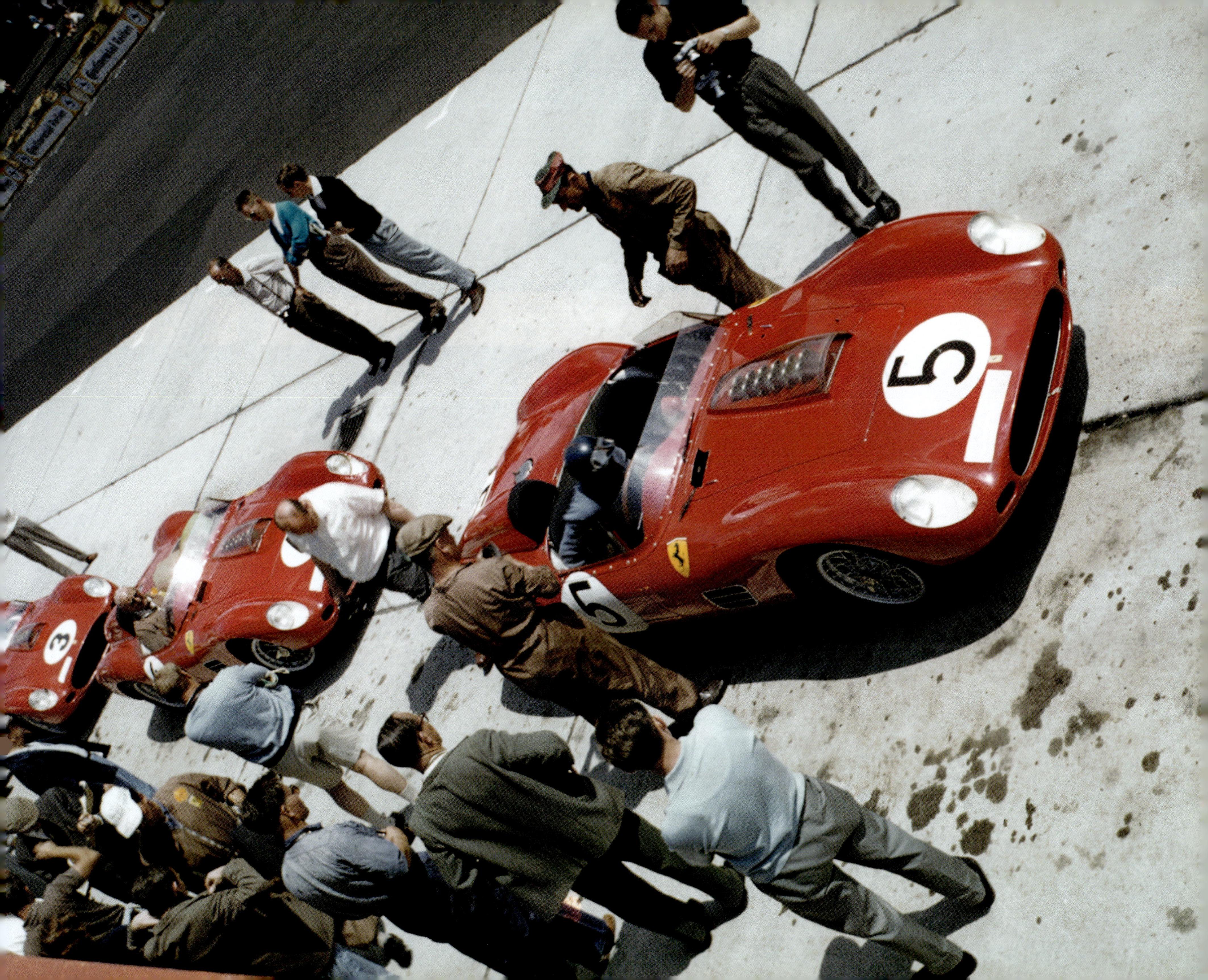
5
3

carburettors. Hill and Gendebien were once again in 0766.

Moss had Aston Martin DBR1/1, with Jack Fairman to back him up and for the first time the works car was to be supported by the privately-entered DBR1/5 of Graham Whitehead, who had Brian Naylor as his co-driver.

Porsche also had the same drivers, Maglioli/Herrmann and Bonnier/von Trips, in their 1600cc RSKs, both cars now fitted with the latest wishbone independent rear suspension. The 1500cc car was in the hands of Barth/de Beaufort.

The Ferrari drivers did not like the handling of the Testa Rossas, and a lot of tuning of springs and shock absorbers was done during practice, which saw Phil Hill pay a visit to a hedge.

"It was a classic Ferrari shock absorber problem." he says. "I went up in the air at Flugplatz, and the rebound was set so tight on the rear that it just lifted the rear wheels off the ground. I already had some turn on the front wheels so the car spun. At the Ring we were always beaten by the chassis going away and the roadholding deteriorating. With all the leaps and bounds on that circuit you had to know that you had something underneath you, and we didn't."

On the first official day of practice Behra did 9' 55" in the Testa Rossa, and the Porsches were also very quick. First Barth did 9' 58.1", and then von Trips was credited with an astounding 9' 40.5", beating Stirling's 1958 lap record. Nobody believed this, least of all von Trips, but the timekeepers let it stand.

Moss himself was way off the pace, with a best time of 10 mins 06 secs, doing only four laps before asking for a change of gear ratio. After his hassle with Reg Parnell on this subject the previous year the DBR1 was fitted, at Stirling's request, with the 3.62 final drive that he had used to win the 1958 race. Now he decided that an even lower cog would be better still, and so a 3.75 unit was installed.

"More than anywhere else I can think of the Ring was where you wanted to be very low-geared," he explains, " because, apart from the three-kilometre straight, on one 14.2-mile lap you were only near maximum speed on a couple of occasions and for about a quarter-of-a-mile at any one time; once through the Flugplatz (where you only just touched the maximum) and then after Fuchsröhre. If you're low-geared you get to the maximum revs early, so you're going to have to back off and although your outright maximum speed is lower you're better off with the better acceleration.

"The straight at the Ring is a relatively unimportant part of the circuit because although it is long, it is uphill and not very fast. It is far more important to be on or near the limit as often as you can on the rest of the lap."

Next day Umberto Maglioli did 10' 2.9" in the Porsche, and Graham Whitehead recorded 10' 7.1" in his DBR1, just one-tenth of a second faster than Phil Hill in the Testa Rossa. Using the 3.75 final drive Moss got down to 9' 43.1", but on the Saturday morning Jean Behra, Tony Brooks and Dan Gurney were all under Stirling's lap record of 9' 43.0". Behra took the Ferrari round in 9' 37", which gave him pole position for the Le Mans start; Brooks recorded 9' 40.5"; and Gurney was just 0.2 secs slower. Phil Hill did 9' 44.2"; and Jack Fairman was on 10' 17" with the DBR1.

If Scuderia Ferrari had hopes of winning this race they were banished by Moss virtually at the drop of the flag. The master of the run and jump was off and away almost before anyone else had begun to move. Denis Jenkinson noted that: 'the Aston Martin took off so quickly it looked as though no one else was going to race. Obviously,' he went on, 'Aston Martin were planning an identical race to last year, with Moss going as hard as he could from the start, making up sufficient time for his slow co-driver to do his stint without losing the lead, for the rules of the race forbade any driver to drive for more than three hours at a stretch. Thanks to Moss this tactic had worked in 1958, but just why he should be made to do the same thing again this year was hard to understand.'

Jenks was not the only journalist to criticise Astons' tactics and Stirling's choice of co-driver, but they had all failed to do their homework. Had they bothered to ask they would have discovered that Moss wasn't made to do anything – the race tactics were all his own, as was his choice of co-driver. "I chose Jack Fairman because I wanted someone who would do just what I asked him to, and Jack was prepared to do two laps and then come in, if necessary." says Moss. "He was a steady driver who would drive sensibly and keep it on the island, which was all I needed."

When entering the Aston Stirling had made the conscious decision to do as much of the driving as the rules would allow and to try and win the race almost singlehandedly. This he proceeded to do in the most amazing fashion with a drive so remarkable that it even eclipsed his stunning performance of the year before.

At the end of the first lap he was 15 seconds ahead of Dan Gurney, who was a further 15 seconds ahead of Phil Hill. His lead had been 18 seconds when he reached the three-kilometre straight, but the Aston was only pulling 144mph @ 6,200rpm and the much more powerful Ferrari had regained three seconds by the time it reached the pits. Third was Graham Whitehead, who was followed by the Porsches of Herrmann and Barth and the Ferrari of Brooks.

Moss simply drove away from everybody. After two laps he was 19 seconds ahead of Gurney; after four the gap was 38 secs and Stirling had lapped in 9 mins 47 secs. On lap seven he set the first of his new lap records with 9' 41" and was now over a minute ahead of Gurney. Two laps later his time was down to 9' 33", and his lead up to 1' 21". Another two laps and the incredible Moss had reduced his 1958 lap

Dan Gurney drifts through the curves between Brünnchen and Pflanzgarten in TR 0770, which he shared with Cliff Allison.

record by 11 seconds, with a time of 9' 32".

Gurney was now slowing due to a slipping clutch and on lap 12 he brought his Testa Rossa in with the news for Cliff Allison. "The next thing I know Cliff is running pretty good lap times," says Dan, "and I thought, 'How in the world is he doing that with the clutch slipping?' Simple – he was shifting gears without using the clutch."

At the end of that 12th lap Graham Whitehead was in a very fine fourth place when he stopped to let Brian Naylor take over the DBR1. The Ferrari pits were suddenly very busy as as Phil Hill and Tony Brooks arrived almost together to hand over to Olivier Gendebien and Jean Behra. Brooks admits that he was not at his best that day.

"I'd been sick early that morning and was very off-colour, so I didn't do myself justice in that race. But anyway, it would have been difficult to have done anything about Stirling in the Aston.

"The Testa Rossa was pretty good round the Ring. It didn't handle as well as the DBR1, but it had more power and a much better gearbox, which was helpful, because you have to change gear a lot there."

On lap 14 the von Trips Porsche failed to come round, having lost a rear wheel near Döttinger-Höhe. The enterprising Taffy walked to a nearby garage, borrowed some tools and fitted the spare, before driving back to the pits two laps down.

Brooks on the approach to Flugplatz with 0768, which Behra had rolled in Sicily.

Having slid off the damp track into a ditch, Jack Fairman borrows a wooden fence post with a view to levering the Aston back onto all four wheels.

But the post snaps in two. Leaving the bits beside the car, Jack climbs aboard and presses the starter, in the hope that he can drive the Aston back onto the road.

Bonnier took over. It was their second piece of bad luck that day, for early in the morning the engine had dropped a valve when being warmed up by the mechanics. In 30 minutes they had changed it for a 1500cc unit and the car had been driven onto the grid just five minutes before the start.

Bad luck also dogged the privately-entered Aston Martin. Brian Naylor managed only two laps in the DBR1 before the gear lever broke off in his hand. As the same thing had happened to Shelby at Sebring, it was inexcusable that Astons had failed to pass on the modification to Graham Whitehead.

After lapping relentlessy in times well under 9 mins 40 secs Moss had built up a stupendous lead of five minutes and 40 seconds when, at the end of lap 17, he stopped to let Jack Fairman take over. In 67 seconds the rear wheels were changed, the Aston was refuelled, and Jack was away. As he left the pits it began to rain.

Fairman was in no hurry and the Ferraris began to make up time on him. They were now second, third and fourth, in the hands of Gendebien, Allison and Behra, with the French champion going like the wind in the very wet conditions. By lap 22 Gendebien had closed to 4 mins 10 secs behind Fairman, but both Behra and Maglioli in the Porsche had overtaken Allison.

Then Fairman went missing! Moss was waiting impatiently for him to complete

Nothing doing, so now he tries brute strength, physically heaving the DBR1 out of the ditch.

Success! The Aston is on all four wheels again and Jack is about to get back in the race, but Olivier Gendebien has just gone by and into the lead. Stirling will not be pleased!

his sixth lap, but of Jack there was no sign. Some four minutes after he was due the Ferraris of Gendebien and Behra went by, now in the lead. As Olivier passed the anxious Aston Martin team he made a spinning sign with his hand. The seconds continued to tick away until, suddenly, the Aston mechanics were galvanised into action as the DBR1 breasted the rise and Fairman headed for the pits.

"He'd been gone so long," recalls Stirling, "I was convinced he'd really stuffed it and was out of the race, so I had packed up my helmet, gloves and goggles and was just about to take off my overalls when they yelled that he was coming in. I pulled everything on again, yanked Jack out of the car almost before it had stopped rolling and was off."

A breathless Jack Fairman was left to explain himself to Reg Parnell. On the very slippery right-hander leading to Brünnchen he had lost the Aston, which had slid across the track and finished up with its left rear wheel in the ditch and its right front in the air. Many people would have left it at that, but the man known as Fearless Jack was not about to walk away. He bodily heaved the car out of the ditch (denting the rear bodywork in the process) and drove on. He had lost a lot of time, but he had refused to give up the race.

Which was now in the hands of the amazing Moss, who relished the challenge before him. "Here was a great chance for me to have a go at the sort of motor racing I enjoyed the most – one Aston Martin against the full Ferrari team."

In *Autosport*, Martyn Watkins described 'a chase which will never be forgotten by anyone who saw it.' By the 26th lap Moss was 22 seconds behind Behra and only 29.6 seconds behind Gendebien. The two Ferraris were trying everything they knew, and on lap 27 Behra took the lead between Bergwerk and Pflanzgarten. As the leaders passed the pits Moss was 12.5 seconds behind Gendebien and 17 seconds behind Behra and on lap 28 he took second place from Gendebien, passing him on the downhill swoop into Adenau. At the pits he was 11 seconds behind Behra. Next time round Behra and Gendebien called at the pits together as Moss swept past into the lead and there followed simply fantastic pit work as both Ferraris had all four wheels changed, took on oil and fuel and went away with fresh drivers – Brooks and Hill. The cars arrived together and left together, the stop on each car having lasted a tremendous 1 min 5 secs! Yet even this could not prevent Stirling from leading by 2 mins 22 secs on the next lap, the order now being Moss, Brooks, Hill, Gurney and Maglioli, with Hill rapidly catching Tony Brooks.'

Above: watched by Mino Amarotti (in raincoat) Phil Hill refuels TR 0766 as Ferrari mechanics change the wheels and add oil. Hidden by car 4 is the Brooks/Behra Ferrari.

Opposite: Hill drifts the Ferrari over the bridge at Breidscheid with the tower of Nürburgring Castle on the horizon.

Once again, Stirling's progress was simply phenomenal, and on lap 33 he arrived at the pits with a lead of 2 mins 43 secs. That was reduced to 1 min 47 secs as the Aston was refuelled and Fairman took over for his final stint of two laps. Phil Hill was now on a charge and took a minute off him on the first, and as the Aston stopped at the pits at the end of the second, Hill roared by into the lead.

After a 59-second stop for fuel and oil, Moss set off 19 seconds behind the Ferrari. One lap later and the gap was down to 12 secs; another lap and it was five! Going into the 39th lap just 2.5 seconds separated the Ferrari from the Aston. As Bernard Cahier wrote in *Road & Track*:

MOSS, THE DBR1 AND THE GREATEST DRIVE

With the Hill/Gendebien Ferrari behind him, Moss is about to blast past the Lotus of David Piper/Keith Greene as he accelerates the Aston down the back straight towards the North Turn.

'Moss was wildly encouraged by the crowd, and each one of his spectacular comebacks in the race was an extraordinary sight. The people were on their feet shouting and yelling, and on the entire circuit you could see handkerchiefs and scarves waving as he went by. Although he was busy driving, he still found time to wave back at the crowds, delighting them even more. The thunder of the crowd was something to hear when Stirling passed Hill, his last adversary of the day, on the North Turn, facing the grandstands, just as Fangio did with Collins two years ago in the German GP. Hill was driving extremely well, but he could do nothing against Moss.'

In fact Moss did not manage to pass Hill at the North Turn, but had to follow the Testa Rossa through Hatzenbach and Quiddelbacher-Höhe before he could get by at Flugplatz. He then increased his lead over the remaining five tours, taking the chequered flag to thunderous applause from the packed grandstands 41 seconds ahead of Phil Hill. The American had driven the Ferrari superbly, but they were no match for Moss and the Aston on the Ring. After the race journalist Denise McCluggage offered consolation with the words, "Don't feel too bad about it, Phil. You were the first human being to finish."

Tony Brooks was third, some three minutes behind Hill, and the only other car to complete the full distance of 44 laps was the Porsche of Maglioli/Herrmann. In fifth place was the third works Testa Rossa of Gurney/Allison, one lap behind due to that slipping clutch.

As at Sebring, the Carveth/Geitner prototype was destined not to finish. "We were in eighth place when Gil crashed at the Karussell on the very last lap." recalls Carveth. "He pretty well wiped out the car and I was very unhappy about it. We really didn't talk to one another after that."

The race was a triumph for Stirling Moss and Aston Martin, each recording their third win in this hugely demanding race, and Feltham had scored a hat-trick with three different cars: DBR1/2 in 1957; DBR1/3 in 1958 and DBR1/1 in 1959.

The Aston had performed superbly (afterwards Stirling said he reckoned it could go on forever), as had the mechanics. Jack Fairman came in for much uninformed criticism after the race, but he, too, had done a tremendous job, particularly during his first stint in heavy rain. And few people would have had the determination – or the physical strength – to have pushed the Aston out of that ditch.

Juan Fangio's epic drive in the 1957 German Grand Prix has rightly passed into legend, but was it really more remarkable than Stirling's in this 1,000 Kms race? I think not. Consider the facts:

After a lengthy pit stop which cost him his lead, Fangio in his 250F Maserati made up almost a minute in 11 laps to catch and pass the Ferraris of Mike Hawthorn and Peter Collins and during the 22-lap race he broke his 1956 lap record ten times.

That was a fabulous performance, to be sure, but get this: in the 1959 1,000 Kms race Moss drove for 36 of the 44 laps and had to regain his lead not once, but twice. In the process he broke his 1958 sportscar record on no fewer than 16 occasions and put 5 minutes and 40 seconds – approaching eight-and-a-half miles – between himself and the leading Ferrari in the opening 17 laps, which almost defies belief. Surely Stirling's performance that day surpassed even that of Fangio in the pantheon of Great Drives, and I cannot think of anyone who has even approached either since.

Fittingly more than 230,000 people – the largest number of spectators to attend a race since the great pre-war days of Mercedes-Benz and Auto Union – were crowded around the Nürburgring to see that exhibition of sustained genius by Stirling Moss – truly a man apart.

CHAPTER NINETEEN

"Such a Stunning Car!"

Moss on the Aston Martin DBR1; the Mercedes-Benz 300SLR and the Nürburgring

"I won from way back in the field several times in my career and I regard the 1000 Kms at the Ring in 1959 as my greatest Comeback Race. If everything is going right you get into a rhythm and the car just flows around the circuit. I felt really inspired that day and having to chase and catch the Ferraris with the Aston undoubtedly had something to do with it! Also, I was given carte blanche by Reg Parnell to drive any way I liked to catch the buggers, all of which kept the adrenalin flowing.

"The DBR1 was one of the most driveable cars you could find. If you knew what you were doing you could position it on the throttle and although it wasn't as quick as the Testa Rossa in a straight line it would allow you to get your foot on the throttle earlier and go through the corners faster because it was so agile. That's what made it such a stunning car!

"The DB3S and DBR1 Astons were very user-friendly. For instance, at the Flugplatz in those days the cars almost took off and the DBR1 would land (not necessarily in a straight line) and give a little twitch, but not a serious one, so you could keep your foot on the throttle, whereas other cars would twitch badly and you would have to back off and correct the steering. The Aston didn't have those nasty traits, which made it such a nice car to drive.

"Although it was not very quick in a straight line you could gain time at Flugplatz (which was very fast) and then down Fuchsröhre, because you could hold it much closer to the limit than something that was not so user-friendly. Then there was the descent to Adenau, with several corners that weren't quite flat where you had to roll off the throttle in second or third. All the way down there the Aston was very, very good and, I would say, much better than the Ferraris.

"The key to going really fast at the Ring was to use the brakes as little as possible. There were very few places where you had to brake really hard - about two or three, as I recall. Mostly, I used just a light touch on the pedal to position the Aston, for if you touch the brakes when you are in a manoeuvre it will accentuate what you are doing.

"Another key was to throw the car into a corner to set it up, followed by a slight application of the brakes not to slow the car, but to position it. Braking is the most difficult manoeuvre in racing, although it seems so simple - you brake to slow down, but I believe that as you improve your driving skills you learn to use the brakes for other things. Their most important function, obviously, is to slow you but also, they're like a trim, they alter the balance of the car and you can utilise that to your benefit, providing you get it right.

"The downside to the DBR1 was that bloody awful gearbox; the fact that it hadn't got much power and had a bad torque curve. There were quite a lot of things wrong with the car, but the handling was superb. The Ring was one of my favourite circuits and the Aston would always shine there.

"In 1955 I drove a Mercedes 300SLR in the Eifel race and set fastest lap with a time of 10 mins 10.8 secs. My new lap record with the Aston DBR1 in 1959 was 9' 32" - more than 40 seconds quicker, which is astonishing. Of course, I wasn't racing Fangio in 1955, just following him closely (that was the only time in my career with Mercedes when I came under team orders - Alfred Neubauer said that it would be nice if Fangio won - and I got the message!) whereas in 1959 I was in a real race and trying to make up for lost time. But that is an amazing difference and shows just how good the Aston really was.

"Comparing the Mercedes with the Aston - if you wanted to win Le Mans you took the 300SLR. It was reliable and strong, but not nearly as nice to drive or as sympathetic to the driver as the DBR1, which was much more user-friendly. In other races, such as the Targa Florio or at the Ring, driving the Aston was a much easier task. The SLR was a superb machine which would do everything you asked of it, but it was not that easy to drive.

"In 1959 I took the Aston to the limit all round the Ring all the time and it didn't bite me. If I'd driven the 300SLR in the same fashion - providing my concentration was at 101% all the time - I think I would probably have got away with it, but it wouldn't have been easy, as it was with the Aston. The Mercedes was so much more demanding."

Above: Juan Fangio (1) leads Karl Kling (2) and Stirling Moss (3) through the South Turn in the 300SLR Mercedes moments after the start of the 1955 Eifel race.

Right: with Adenau in the background, Stirling drifts DBR1/3 through Kallenhard on the way down to Wehrseifen during the 1958 1000 Kms.

Below: on his way to Astons' hat-trick in 1959 with DBR1/1.

148

CHAPTER TWENTY

Astons, at long last Le Mans

Falling into victory

Having determined not to develop the DBR1 mechanically for Le Mans, Astons went looking for some extra miles per hour in the wind tunnel during the winter months. Using a quarter-scale model at the Royal Air Force School of Aeronautics at Cranwell they experimented with several modifications to the rear of the DBR1, raising the bodywork in an attempt to get a smooth airflow from the top of the windscreen to the top surface of the rear. A high, rounded tail was tried, as was a long flat, sloping rear culminating in a Kamm cut-off. Neither used a head-rest.

The most efficient shape proved to be the very rounded rear-end, but when Jack Fairman tested the full-size version at Silverstone and on the Motor Industry Research Association's test track in the spring of 1959 he found difficulty in breathing, as the airflow tended to suck the air out of the cockpit. Furthermore David Brown didn't like the look of it at all.

In the end a compromise was reached and the rear bodywork was raised between the wheelarches with a higher, but less substantial headrest. A plastic tonneau cover was fitted over the passenger seat from the top of the windscreen to the rear deck. More aerodynamic improvements were made by bringing the metal of the front wheelarches further down over the wheels and by fitting quick-release spats that covered the rear wheels down to the knock-off hubs. Fully-enclosing spats were tried, but they brought a dangerous increase in tyre temperature.

Previously all racing Astons from the DB3 onward had an exhaust system which exited under the driver's door. From its beginnings with a 2.5-litre engine, the DBR1 had been a very noisy car indeed, and several drivers had complained of their right ear being deafened during a race, so for Le Mans the twin pipes were run right under the Aston to the back. This reduced the noise, but the slight rerouting of the pipes was to bring driver overheating problems in its wake.

Le Mans was the one race David Brown had wanted to win above all others ever since he had bought Aston Martin back in 1947. The Nürburgring was a far greater test of man and machine, and three consecutive victories there were very nice, thank you, but in the eyes of the public at large, Le Mans was the Big One, with a worldwide reputation that was out of all proportion to its real value.

Aston Martin had been to the Sarthe 10 times and and had finished second on two occasions, but outright victory had always eluded them. Nothing had been said officially, but there was a feeling in the air at Feltham that this was the team's last opportunity to win and so, having done his utmost to make the cars reliable, Reg Parnell selected his drivers for their age and experience rather than youth and outright speed. His pairings were: Salvadori/Shelby (DBR1/2); Moss/Fairman (DBR1/3); and Trintignant/Frère (DBR1/4). Graham Whitehead and Brian Naylor were again in Aston Martin DBR1/5.

Opposite: Carroll Shelby in DBR1/2, on his way to realising David Brown's dream of winning Le Mans.

1959

In the absence of Tony Brooks Scuderia Ferrari brought in the Franco-Brazilian driver Nano da Silva Ramos, who had driven for the Gordini Grand Prix team in the mid-1950s. He was paired with Cliff Allison after Jean Behra had pulled rank as self-styled team leader and demanded Dan Gurney as his co-driver. They were given a brand-new Testa Rossa (0774), while last year's winners Hill and Gendebien continued with 0766, (which they had driven all season) and Allison/da Silva Ramos were given 0770.

Works, 1600cc RSK Porsches were present in the hands of Taffy von Trips/Jo Bonnier and Umberto Maglioli/Hans Herrmann and there was a 1500cc version for Edgar Barth/Wolfgang Seidel. Backing them up were the privately entered 1500cc RSKs of Hugus/Erickson and de Beaufort/Heinz. There were Lister-Jaguars for Ivor Bueb/Bruce Halford and Walt Hansgen/Peter Blond; Ecurie Ecosse had a D-type Jaguar for Innes Ireland/Masten Gregory and a Tojeiro-Jaguar for Ron Flockhart/Jock Lawrence.

There were three privately-entered Testa Rossas, for E.D. Martin/Bill Kimberly (0730); the Ecurie Francorchamps car (0736) for Lucien Bianchi/Alain de Changy and the NART 0666 (Rod Carveth/Gil Geitner), which had been back to the factory for repairs following its crash at the Ring. In common with the works cars, all would fail to finish.

At scrutineering the weighing machine revealed that the 1959 Testa Rossas were considerably lighter than the 1958 cars. The heaviest was the brand-new 0774, which scaled 1885 lbs, whereas the previous year the lightest had been 0704 (the second prototype) which had weighed in at 2,215lbs. The Aston Martins too had lost weight, DBR1/2 checking in at 1,894lbs (1,960lbs in 1958), and DBR1/3 weighing 1,883lbs (2,017lbs in 1958). The newest car, DBR1/4, was the heaviest at 1,900lbs, but Ted Cutting notes that, "After 1956 no-one at Aston Martin believed the Le Mans weights. Our DBR1s got lighter every year!"

In practice it soon became apparent that the Ferraris were still undergeared, despite the lessons of the Test Day. In his autobiography, *Starting Grid to Chequered Flag* Paul Frère wrote:

Opposite: the Testa Rossas lined up for practice, with Olivier Gendebien ready to set off in 0774.

Right: Scrutineering provided the first view of Astons' modification to the DBR1 bodywork in their search for more speed.

'Although our cars were definitely slower than the Ferraris, our hopes lay in the fact that it seemed as if a deadly rivalry had sprung up between the drivers of the Italian cars, only Hill and Gendebien had seemingly decided to repeat the waiting game which had given them victory a year ago.

'Even during practising it seemed that each one wanted to show his team-mates that he was capable of driving faster than they, and after each of the two practice sessions the cars went back to the garage with bent valves.'

Dan Gurney was fastest of all, with a time of 4 mins 03.3 secs and Behra was 0.3 secs slower in the same car, but the maximum revs needle was on 8,900rpm! Gendebien did 4' 05" and Masten Gregory proved that the D-type was still a very good Le Mans car by recording 4' 9.7".

Inevitably Stirling Moss was fastest of the Aston Martin drivers with a time of 4' 10.8", but only just, as Paul Frère did 4' 11"; Roy Salvadori 4' 12"; Jack Fairman 4' 16"; and Carroll Shelby 4' 21". Salvadori and Shelby completed seven and 10 laps respectively on the first day of practice and decided that was enough, "So we parked the car and played gin rummy." says Carroll.

At Stirling's request, DBR1/3 had been fitted with a four-bearing engine giving

Seconds after the start and the Astons of Trintignant (6) and Salvadori (5) have not begun to move, but Moss (4) is well under way, as is Innes Ireland in the D-type.

255bhp, whereas the seven-bearing units in the other two cars had been detuned in the search for reliability and produced just over 240. The latter could be run at higher revs for longer periods, but the former gave more power, due to lower frictional and pumping losses.

"A four-bearing unit was the last thing I would have chosen for a 24-hour race," says Roy Salvadori. "It certainly gave more power, but it was also going to be less reliable, particularly if you were going to rev it over 6,000."

That clearly did not bother Moss, but after the first practice he was unhappy with the car's 3.24:1 final drive ratio, so overnight it was changed to 3.19:1. This did not prove any better, so it was changed back to the lower ratio for the race.

Astons also experimented by running with and without their rear-wheel spats and tonneau covers. The spats added around 100rpm/3-4mph on the Mulsanne straight, and the tonneau cover was worth 300rpm/9mph. Together, they brought the DBR1's top speed up to 165mph, but this was still way short of the Ferraris, which were hitting 174 almost as soon as they reached the straight, for they were still undergeared.

Graham Whitehead was unlucky, in that a big end failed on his four-bearing engine during the first practice session. Reg Parnell promised him Astons' spare, a seven-bearing unit, but Graham had to wait until the last session was over before Reg would release it.

In time-honoured Aston Martin tradition, Parnell did his sums (advised by John Wyer) and came up with target lap times for his drivers. Apart from Moss, that is,

As Moss heads up towards Dunlop Bridge, many cars are not even moving. Stirling is followed by the Ireland/Gregory D-type (3); the Flockhart/Lawrence Tojeiro-Jaguar (8); and the Trintignant/Frère Aston Martin (6).

for it was agreed that his car would be semi-expendable and that he would drive at the speed he thought best. The Testa Rossas were clearly much faster than the DBR1s, and Reg confidently expected them to race among themselves early on, so Stirling was assigned the task of forcing their pace in the hope that one or more would blow up, even if Stirling's car did likewise.

Salvadori and Shelby were to provide close support to Stirling, with a target overall lap time of 4 mins 20 secs, bearing in mind that the fastest winner to date had been the Flockhart/Bueb 3.8-litre Jaguar in 1957, with an overall lap time of 4' 24.5" under perfect conditions. Frère and Trintignant were to hold themselves in reserve with an average time of 4' 22".

At 4pm in the afternoon of Saturday, June 20 Stirling Moss made his usual copybook Le Mans start and was first away, followed by Innes Ireland in the D-type. Last to leave was Jean Behra, who stalled his Ferrari twice.

At the end of the first lap Moss came howling past the pits with the Testa Rossas of Olivier Gendebien and Nano da Silva Ramos hard on his heels. Behra was up to 16th place and going like the proverbial clappers, paying no attention to his rev-counter. He was the Champion of France in front of his home crowd and he was going to show them where he belonged – in the lead.

After three laps he was in 10th spot, after five he was fifth and on the tenth he passed Ireland into fourth place, with the other two Ferraris between him and Moss. With just over an hour gone Behra was in second place and had set a new record for three-litre cars with a time of 4 mins 3 secs. He caught up with Moss as the two cars

Jean Behra at Mulsanne in the brand new Ferrari, 0774. In an attempt to make up for his poor start, Behra thrashed the car to within an inch of its life and it later expired during the night.

fled past the pits to the roars of approval from the excited spectators and the Ferrari passed the Aston on Mulsanne.

"I tucked in behind him and got 6,050rpm at the four-kilometre post," said an impressed Moss, later.

He hadn't been hanging about either, as Paul Frère recalled in amazement: "In practice I had done 4 mins 10.5 secs and felt that in the race I could get down to 4 mins 6 secs, but now Stirling was doing 4 mins 3 secs, and without the help of slipstreaming. This performance left me utterly speechless."

Behra completed the lap he passed Moss in 4' 1.9" (the first-ever at over 200kph by a three-litre car) but he wasn't through with the lap record yet. Going away from Moss he covered his 29th tour in 4' 0.9", which would stand as the fastest lap of the race.

Then there was chaos in the Ferrari pits as all three Testa Rossas came in at once, and Gurney, Hill and Allison replaced Behra, Gendebien and da Silva Ramos. The tell-tale on Behra's rev counter reportedly stood at 9,300rpm. Moss now was back in the lead, but at 6.30pm he made his scheduled stop, and Jack Fairman took over, getting away still in first place. However, Dan Gurney was really motoring and putting in many laps very close to Behra's record. Fairman, on the other hand, was going round in 4' 12" or thereabouts, setting his own personal fastest lap of 4' 08" in the process.

After four hours' racing Gurney led from Fairman; Gregory (D-type); Shelby (Aston Martin); Lawrence (Tojeiro-Jaguar); Bruce Halford (Lister-Jaguar); Frère (Aston Martin); and Hill (Ferrari). The Allison/da Silva Ramos Testa Rossa was brought in to retire after it kept jumping out of gear which led to a dropped valve. First blood to Aston Martin.

Phil Hill had been slowed by a lengthy pit stop to investigate what appeared to be flooding carburettors, but which proved to be water leaking through the cylinder head gaskets into the combustion chambers. This problem resolved itself temporarily as the level of water in the cooling system fell, but it would prove to be the car's downfall.

There were more problems for Ferrari when Dan Gurney was black-flagged by officials for having only one headlamp working, and his stop to correct this allowed Fairman back into the lead. It was short-lived, however, as just a few laps later Jack brought DBR1/3 in to report fluctuating oil pressure. Parnell sent him out again to complete his stint as all cars had to complete 30 laps before any liquids could be added. Two laps later Jack was back, and Moss took over but he found that the Aston was seriously down on power and after a couple of slow laps came in to retire. It was later discovered that a large part of the head of an inlet valve had broken off. Aston Martin and Ferrari were now down to two cars each as Brian Naylor had earlier crashed the Whitehead DBR1 at White House, happily without serious injury, but the car was badly damaged at the rear.

Although his race was run, Moss refused to leave the pits, and whenever a Ferrari made a stop he would wander over to see what was going on before reporting back to Reg Parnell. It was very clear that the Testa Rossas were all using a lot of water and *Autosport*'s John Bolster reckoned that about one-and-a-half gallons were usually added at each stop. This was comforting news to all in the Aston Martin pits for clearly, all was not well with the Ferraris.

At 10pm the Behra/Gurney car had completed 85 laps, one more than both the Ireland/Gregory Jaguar and the Salvadori/Shelby Aston Martin, which were in close company. Then came the Flockhart/Lawrence Tojeiro-Jaguar; the Bueb/Halford Lister-Jaguar and the Trintignant/Frère Aston Martin, all on 83 laps, with the Hill/Gendebien Ferrari a further lap behind.

After a very fine drive Innes Ireland and Masten Gregory were forced out when their D-type suffered a broken conrod and, not long afterwards, the Bueb/Halford Lister suffered the same fate.

Different strokes: Stirling Moss blasts through the second part of the Esses with DBR1/3 in a beautiful four-wheel drift, while Olivier Gendebien is more restrained in TR 0766.

Trouble hit Ferrari around midnight when the gear lever of the new Testa Rossa (0774) came off in Dan Gurney's hand. He stopped at the pits but found nobody able to help, so he did another lap – in second gear – before coming in again and this time a mechanic produced a piece of tube which fitted over the broken lever. Dan was able to continue, but he was now in second place behind the Salvadori/Shelby Aston Martin.

This shortly became third, for the Ferrari was now overheating badly, and the Hill/Gendebien car moved ahead of it. At 1.25am Jean Behra brought the car in with steam coming from its nearside exhaust pipes, and the Testa Rossa was withdrawn.

Just before 2am the Hill/Gendebien car moved into the lead when Carroll Shelby brought the DBR1 in for a stop of 5 mins 27 secs, during which time all four brake pads were changed, 141 litres of fuel were added and new rear wheels fitted. Salvadori rejoined the race 3' 50" behind the Ferrari.

At half-distance Hill and Gendebien were two laps ahead of the Salvadori/Shelby Aston, which was a further two laps ahead of its team-mate. Three laps behind that were the Porsches of von Trips/Bonnier and de Beaufort/Heinz with the Barth/Seidel car next up, seven laps further back. Porsche were leading the race on Index of Performance and were ideally placed for an overall win should the leading cars fail.

And suddenly Roy Salvadori was in trouble, as he vividly recalled a few days after the race. "The first thing that happened was that going down Mulsanne a nasty tapping set in, which I immediately thought was a bearing: tap, tap, tap. I switched off the engine. No change. So I restarted the engine and noticed that the oil pressure was perfect. The tapping was still there, then suddenly it ceased."

When the tapping returned a few minutes later he called at the pits to report what he thought must be a problem with the gearbox or transmission. A quick look round

Night work. Above: having at last discovered the Aston's thrown tread, mechanics change the rear wheel. Right: Dan Gurney looks on as mechanics try to repair the broken gear lever on his Testa Rossa.

revealed nothing, and he was sent on his way.

Two more laps and the vibration was back. "At one particular period it was terrible. The whole car darted around in the corners and seemed as though it was shaking itself apart, so I called in for a second time."

Again, nothing amiss could be found, so Reg Parnell told Roy to do five more laps to complete his tour of 30, when the car could be refuelled and then a proper inspection would be made.

"Those five laps were terribly slow – about six and a half minutes – with the car vibrating to hell," says Roy who then came in once more, convinced that either the de Dion tube or the transmission was broken. Reg got in the Aston, had it jacked up at the rear and put it in gear. It was then that mechanic John King spotted that a large piece of rubber was missing from the tread of the off-side rear tyre. A new

wheel was fitted, the car was refuelled, and Carroll Shelby drove back into the race, but the three stops had taken just over seven minutes in all and appeared to have cost Astons all chance of victory. By 5am Hill and Gendebien were three laps ahead of the DBR1, lapping comfortably in 4 mins 15 secs and looking set to repeat their victory of 1958.

And the Porsches were still very much in the picture, but suddenly – within minutes almost – the three works cars were out. The von Trips/Bonnier car broke a crankshaft; that of Barth/Seidel dropped a valve; and the de Beaufort/Heinz car suffered clutch failure.

At around 10am the Testa Rossa was in the pits for a change of pads on its Dunlop disc brakes. Romolo Tavoni recalls that this was the second change of the race.

"We had done our testing at the Modena Autodrome, instead of at Monza, where the cars reach high speed, so the brakes were not tested sufficiently. On the second stop the pads were worn completely; it was metal to metal."

Olivier Gendebien continued, but the Ferrari was now in deep trouble with over-

ASTONS, AT LONG LAST LE MANS

Olivier Gendebien cruising to victory (or so he thought) in TR 0766.

heating. It had only lasted as long as it did because Hill and Gendebien had refused to be drawn into the flat-out blind at the beginning of the race and had also been slowed by the apparent flooding of the carburettors. Now Olivier found the water temperature rising, and the oil pressure falling. He stopped at the pits but he hadn't completed his 30 laps, so no more water or oil could be added. He managed a couple of very slow laps before stopping once more and the Testa Rossa was pushed away.

The Aston Martins of Salvadori/Shelby and Frère/Trintignant were now first and second and a handy 25 laps ahead of the third-placed car, which was the 250 GT Ferrari of 'Beurlys'/'Elde'. However, there were still more than four hours to go, and no DBR1 had ever completed the 24 Hours in three previous attempts.

Paul Frère had taken over from Maurice Trintignant with instructions to match the times of the Salvadori/Shelby car, which should have been lapping at around 4 mins 45 secs, but Carroll was so anxious to finish that his times dropped to between 4 mins 50 secs and 5 minutes. Frère very soon caught up and became frustrated at having to hold station behind him. At the risk of incurring the wrath of Reg Parnell he eventually overtook the American, moving onto the same lap.

On his final tour Carroll deliberately slowed even more, in order to time his victorious arrival at the start/finish line for a few seconds after four o'clock. His timing was spot on, but the man with the chequered flag was French and he had other ideas. He ignored the Aston and waited instead for the winner of the race on Index of Performance, a French DB-Panhard, what else? Carroll had to do one more lap in order to take the flag and put the seal on David Brown's long-sought victory.

Above: mission accomplished - an exhausted Carroll Shelby drives Roy Salvadori, David Brown and Stirling Moss through an admiring throng after Astons' long-sought victory.

Opposite: lights blazing, Salvadori hustles DBR1/2 through the Esses early in the race, sandwiched between the Lister-Jaguar of Ivor Bueb/Bruce Halford and the Stanguellini of Delageneste/Guiraud.

Carroll's fine achievement brought him little pleasure at the time – he was just damn pleased to get the whole thing over and done with – for he had caught a stomach bug just before the race and had a thoroughly miserable 24 hours. The same had happened the year before, and he had dropped out before the start, but this time he went through with it, existing on a couple of strawberries and a few bottles of Coca Cola. By the end he was exhausted.

Roy Salvadori was also in poor shape due to a heavy cold – his race diet had been aspirins – and he was driven quickly back to Astons' HQ at La Chartre even before the official presentation which Carroll, virtually out on his feet, attended with a delighted David Brown. Later DB drove his victorious DBR1 back to the hotel.

"The reception I got along the way was unbelievable, with people waving and cheering and urging me to go faster," he later recalled. "In previous years I'd driven our highest finisher home after that race and the brakes were non-existent, the shock absorbers were useless and sometimes the Aston was almost undriveable. But that DBR1 could have done another 24 hours and no doubt about it!"

Which is more than could be said for the team. They were all exhausted, and the victory party at La Chartre petered out almost before it had begun. The previous year's débâcle had led to a monumental bunfight, but this time, with DB's ambition realised, they were all too tired to care.

1959

CHAPTER TWENTY-ONE

Post Mortems

Le Mans afterthoughts

Le Mans had been a disaster for Scuderia Ferrari. For the second time in three races the works cars had failed to finish and on this occasion so had the customer Testa Rossas. It was only thanks to privateers 'Beurlys' and 'Elde' that Ferrari were still in the Championship race, for their 250GT had finished a splendid third overall, scoring four invaluable points. Ferrari still led the Championship, but only by two points, having 18 to Aston Martin's 16 and Porsche's 15.

Afterwards it was commonly agreed among writers covering the event that the failure of the Ferraris was due to the fact that the team was something of a shambles from start to finish. Jesse Alexander of *Sports Cars Illustrated* was a friend of both Phil Hill and Dan Gurney and he had paid particular attention to the Scuderia on behalf of his American readers. He reported that:

The Ferrari team in the pits before evening practice. Nearest the camera is the Behra/Gurney car with Jean Behra (left) talking to an official.

'The defeat actually started back in April when the Maranello team travelled all the way to Le Mans for a single day of practice in which gear ratios and handling were to be sorted out . . . Ferrari handling left something to be desired, but the engine and Dunlop-Mintex disc brakes were the best part of the car . . . at least in the minds of several of the drivers. With plenty of time to put it right and to fit a higher axle ratio it was felt that Ferrari would have no trouble winning Le Mans hands down. But as Phil Hill put it: "We might just as well have not bothered coming in April, for all the good it did us."

'Just what was the Ferrari problem? First of all the cars were still undergeared; 8,000rpm worked out to 180mph, 8,000 coming up within the first two miles of the Mulsanne straight. "We're not far from flat out all the way down the straight," said Cliff Allison. The Ferrari engineers restricted their drivers to 7,500rpm, but not all obeyed these orders religiously, least of all Behra.

'The second factor that contributed to their downfall was a serious lack of organisation on the part of the team managers. To the observer, Ferrari team organisation was the most haphazard of any. No-one to our knowledge kept a serious

The Aston Martin pitwork was superb throughout the 24 hours. Here on the Sunday morning the watch on Eric Hind's wrist shows 11-40 as Reg Parnell directs operations through his loud-hailer and Carroll Shelby gets out of the car.

As Roy Salvadori settles into the cockpit the Aston has taken on 119 litres of fuel and 1.5 gallons of oil in 62 seconds. Opposite: Phil Hill and Olivier Gendebien (seen here at Arnage) were convinced that they had the race in the bag, until....

lap chart nor could one find out in the Ferrari pits, at any time, what the positions of their cars were or the gaps between them . . . Another headache in the Ferrari camp is the huge gap presented by the language barrier. Phil Hill and Behra just get by in Italian; Tavoni speaks a limited amount of English and perhaps understands more than he admits, but it is still a considerable barrier to constructive organisation. Most of all Ferrari lack an engineer who can also drive.

'The Italian failings were made all the more conspicuous by the mere presence of Aston Martin and Reg Parnell. The Aston pit stops were thrilling to watch; once the brake pads on all four wheels were changed on two cars during the race, the car was refuelled, oil tanks topped up and rear wheels changed. In each case it took slightly over five minutes to do all this. The less said about the Ferrari pit stops the better.'

The Autocar made the same point: 'As always, these (Aston Martin) pit stops were models of efficiency, with hardly a word spoken, and lasting no more than about 55 seconds. They were in marked contrast with the near Pandemonium of the pit work on the works Ferraris earlier, a similar routine taking on the average 1 min 33 secs.'

It hadn't been all beer and skittles in the Aston Martin camp, however. Whereas with Ferrari it was the engines that became overheated, with Astons it was the drivers. The re-routing of the exhaust pipes under the cars meant that the pedals became very hot indeed and all the drivers of the two victorious cars suffered from burnt feet to one degree or another. Early on the Sunday morning Maurice Trintignant very nearly had to give up, so painful was his right foot. The reserve driver, Henry Taylor, was put on standby, but Maurice decided to tough it out, explaining afterwards that there was a lot of fresh oil on the circuit which Taylor knew nothing about.

"We used to take air from the front of the car and so get a tremendous amount of ventilation in the cockpit," explained Roy Salvadori. "But this year there were three vents on the top of the car, just in front of the windscreen. They were utterly useless and every driver just got completely cooked."

It was the engines that were cooked at Ferrari and Roy was not surprised. "Those (practice) times weren't their true form because they were over-revving terribly to get them. It wasn't a true speed, and the cars were being stressed far too much. Their laps at fractionally over four minutes were forced to such an extent that they simply couldn't have got through the race . . . The only advantage Ferrari had over us was extra speed, and they only had that by straining themselves. Until we had tyre trouble we were never matched on continuous speed. The Italians were making faster laps perhaps, but they weren't going as quickly over a long period as we were. And if we hadn't had the tyre trouble, I'm quite confident that at no time would we have dropped out of the lead, because after we got going again we were gaining on them all the time."

Phil Hill is having none of that! "We were cruising to an easy victory, even though Roy always claims that it was a big battle and that Astons didn't have it as easy as they in fact did. Never before had I ever sat back in the middle of a race and counted the prize money, but that is what Olivier and I were doing, we were so certain of winning.

"It was the easiest Le Mans I have ever been involved in, and I've always resented the fact that the team didn't let us know that the other car had had trouble losing water during the night. Had we known about that we would have been on the lookout and changed our driving methods a little by using the brakes more, cornering harder and not staying on the throttle so much. I don't know whether the Testa Rossa would have lasted or not, but I would have had the spark plug out so that there would have been no combustion in the cylinder that had the leak. We could have finished the race on 11 cylinders, we were having it that easy."

Maybe, but there can be no doubt that the Ferraris were driven very hard indeed early in the race, and the fastest laps of both teams makes interesting reading:

ASTON MARTIN
Moss: 4 mins 03.3 secs DBR1/3
Salvadori: 4 mins 05.0 secs DBR1/2
Naylor: 4 mins 08.9 secs DBR1/5
Trintignant: 4 mins 11.2 secs DBR1/4
FERRARI
Behra: 4 mins 00.9 secs TR/0774
Hill: 4 mins 02.1 secs TR/0766
da Silva Ramos: 4 mins 02.5 secs TR/0770

All three Ferraris were driven harder and faster than the fastest Aston Martin, and this undoubtedly played a part in their eventual failure. There can be little doubt too that Stirling Moss had a lot to do with this although, clearly, the Ferrari drivers didn't need much in the way of outside assistance when it came to driving their under-geared Testa Rossas into the ground.

In his Race Report Reg Parnell stated that: 'It is difficult to estimate accurately the part played by Moss in our success at Le Mans. According to plan, he set a very high average speed for the opening hours of the race in an attempt to break up the Ferrari opposition (at the time of its retirement, car no 4 had run at an average lap time of 4 mins 13 secs), and his performance was without doubt responsible for the failure of the Behra/Gurney Ferrari.

'Salvadori and Shelby drove extremely well together, but it was disappointing that Salvadori was unable to identify the tyre trouble during the night session. Trintignant and Frère were reliable and consistent and, despite the former's blistered foot, it is felt that these two drivers were in the best physical condition at the end of the race. All the drivers conformed to the plan arranged, and our success can justifiably be described as the results of a team effort.'

Reg's words should have been compulsory reading for Scuderia Ferrari, but he was, perhaps, a little hard on Roy Salvadori regarding the tyre problem. Roy had been with the team since 1953, long enough for everyone to know that mechanical sympathy was not his strong point.

As usual, Moss was superb. His car was regarded as expendable by Astons, in the hope that he could make the Ferrari drivers over-extend the TRs early in the race.

Reg Parnell and mechanics Eric Hind and Jimmy Potton congratulate Carroll Shelby on a fine drive.

In the circumstances, one would have thought that with all the racing experience available in the Aston Martin pits, someone would have had the presence of mind to remove the quick-release rear wheel spats on the DBR1 and run a hand around the tyres – on Roy's initial stop, not his third.

However, the fact remained that Astons had won the Big One and, as a result, would have to make their third and final diversion from their 'Le Mans only' policy, for they now had a very real chance of winning the World Championship. The final round was the Tourist Trophy, to be held at Goodwood. This provided a major advantage over their rivals, as neither Ferrari nor Porsche had officially entered a team of cars in a long-distance event there (the three Ferrari 750 Monzas which took part in the 1955 Nine Hours race were 'private' entries), whereas Astons frequently used Goodwood for testing and had won all three Nine Hours events and the 1958 TT at the Sussex circuit.

But that was in September, more than two months away. Meanwhile Scuderia Ferrari prepared no fewer than six cars for the French GP meeting at Reims (which always carried a large amount of prize money), five for the Grand Prix itself and one for the F2 race which followed it. The big surprise was that one of the GP cars was for Dan Gurney.

The young American was already looked upon as the sensation of the season, by virtue of his sportscar drives for Ferrari. The way he had mastered the tortuous Targa Florio and Nürburgring circuits in particular with such ease had impressed everyone, as had his tremendous natural speed. Enzo Ferrari was clearly so impressed with his latest import from the USA (whom he had signed for very little money) that he decided to give him his chance in a Grand Prix. But first there would be a test drive, so just days after Le Mans Gurney found himself at Monza, where his budding career almost came to a premature end.

"I'd only been round the circuit in the wet," he recalls, "so I took out a Volkswagen in an attempt to learn the course. Jean Behra spent most of the day driving the latest version of the Grand Prix car and set a new, unofficial lap record with it.

"Along about five o'clock they told me, 'OK, now you get in this car.' I was a basket case by then anyway, but I did 10 laps and then they called me in and told me that they wanted me to try some different front tyres, 'so be cautious!'. They didn't say anything else.

"They replaced the 15-inch wheels at the front with 16-inch ones and I did a couple of laps to make sure that they were OK. On my third lap I got to my braking point for the Parabolica Curve, and the front wheels locked up. I unlocked them, but they locked up again, and by then I was going way too fast and I backed the Ferrari into the earth bank which was there at the time. It had maybe a 45° incline and the car flipped, landing back on its wheels. I stayed in it but I had grass all over my ankles and down my back so I must have come out of the cockpit quite a way. Apart from a few bruises I was unhurt and the car was not badly damaged, but all I could think was, 'There go my chances in Formula 1.'

"However, the Ferrari people asked me what happened and I said that I had made a mistake. They seemed rather surprised at this and then told me that in my first 10 laps I had broken Phil Hill's 1958 lap record and come within a second of Behra's best time. That, and my being honest about my mistake, must have impressed them, because within a week I was driving my first Grand Prix at Reims."

This must have come as a shock to his team-mate Phil Hill who, the previous year, had almost given up hope of ever getting a GP ride with Ferrari. So much so that in

Dan Gurney (seen here in the Nürburgring 1000 Kms) made a huge impression during his first full season in Europe. Unfortunately, he left Ferrari to join BRM....

the French GP he had elected to drive Jo Bonnier's 250F Maserati in defiance of Enzo Ferrari, who had steadfastly refused to give him a chance in single-seaters. Phil had been driving for the Scuderia, off and on, since 1955, putting up some superb performances in sportscars yet being constantly overlooked for Formula 1. It had taken the tragic loss of both Luigi Musso and Peter Collins to get him a regular seat in Ferrari's F1 team after almost four years, and here was Dan Gurney sitting behind him on the grid of the French GP after four races.

Along with Gurney, Ferrari nominated Tony Brooks, Jean Behra, Phil Hill and Olivier Gendebien to drive in the Grand Prix, with Cliff Allison getting the F2 ride. Gurney's first GP drive was also to be Jean Behra's last.

It was the arrival of Tony Brooks at Ferrari which changed things drastically for Behra. Jeannot, as he was known, was undoubtedly a fine driver with a wealth of experience, but that included a number of big accidents and a reputation as a fiery and often argumentative personality. It did not include the sublime talent possessed by Brooks, and although Behra beat him in their first F1 race at Aintree, the Englishman soon established his superiority.

Pina Brooks recalls that, "Ferrari was the happiest team Tony was ever in. There was no animosity at all except from Behra, who always complained that Brooks had a faster car."

The Frenchman's complaints came to a head at Reims, as Romolo Tavoni sorrowfully recalls: "Ferrari always said, 'In Formula 1 all my drivers are equal,' meaning that they all had the same equipment, but Jean Behra always thought that he ought to have the best equipment.

"When he was not angry, Behra was a very kindly man, a very funny man, but once he got in a car he was Champion of France and he was in a battle with himself. At Reims after the French GP he complained that his car had not lasted the race because he had been given a broken engine.

"We discussed this in the bar with the French Dunlop representative, Henri Lallement, translating for me. I said, 'Mr Behra, it is not right for a driver of your standing to talk like this, you know it is not correct.' Behra took a glass of Coca-Cola and threw it in my face. I called him a bloody bastard and he hit me!

"Now I am sorry, because he was not a bloody bastard, but if he said, 'I am angry because . . .' and left it at that I was in a position to get between him and Mr Ferrari. But he was so determined and he was always complaining, 'My car loses 10 metres to Tony Brooks in this corner . . . my car is not as good as his.'

"I remember Tony Brooks with a very nice spirit; he was a very kindly gentleman and a very fast driver, but not a very strong personality, which Behra was. If he had 10% of the determination of Jean Behra he would have won a couple of World Championships."

He might also be dead, for it was that determination to succeed at all costs that led Behra to his untimely death a month later. Both men were Roman Catholics, but whereas the Englishman's religious upbringing had imbued in him a firm belief in the sanctity of life, the Frenchman's, apparently, had not. Brooks was simply not prepared to take the kind of risks in motor racing that Behra took on an almost daily basis.

This caution may well have cost him the 1959 World Championship in the final round at Sebring, when he called at the pits after being shunted up the rear by his new team-mate, Taffy von Trips, on the first lap, rather than risk continuing with the damage unchecked. Brooks may not be a World Champion, but he is still here.

Enzo Ferrari fired Jean Behra for hitting Tavoni, and the pugnacious Frenchman died at Avus when his Porsche went over the banking during a sportscar race the day before the German Grand Prix. Dan Gurney and Cliff Allison remember him with affection.

"He was a terrific guy," says Dan. "I drove with him at Le Mans and I thought that just being able to share a car with the great Jean Behra was fabulous. We got along very, very well. Then he had that falling out with Tavoni at Reims and I thought it was very sad and uncalled for. He did hit Tavoni, but you can only take so much abuse and then you have to react. I never found out what the heart of the matter was but I felt that his sacking was very unfair. Tavoni was seen as the good guy on the team and a good Team Manager, and everybody got along with him, but

Jean Behra with Mino Amarotti at the Nürburgring.

Behra's reputation didn't include being unreasonable or anything else, so I was amazed by the whole thing – I still don't know why it happened. It was very sad for him and some kind of a political thing, as often happened with Ferrari which probably had 10 times the intrigue of most teams."

Cliff has a slightly different recollection: "I drove with Behra at Sebring, and he was smashing, no problem, but he was a very deep person who didn't tell you what he was thinking and he wasn't the easiest person to get along with at all times. He got a bit upset before he left Ferrari, and I'm not sure that some of it wasn't his own doing. He was a bit of a prima donna."

167

1959

Stirling Moss harries Tony Brooks out of the chicane during his epic drive in DBR1/2, after his original Aston caught fire in the pits.

CHAPTER TWENTY-TWO

Goodwood on a Summer's Day

The Championship goes to Feltham

'Tomorrow sees the 24th edition of the RAC Tourist Trophy Race, taking place, as it did last year, at Goodwood. This is the final event counting towards the World Sportscar Constructors' Championship. If anyone has any fear that the race, now of six hours' duration, will be a rather boring procession, as it was last year, he should think again and then look at the Championship table and the entry list. Ferrari have 18 points, Aston Martin 16 and Porsche 15 and all three marques are fielding full teams in a desperate bid for the Championship.'

'The main issue then, should be between Ferrari and Aston Martin, and on paper it looks as though there will be a battle royal between these two teams, with the Porsches waiting to pick up the pieces, if any. Scuderia Ferrari have won the Championship every year since its inception and it would be fine indeed if the Feltham équipe could be the first to defeat the previously all-conquering red cars, but we can on no account overlook the Porsches. It will be a three-cornered battle and you can be sure that it will be much more exciting than last year's race.'

Those were the opening and closing paragraphs of my preview of the TT in *Autosport*. My prediction of an exciting race was hardly the stuff of Nostradamus, but it was to be proved correct way beyond my wildest dreams. Another prediction that was to be fulfilled in due course was as follows: 'This is the first appearance in England of the phenomenal Dan Gurney, who has shot to stardom with the rapidity of a rock'n'roller', if he'll pardon the comparison! His experience, compared with the rest of the Grand Prix men, is very limited and his wonderful performances for Ferrari this season would seem to indicate an enormous potential ability.'

If you had to choose a really demanding location for the final round of a three-way fight for the Championship you would have needed to look no further than the Nürburgring or Spa. Goodwood was simply not in the same league as these giants, being a flat, 2.4-mile course formed around the perimeter track of the old Westhampnett Airfield, which had been a fighter base during World War Two. Described by someone as 'like racing round a field', it had nevertheless developed a unique, garden-party atmosphere, and its three Nine Hour races, held in 1952, 1953 and 1955, had all proved to be very demanding and exciting events. However, no Hollywood scriptwriter would have dared to dream up the drama and excitement that was to be produced there by the battle for the 1959 Tourist Trophy.

Aston Martin had been having a disastrous season with their Grand Prix car which, after a most heartening second place in Silverstone's International Trophy race in May, had performed dismally ever since.

Preparing the successful DBR1s for the Tourist Trophy must have provided a welcome break for all concerned as here they had a proven winner. Furthermore, their team was once more going to be led by the finest driver in the world on a circuit which Astons had made their own since 1952. The Championship was theirs for the taking (but then they had thought that in 1958).

The three cars which had run at Le Mans were prepared for the race with no mechanical alterations (apart from a change of final drive ratio from 3.25:1 to 4.03:1), although all reverted to the original side exhaust system. The high rear bodywork remained the same, but the wheel spats were removed and air ducts were cut into the rear wheelarches, as Goodwood was known to be very hard on tyres. The front wheel fairings were returned to their normal shape.

Aston Martin faced formidable opposition at Goodwood, in the shape of the works Ferraris (left) and Porsches.

After their humiliating defeats in the Targa Florio and at Le Mans there was no question of Ferrari giving the Tourist Trophy a miss this time. In the months before the race Carlo Chiti made numerous changes to the Testa Rossas. They had suffered from fluctuating oil pressure in previous races, and to overcome this Chiti devised a dry-sump lubrication system similar to that on the Grand Prix cars. In an effort to improve their handling 1.5° of negative camber was applied to the rear wheels.

Initially Ferrari's driver pairings for the Testa Rossas were given as Tony Brooks/Olivier Gendebien; Phil Hill/Dan Gurney and Cliff Allison/Giulio Cabianca, the last-named replacing Nano da Silva Ramos. There was also a two-litre Dino for Giorgio Scarlatti and Ludovico Scarfiotti.

The team arrived on the Wednesday before the race and went straight to work, trying to tune the suspension to the circuit. Of all the Scuderia's drivers, only Tony Brooks and Cliff Allison had seen Goodwood before, so Brooks was nominated to act as instructor and chauffeured the others around in his Testa Rossa to show them the correct lines for the corners.

Porsche showed up with three 1.6-litre RSKs for Taffy von Trips/Jo Bonnier; Umberto Maglioli/Edgar Barth and Hans Herrmann and newcomer Chris Bristow, a young Englishman who had been making a considerable name for himself. Aston Martin retained their Le Mans driver line-up and brought along DBR1/1 as a practice car. This was fitted with (whisper it!) a five-speed Maserati transaxle gearbox which was a remarkable 50lbs lighter than the David Brown CG537 unit and, as all who tried it discovered, a delight to use. Although the reliability of the CG537 had been considerably improved, it was never the easiest to operate and when Moss tried R1/1 in the first official practice session on the Thursday he announced that the right-hand change Maserati box was 'Fabulous!' To make the point he improved upon his own lap record of 1' 32.6" with a time of 1 min 31.2 secs and then did 1' 31.4" in DBR1/3, his race car. Roy Salvadori was also very quick in R1/1, equalling Stirling's lap record. He then did 1' 33.8" in R1/3 and 1' 35.8" in R1/2.

Paul Frère had driven round Goodwood countless times over the years in his capacity as a journalist, but to his surprise he found he could barely get under 1 min 40 secs in the DBR1 to begin with, and nor could his co-driver, Maurice Trintignant. Salvadori was going very fast right off the bat, so Paul sought his advice and then followed him for a couple of laps.

"Roy took the bend leading to St Mary's in quite an unorthodox way, but it turned out to be much quicker than the 'right' way," says Paul, whose times immediately dropped to under 1' 36".

As expected, Tony Brooks was fastest of the Ferrari drivers and, with 1'32", second only to Moss overall, but the real surprise was provided by Edgar Barth and Graham Hill, who lapped the 1.6-litre Porsche and the two-litre works Lotus respectively only one second slower than the Ferrari. Next came Gendebien (1' 33.2"); Allison (1' 33.4"); Phil Hill (1' 33.6"); and Gurney (1' 34"). Jack Brabham was sharing a Cooper Monaco with Bruce McLaren and got down to 1' 32.8", faster than Trintignant (1' 35.2") and Graham Whitehead, who managed 1' 35.4" in his DBR1/5.

The next day's session was used by most teams to set up their cars for the race. The Ferrari drivers were complaining of excessive understeer, so shock-absorber settings were changed, the anti-roll bars were removed and experiments were conducted with spacers on the springs, first on one side and then the other, but this didn't seem to make any difference and the drivers still weren't happy. "I didn't really feel like trying hard in the car – as hard as I know how.' said Cliff Allison. "I wanted it to give something to me."

Late in the afternoon, when no-one else would have time to copy him, Reg Parnell produced his ace – on-board jacks. Carroll Shelby was called into the pits, a mechanic connected an air hose to a valve let into the side of the Aston, and four jacks descended from the chassis to push the car about six inches off the ground. All four wheels were changed, the car was refuelled, dropped to the ground and Carroll was off in just 33.4 seconds!

Astons' three victories in the Nine Hours races had taught them that Goodwood was a tyre-killer. Reg Parnell had given this a great deal of thought and concluded that the cars would have to make two and probably three wheel changes during the race. (In the event, the winning car made four.) So too would the Ferraris, but the Porsches, being much lighter, might just get away with two changes, although they would be slowed by their bolt-on wheels.

Reg had recently seen a film of the Indianapolis 500 race, in which many cars used on-board jacks operated by compressed air. In an attempt to give Astons the edge

Aston Martin demonstrate their demon tweak – on-board hydraulic jacks. The small hose plugged into the side of the car supplies the nitrogen gas that actuates the four jacks. Eric Hind and Ian Murray change the rear wheels while Bryan Clayton refuels the Aston. Jack Fairman waits on the pit counter to take over.

over their rivals, he decided to employ a similar system. As Ted Cutting recalls: "We went to Smiths, who made the 'Jack-all' hydraulic jacking system, and we fitted four to each car, piped up to a central, plug-in tap in front of the driver's door. Instead of using hydraulic fluid, we used nitrogen gas and the moment the mechanic plugged in, the 1,000lbs pressure raised the car almost instantaneously.

"When we had equipped the first car at Feltham, Reg got different teams of people to do wheel changes, to see how fast it could be done. One team comprised draughtsman Steve Stephens, myself and a couple of other blokes who'd never changed a wheel in their lives, and we jacked up the DBR1 and changed all four wheels in under a minute!"

After Friday's practice both Aston Martin and Ferrari reshuffled some of their driver pairings. Although Reg Parnell left Paul Frère and Maurice Trintignant together in DBR1/4, he put his two fastest men, Stirling Moss and Roy Salvadori, in DBR1/3 and gave DBR1/2 to Carroll Shelby and Jack Fairman. Ferrari now partnered Brooks with Gurney in 0770; Hill with Allison in 0774, and Gendebien with Cabianca in 0766. The Porsche team was unchanged.

Race day was hot and sunny, but a disappointingly small crowd turned up to watch

1959

The start – and time and Moss wait for no man! The official starter still has the Union Jack held high, but Stirling is already beside his Aston, having synchronised his watch with those of the official timekeepers. The other drivers are not sure whether to wait for the flag to fall or to follow Stirling. Under the figure 1 on the pit roof (extreme left) are Bruce Halford and Masten Gregory and crouched in front of Masten is the author, taking the pictures below . . .

Tony Brooks brings the brakeless TR 0770 to a halt at Lavant, having deliberately spun it across the grass from the right of picture. The Sieff/Blond Lister-Jaguar takes avoiding action.

the 24th Tourist Trophy. The cars were lined up for the Le Mans-type start in order of practice times, so it was Aston Martin; Ferrari; Porsche; Lotus; Ferrari; Ferrari; Aston Martin; Cooper-Climax, with Moss, Gurney, Barth, G. Hill, Gendebien, P. Hill, Shelby and Brabham as first drivers.

The race was sponsored by the *News of the World* and one of the paper's directors was given the honour of dropping the flag at noon. Somewhat embarrassingly Stirling Moss was halfway to his Aston almost before the flag had been raised and, seeing Moss on the move, most other drivers followed suit. Many onlookers wondered if Moss (among others) should be penalised for jumping the start but in fact Stirling was not guilty of this offence. Punctilious as always, he had synchronised his watch with those of the time-keepers and at precisely midday he ran for his Aston, whereas at the same moment the official was just raising the flag instead of lowering it. The result was that many cars were well on the move before the flag hit the ground.

Dan Gurney's Testa Rossa was not among them, as it refused to fire on the button and he got away in the middle of the field. Moss and Shelby made superb starts, and at the end of the opening lap the two Astons led from the Lotus of Graham Hill, the Aston of Graham Whitehead, the Porsche of von Trips and the Ferrari of Gendebien. Gurney was back in 12th spot and Phil Hill even further behind, his car sounding very rough. The Ferrari had dropped a valve and retired after one more lap.

Jack Brabham's Cooper Monaco was out with a broken stub axle before 10 laps had been completed, and Dan Gurney was charging though the field, making up for his bad start. In no time at all he was third, behind the two Astons.

Graham Whitehead brought his DBR1 to a halt at Lavant with a small fire in the battery. It was extinguished and he drove back to the pits where a new battery was fitted and co-driver Henry Taylor took over.

Moss was really pressing on, equalling his own lap record and stretching his lead all the time. He lapped team-mate Maurice Trintignant after just 35 minutes and at 1pm was 30 seconds ahead of Shelby, who was just six seconds ahead of Gurney. Dan was the first to make a scheduled pit stop and at the end of lap 38 the Ferrari mechanics refuelled the Testa Rossa and fitted four new wheels before Brooks rejoined the race.

"Our problem was the Ferrari's lack of agility at Goodwood, which was very much an Aston circuit," says Tony. "I wasn't helped by the fact that the mechanics managed to leave the pins out of a front brake pad and on my first lap I got to Lavant and the brake pedal went to the floor. I literally had no brakes and I had to spin the car to a halt. I went back to the pits where they removed the front wheels and put in new pads."

Carroll Shelby was the first of the Aston Martin drivers to stop (after 44 laps) and the hydraulic jacks pumped the DBR1 into the air. Both rear wheels (with tyres worn down to the canvas) and the nearside front were changed, and the car was refuelled, all in 32.2 seconds. Reg Parnell's 'secret weapon' was already paying dividends.

But for once the Ferrari mechanics were very efficient – the Gurney-Brooks change-over had only taken 39.2 seconds, and now Gendebien handed over to Phil Hill (instead of Cabianca) in 44 seconds. After 47 laps Moss stopped and Salvadori took over DBR1/3 in 41.5 secs without losing the lead, but Taffy von Trips was now in second place with the Porsche, ahead of Fairman and Trintignant.

Tony Brooks' two stops had left him some way down the field, and he was trying hard to make up lost ground. At one point he had to take the escape road through the chicane to avoid a slow car. Jack Fairman had a spin at Madgwick but continued in third place.

Ten laps after Moss had stopped, Trintignant came in for fuel and three new wheels, Paul Frère getting away after just 27.2 secs. By contrast the Porsche pit stops

173

1959

Aston Martin virtually owned Goodwood in the fifties,
winning all five endurance races held there.
Roy Salvadori exits the chicane in DBR1/3 during the opening laps of the TT.

were positively pedestrian, and by the time Bonnier and Maglioli had taken over from von Trips and Barth Aston Martin were running one-two-three in the order Salvadori, Fairman and Frère.

Phil Hill and Tony Brooks were now lapping at around 1 min 35 secs, but were still not back on the leader board. Shortly after 2 pm Gurney replaced Brooks, and then Allison took over from Hill. Then came real drama, as the author (covering the race from the pits for *Autosport*) reported:

'At 2.35 Roy Salvadori was called in. He came rocketing down the pit road, the Aston's exhaust pipes belching flame on the overrun. The mechanics were standing by and as the car screamed to a halt somehow some fuel spilt over the side of the car and on to the hot exhaust pipe. There was a whoomph, and suddenly the car was a mass of flames – and so was Roy! He threw himself out of the car landing head first on the grass and rolled over and over to put out the flames . . . By now the Aston Martin pits were aflame, and the 50-gallon drum of fuel mounted on a steel tower came crashing down on to the pit roof as the tower buckled under the heat.'

The Goodwood Fire Brigade went into action and extinguished the blaze very quickly. Roy Salvadori was the only casualty, with what happily proved to be minor burns to his face and right hand. DBR1/3 was in a very sorry-looking state, however, its British Racing Green paintwork now covered in dirty grey extinguisher foam. Well aware that Jack Fairman was shortly due to hand over DBR1/2 to Shelby, Moss had a quick chat with Reg Parnell. Ten minutes after Salvadori's flaming entrance, Fairman made his scheduled stop. This time the refuelling was uneventful, all four wheels were changed, and the Aston went back into the race 56 seconds later – with Moss at the wheel and to thunderous applause from the grandstands.

The Aston Martin mechanics were now able to have a good look at their pits, which were a smouldering shambles. Graham Whitehead came to their rescue by giving them his, bringing in Henry Taylor and retiring DBR1/5. Although the car was way out of the running due to its earlier battery fire, it was nonetheless a very sporting gesture by Graham, which David Brown later acknowledged with a cheque for £50.

Despite all their dramas, Aston Martin still held the lead with the Trintignant/Frère car, which was ahead of Bonnier (Porsche), Allison (Ferrari) and Moss. The fact that Stirling was back in fourth place was wonderful news for all the spectators, who now eagerly anticipated yet another Moss Special – a demon drive

The race-leading DBR1/3 of Moss/Salvadori blazes in front of the Aston Martin pits as the Goodwood Fire Brigade goes into action. A stunned Bryan Clayton, who was refuelling the car, stands under the figure 4.

1959

Above: Moss (in his second Aston of the day) leads Olivier Gendebien's Ferrari and the Ecurie Ecosse Jaguar of Ron Flockhart through St Mary's.
Opposite: Tony Brooks leaves the pits in TR 0770, having taken over from Dan Gurney.

that would produce victory against all the odds. They were not to be disappointed.

At just after three o'clock Paul Frère took over DBR1/4 from Maurice Trintignant and briefly had a close-up view of Maestro Moss at work, as he later recalled.

'This was the Nürburgring 1,000 Kms race all over again. The task seemed an impossible one, which only Moss was capable of achieving and he knew it. Only he could, as indeed he was now doing, gain two or three seconds on each lap for hour after hour, and the spectacle of this virtuoso surpassing himself gave everyone who was present some unforgettable moments. Stirling lapped me and despite all my efforts in trying not to drop back too quickly I saw the gap between my car and his increase at every corner. In two laps he had gone out of sight. It was fantastic.'

Moss soon disposed of Allison and was gaining two or three seconds on Bonnier every lap. Gurney stopped to hand over Testa Rossa 0770 to Brooks, complaining of a locking front brake, and then at 3.30pm Bonnier came past the pits with Moss right behind him, the Aston taking the lead at St Mary's to wild applause.

"I could sense that the spectators were with me," says Moss, "which was always a help. The psychology in racing is very much more important than many of those taking part perhaps realise. Just as actors are encouraged by a good audience, in motor racing you do know when the spectators are appreciating what you are doing."

At five minutes to four Moss brought the Aston in for three tyres and fuel and was away again after 38.6 seconds, now in second place, 24 seconds behind Jo Bonnier. Eleven minutes later it was the Porsche's turn to stop, and Jo got a tremendous ovation from the crowd for a really superb drive, but the stop took 2 mins 26 secs and this let Phil Hill into third place with the Ferrari.

Cliff Allison swings 0774 into Woodcote early in the race.

Brooks was back in sixth position and motoring very fast indeed, setting a new sportscar record on lap 154 with a time of 1 min 31.8 secs (94.12 mph). At 4.15pm Barth took over from Maglioli, the Porsche still in fifth place; Frère took over from Trintignant, and then Brooks handed Testa Rossa 0770 back to Gurney.

If Tony thought that his day's work was done he was mistaken, for just before five o'clock Phil Hill brought 0766 in for its final stop, and it was not Allison, but Brooks, who took over. Ferrari's chances of catching Moss were nil, but Romolo Tavoni knew that they could equal Aston Martin on Championship points by finishing second. Brooks was the Scuderia's fastest driver – and the one with the most experience of Goodwood – so Tavoni now gave him the task of catching Taffy von Trips in the Porsche, a move which turned the final hour of the Tourist Trophy into an unforgettable chase.

Roy Salvadori had returned to the Aston Martin pits after receiving hospital treatment for his burns, and when Moss stopped at 5.03pm he offered to do the final stint. Stirling was well in the groove, however, and continued on his winning way. A few laps later Porsche suffered another blow when the Barth/Maglioli car expired with engine failure, Edgar Barth parking it just before the start/finish line.

Barring another fire, perhaps, Astons had the race sewn up, and all eyes were now on Tony Brooks. With one hour to go he was only 20 seconds behind von Trips but curiously appeared to be making little or no effort to catch him. It later transpired that he had been getting pit signals showing a plus in front of the number of seconds between the Porsche and himself.

Brooks of course was new to this particular Ferrari and its position in the race relative to the opposition, and he took the signals to mean that he was ahead of von Trips, whereas Tavoni was trying to tell him that the opposite was true.

Eventually Tony got the message, and the Testa Rossa began to fly. With 40 minutes to go he had reduced the gap to 14 seconds, but there was no mistaking the message in the signals Jo Bonnier was showing Taffy, and the German responded magnificently. Stirling Moss now became part of the equation, as he was between the two cars and maintaining station some 75 yards behind the Porsche. At 5.30pm Brooks was 23.5 secs behind von Trips. Then it was 11.5 seconds, then 12, then 11.5 again. As I wrote in *Autosport*:

'Tony then got the "flat-out" signal from his pit and next time round the distance was 10 seconds. Then it was 9.6 – 9 – 8.4 – 8.2 – 8, then 7. Taffy was well aware of the danger now and was driving quite brilliantly while Stirling was taking considerable interest in the goings on, and Tony had quite a job to pass him, which he managed to do at Fordwater.

'With seven minutes to go Tony was only six seconds behind the Porsche. The excitement was intense with the crowd cheering both cars on as they passed the pits. Four laps to go and the distance was was four and half seconds, with both drivers trying all they knew. Tavoni and Bonnier had a mock battle in front of the pits, each making urgent "slow down" signals, Bonnier to Brooks and Tavoni to von Trips!

'The tension on that last lap was terrific. Down to Woodcote they came with the Ferrari seemingly on the Porsche's tail. Through the chicane, they shot and the Porsche scuttled across the line just two seconds ahead of the Ferrari.'

Almost unnoticed amid this excitement, Dan Gurney had also been driving very fast indeed. Lapping consistently at around 1 min 33 secs, he passed Paul Frère into fourth place and was 16 seconds ahead of the Aston when, on his penultimate lap, a tyre blew at St Mary's and he motored slowly round to park the Ferrari behind the Barth/Maglioli Porsche. When von Trips and Brooks had completed that last, decisive lap, he and Barth drove slowly across the line to qualify as finishers.

Then Moss toured in to rapturous applause from his delighted fans, which meant just about everyone. Once again he had snatched victory from defeat for Aston Martin and, thanks very largely to his extraordinary skills the Feltham team had won the World Championship, with a total of 24 points to the 22 of Ferrari and the 21 of Porsche.

Results

1959
SPORTSCAR WORLD CHAMPIONSHIP

	Sebring 12 Hrs	Targa Florio	Nürburgring	Le Mans	Tourist Trophy	
1. Aston Martin	0	0	8	8	8	24
2. Ferrari	8	0	6	4	4	22
3. Porsche	4	8	3	0	6	21

SEBRING 12 HOURS
March 21

1) P. Hill/O. Gendebien/
   D. Gurney/C. Daigh   (Ferrari TR59/0766)   188 laps, 977.6 miles at 80.26 mph
2) J. Behra/C. Allison   (Ferrari TR59/0768)   187 laps
3) W. von Trips/J. Bonnier   (Porsche RSK)   184 laps
4) R. Holbert/D. Sesslar   (Porsche RSK)   182 laps
5) J. Fitch/E. Barth   (Porsche RSK)   181 laps
6) E.D. Martin/L. Reventlow   (Ferrari 250TR/0730) 174 laps

Fastest lap: C. Allison (Ferrari TR59) 3 mins 21.6 secs, (92.86mph)

TARGA FLORIO
May 24

1) E. Barth/W. Seidel   (Porsche RSK)   14 laps in 11 hrs 2 mins 21.4 secs (56.7 mph)
2) Strahle/Mahle/Linge   (Porsche RS)   11 hrs 22 mins 20.4 secs
3) H. von Hanstein/Pucci   (Porsche Carrera)   11 hrs 31 mins 44.2 secs
4) Strahle/Mahle/Linge   (Porsche Carrera)   11 hrs 36 mins 10 secs
5) Boffa/Drogo   (Maserati 200S)   11 hrs 41 mins 20 secs;
6) C. Davis/Sepe   (Alfa Romeo GSV)   12 hrs 02 mins 30 secs

Fastest lap: J. Bonnier (Porsche RSK) 43 mins 11.3 secs (62.2 mph)

NÜRBURGRING 1,000 Kms
June 7

1) S. Moss/J. Fairman   (Aston Martin DBR1/1) 44 laps in 7hrs 33 mins 18 secs (82.5 mph)
2) O. Gendebien/P. Hill   (Ferrari TR59/0766)   44 laps in 7 hrs 33 mins 59 secs
3) C.A.S. Brooks/J. Behra   (Ferrari TR59/0768)   44 laps in 7 hrs 36 mins 45 secs
4) U. Maglioli/H. Herrmann   (Porsche RSK)   7 hrs 40 mins 57 secs
5) D. Gurney/C. Allison   (Ferrari TR59/0770)   43 laps
6) Walter/Heuberger   (Porsche 1.5-litre)   42 laps

Fastest lap: S. Moss (Aston Martin DBR1) 9 mins 32 secs (89.17 mph)

LE MANS 24 HOURS
June 20/21

1) R. Salvadori/C. Shelby   (Aston Martin DBR1/2) 4347.9 kms at 112.57 mph
2) M. Trintignant/P. Frère   (Aston Martin DBR1/4) 4337.5 kms
3) 'Beurlys'/'Elde'   (Ferrari 250GT)   4001.6 kms
4) A. Pilette/G. Arents   (Ferrari 250GT)   3991.4 kms
5) R. Grossmann/F. Tavano   (Ferrari 250GT)
6) Fayen/G. Munaron   (Ferrari 250GT)

Fastest lap: J. Behra (Ferrari TR59/0774) 4 mins 00.9 secs (125.0 mph)

TOURIST TROPHY
September 5

1) S. Moss/C. Shelby/J. Fairman (Aston Martin DBR1/2) 224 laps in 6 hrs 00 mins 46.8 secs, (89.41 mph)
2) J. Bonnier/W. von Trips   (Porsche RSK)   223 laps in 6 hrs 00 mins 14.4 secs
3) C.A.S. Brooks/P. Hill/C. Allison/
   O. Gendebien   (Ferrari TR59/0766)   223 laps in 6 hrs 00 mins 16.4 secs
4) M. Trintignant/P. Frère   (Aston Martin DBR1/4) 221 laps
5) C.A.S. Brooks/D. Gurney   (Ferrari TR59/0770)   220 laps
6) P. Ashdown/A. Ross   (Lola)   210 laps

Fastest lap: C.A.S. Brooks (Ferrari TR59 0766) 1 min 31.8 secs (94.12 mph)

Goodwood on a summer's day, and Dan Gurney barrels into St Mary's in the Ferrari he shared with Tony Brooks.

CHAPTER TWENTY-THREE

The End of an Era

Aston Martin withdraw from racing

After the prize-giving Romolo Tavoni phoned Enzo Ferrari to give him the bad news: the Scuderia had lost the Tourist Trophy and the Championship.

"One minute's silence, please!" demanded his boss.

"In 1959 we lost the Championships for Drivers and Constructors in Formula 1 and the Manufacturers title," says Tavoni. "It was the worst year we ever had in the Competitions Department.

"The 1959 Testa Rossa was too different from the 1958 car, and after Le Mans we changed the exhaust systems, the carburettors, the brakes, the shock absorbers – all little things which were not sufficiently tested in Modena or at Monza.

"Aston Martin won the Championship because the DBR1 was a better car than our Testa Rossa and because they had smoothed out all the small problems they had before, thanks to their Team Manager Reg Parnell, who was a very intelligent man and a fine tactician. Ferrari lost the Championship because we had lots of small problems. If we had stayed with the 1958 car it is possible we would have won in 1959."

Those are Tavoni's technical reasons for the Scuderia's poor performance, but it is perhaps instructive to note also that the surviving Ferrari drivers from 1959 look back on that season as one of the happiest they remember. They all got on famously and found the Testa Rossas and Grand Prix cars enjoyable to drive. Yet, as Romolo Tavoni has said, it was the Scuderia's least successful season to date. This must only have strengthened Enzo Ferrari's long-held belief that happy and contented drivers make an unsuccessful team.

From the earliest days of Scuderia Ferrari in the 1930s, Enzo had encouraged rivalry, not amity, between his drivers, playing one off against another and firmly believing that their keenest rivals should be their team-mates, or at least one of them.

This worked well with men of Latin blood, who usually harboured a fierce, competitive spirit, even among friends, but with his Anglo Saxon and American drivers of the 1950s Ferrari found that their friendships dulled their competitive edge. Mike Hawthorn and Peter Collins, for example, were great mates who were simply not interested in racing against each other and their 1957/58 seasons at Ferrari were remarkably unsuccessful.

In 1959, with Brooks, Hill, Gendebien, Gurney and Allison forming a harmonious, English-speaking quintet, Ferrari must have wondered if he had done the right thing by firing the uppity Jean Behra. However, the Anglo–US element was so completely unfazed by the Frenchman's complaints that he was never going to invoke the in-team rivalry that Ferrari sought. The mutual admiration society that existed at Scuderia Ferrari in 1959 was hardly the main reason for the team's lack of success that year, but you can be sure that Enzo Ferrari believed it had a lot to do with it.

By contrast Aston Martin always was, by common consent, a terrific team to drive for. Until the advent of the DBR1 no Aston was a contender for top international honours, but the team still attracted some very fine drivers. They would have had a better chance of winning with several other teams, but racing with the David Brown Aston Martins was fun, free of hassle and as safe as racing could be in those days.

Above: Maranello mates - (l-r) Brooks, Hill and Gurney were part of a harmonious Ferrari team in 1959.

Below: David Brown with his Championship winners and their Tourist Trophy spoils, (l-r) Carroll Shelby, Stirling Moss, Roy Salvadori and Jack Fairman.

Below right: Moss the Master corrects a slide as he negotiates Woodcote early in the TT.

"There was a couple of times I could have driven for Ferrari or Maserati," recalls Carroll Shelby, "but I was always happy to race for Astons because John Wyer ran such a great team."

"Driving for Astons was special," says Stirling, "because it was like being in a club. The drivers were pretty close and David Brown was a very amenable bloke and you could lark about with him, which you could not do with Tony Vandervell, for example. And John Wyer was such a fabulous Team Manager that I always liked to take the piss out of him! All of which made for good relations within the team."

With the introduction of the DBR1 in 1957 Astons at last moved into the big league with a car that was good as, if not better than, anything that the opposition could produce. In the circumstances it is indeed ironic that they should win the 1959 Manufacturers' Championship almost by mistake. Having deliberately set out to avoid it, they had been sucked into it by Stirling Moss' outrageous victory at the Nürburgring. Their long-sought triumph at Le Mans made their participation in the final round inevitable, but it is fair to say that none of their three victories would have been possible without Stirling's extraordinary skills.

Still, it had been a close-run thing and there can be little doubt that if Porsche had not been committed to bolt-on wheels they could have won the TT and the Championship. Astons' on-board jacks meant that they could get the DBR1s re-fueled and re-shod in under thirty seconds on occasion. With their normal, quick-lift jacks, Ferrari were getting the Testa Rossas in and out in under forty, but the Porsche pitstops were disastrous. Undoing four nuts per wheel meant that the first von Trips/Bonnier change-over took 1 min 41.6 secs and the Barth/Maglioli swap took almost half-a-minute more – 2 mins 15 secs! They had lost the race before it started.

THE END OF AN ERA

After the race Tony Brooks came in for some criticism for not trying to catch von Trips as soon as he had taken over Testa Rossa 0766 from Phil Hill, but he should have been better informed of the situation before he got in the car.

"There was confusion over Ferrari's pit signals to me," he says, "and I didn't realise that if I passed von Trips, Ferrari would win the Championship. I failed by about two seconds, and Moss and the Aston won the race and the title. We should certainly have beaten the Porsche, but I don't think we could reasonably be expected to beat a trouble-free Stirling in the DBR1, because it had such superb roadholding. Goodwood was a tight circuit with lots of corners where nice, balanced drifts are what you want and that was not the forte of the Testa Rossa."

Actually, Tony is mistaken when he says that second place would have won the Championship for Ferrari. It would have given the Scuderia the same number of points – 24 – as Aston Martin, but Astons would have taken the title with three wins to Ferrari's one.

The fire in the Aston Martin pits was exciting, dramatic and frightening. The fact that no-one was badly hurt was remarkable and allowed people to make many a sly remark about 'flamin' Astons', the same team having set fire to one of its DB3s during a refuelling stop in the 1952 Nine Hours race, also at Goodwood. But what really happened? Development Engineer Bryan Clayton was the unfortunate man in

Above: Astons brought a new dimension to pit stops in European racing by using on-board, hydraulic jacks in the TT. The Frère/Trintignant DBR1/4 is up in the air as the rear wheels are changed and Frère waits to take over.

Below: Brooks and Moss in a classic eight-wheel drift through Madgwick.

1959

The moment of disaster. John King is already knocking off the wing nut as Jerry Holmes plugs the hydraulic tube into the side of the Aston. Jim Potton holds the new wheel and Roy Salvadori is about to leave the car. Behind him, Bryan Clayton struggles to open the fuel-filler, unaware that petrol is gushing out of the hose and is about to ignite on the DBR1's hot side exhaust...

THE END OF AN ERA

A Ferrari flashes by the blackened hulk of the Moss/Salvadori Aston some time after the fire.
Despite its appearance, DBR1/3 was not seriously damaged.

charge of the refuelling hose.

"Very shortly before the start Reg said to me, 'We need somebody to do the refuelling. Will you do it?' It was never my job normally, but I agreed and tried each fuel hose. They didn't have a 'dead man's handle', just a lever that turned on and off. The lever on one hose was nice and free, and the others were quite tight, so I took the one with the easier action.

"The fuel hose was pretty rigid and quite heavy, with a heavy metal spout and lever. So I had this under my right arm, and a dip-stick in the fingers of the same hand (Reg wanted to know how much fuel had been used between each stop), leaving the other hand free to open the flap covering the filler-cap. I then had to open the cap, dip the tank, put the spout in and fill it.

"Whenever our cars came in, just before the driver got out, there was always a small blow-back of flame through the exhaust. This time, when Roy came in to hand over to Stirling, I rushed forward to start my procedure and, as I did so, somehow the lever got knocked on; I still don't know how. The first thing I saw as I was fumbling with the body flap over the filler-cap, was a flicker of flame running down the back of the car, between the headrest and the wheelarch. I thought, 'That shouldn't be there!' I was staggered, then suddenly it went 'Whoof' and, I must admit, I just dropped everything and ran."

With hindsight it does seem odd that the BARC allowed the large-bore, gravity-fed fuel pipes to be fitted with anything other than a dead man's handle, but they did, despite a warning from John Wyer.

In his autobiography John conceded that Astons' first fire, in 1952, had been their own fault, but claimed extenuating circumstances in 1959 'because the refuelling equipment provided by the organisers was thoroughly dangerous, consisting of ordinary gate-type valves which could all too easily be knocked on and off. I warned the organisers before the race that I considered the equipment to be lethal and threatened to withdraw the cars unless it could be changed, but my criticisms were tempered by the fact that Reg Parnell was a member of the BARC and was anxious not to cause too much trouble.'

In the circumstances Bryan Clayton could not be held responsible for the incident and he certainly didn't deserve to be called a name or two (by Reg Parnell, of all people) once he got back from the Medical Centre. John Wyer, however, was understandably more sympathetic when Bryan apologised after the race.

"I'm sorry, Mr Wyer, but what can I say?"

"Nothing." said John. "I've forgotten it, now you forget it!"

Singed, but happily not seriously burnt, Roy Salvadori watches Moss bring home the bacon for Aston Martin.

Incidentally, the Aston was not as badly damaged as it was at first thought. A thorough inspection back at Feltham revealed that only the off-side of the car had suffered relatively slight damage affecting the body, side screen and windscreen, upholstery, tyres and flexible brake pipes.

DBR1/3's misfortune was DBR1/2's gain, for as a direct result of the blaze this car went on to win its sixth major race for Aston Martin, making it by far the most successful R1 of all, winning at Spa, the Nürburgring and Spa again in 1957; the Tourist Trophy in 1958 and Le Mans and the Tourist Trophy in 1959.

At the end of the season both Dan Gurney and Tony Brooks decided to take their leave of Scuderia Ferrari. Having finished second in Germany and third in Portugal, Gurney was a good fourth in the Italian GP at Monza, but that was to be his last race for Ferrari. In just four Grandes Epreuves and five Championship sportscar races he had made his mark on European racing with a string of fine drives and had astonished everyone with his tremendous speed and intelligent approach to racing.

However, as he is the first to admit, that intelligence deserted him momentarily after the Italian GP, because he left Ferrari and did not even take part in his home GP at Sebring in December.

"I made a wrong move and it was a demonstration of my great judgement about the future." he recalls, ruefully. "Enzo Ferrari treated me extra nicely, and I enjoyed my time there very much, not least because Tony Brooks is one of my all-time great drivers. He was a great team leader who could consistently put us in our places.

"I thought that the Testa Rossa was the best of all the sportscars at that time and superior to the Aston, although Astons had Stirling, and he could carry a car in a way that most of the rest of the guys couldn't. In his hands the Aston was one terrific car, a classic, but I think the general consensus of opinion was that although the DBR1 did handle better the Testa Rossa chassis was pretty good, too, and the Ferrari was definitely the better of the two.

"However, I was paid very little and I could see that the front-engined car was on its way out. Also, you could drive the wheels off a Ferrari and it would stay with you (most of the time) and I assumed that all racing cars had equally good reliability and durability. I joined BRM for 1960 and it was a great shock to me when I only finished three races out of eleven!"

Losing Dan Gurney was a serious blow to Scuderia Ferrari, but worse was to come, for Tony Brooks also left the team. As a result of his coming-together with von Trips in the USGP he had finished third in the race and second in the World Championship, behind Jack Brabham. Leaving the Scuderia meant that he gave up any further chance of winning the title, but that was not such a blow as it might seem for his faith in the Championship had been seriously dented the year before, when Moss had won four Grandes Epreuves, he himself had won three, and the Champion had won one. This did not seem quite right to Tony, for whom winning was the thing.

After the USGP Brooks went to Modena and told Romolo Tavoni that he would not be renewing his contract. He had decided to abandon dentistry and enter the motor trade. In the first week of the New Year he told *Autosport*:

'Because of the immense amount of work involved in setting up my new garage, I have not been able to give as much thought to my future racing career as I should have liked. At the moment I have made no definite plans for 1960, but I can say that I shall not be driving for Ferrari.'

He would not be driving for Aston Martin again either. Six weeks after the TT David Brown gave a dinner in London to celebrate his team's victory in the Sportcar World Championship. Needless to say, Stirling Moss had the place of honour. The celebration was tinged with sadness, however, for DB chose the occasion to announce that he was withdrawing his Aston Martins from sportscar racing. By winning Le Mans and the Championship he had achieved everything he had set out to do back in 1949, and more.

It was a fitting time to make the decision, for the Championship had been won in a blaze of glory (no pun intended) and the last sportscar race of the decade had been one that would long be remembered, both for its high drama and excitement and for Aston Martin's famous victory.

Also, as DB remarked, the FIA was once again tampering with the sportscar regulations, and his DBR1 was already ineligible for the 1960 races. And, as with Formula 1, the mid-engined revolution was on the march, and front-engined machines would soon be obsolete. The end of the decade was also the end of an era, and it was time for Aston Martin to take their leave.

**Dan Gurney drifts 0770 through Woodcote.
It was his last race in a Testa Rossa for Ferrari.**

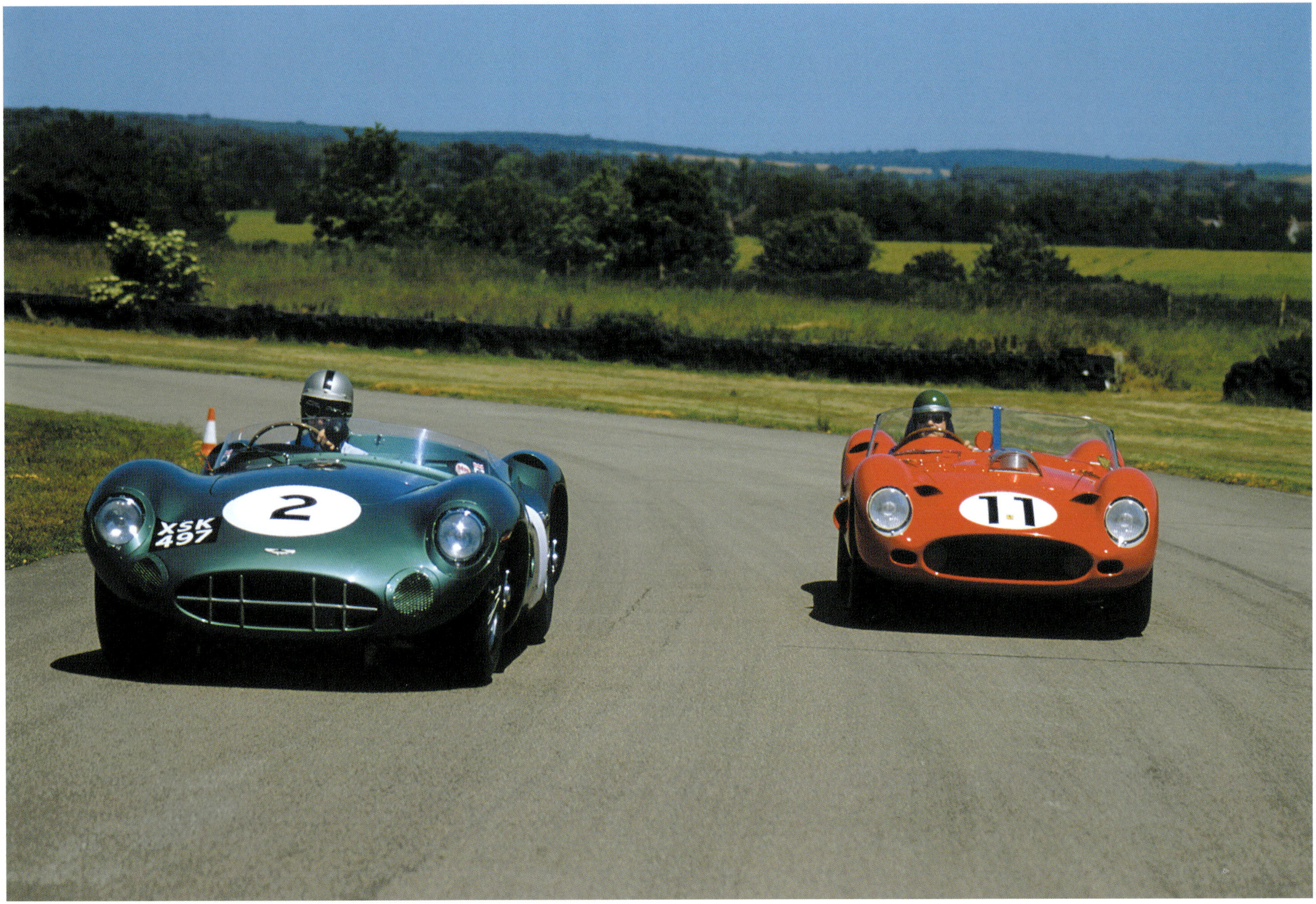
2
XSK
497
11

CHAPTER TWENTY-FOUR

Bouquets and Brickbats

Roy Salvadori tries the cars

After the two years of their rivalry, the Aston Martin DBR1 and the Ferrari Testa Rossas emerged with equal success, winning one World Championship and five Championship races each. In 1958 both teams entered five races, Ferrari winning four (80%) and Aston Martin two (40%). In 1959 Ferrari entered five races and won one (20%), and Aston Martin entered four, winning three (75%).

Scuderia Ferrari was by far the busiest, entering 17 cars in five races in 1958 and 15 in five in 1959, whereas Aston Martin entered 12 cars in five in 1958 and only eight in four in 1959. The Testa Rossa scored 38 points in 1958 and 18 in 1959 (total 56), whereas the DBR1 scored 12 in 1958 and 24 in 1959 (total 36).

Aston Martin's superb first DBR1 victory at the Nürburgring in 1957 must not be forgotten, as it was undoubtedly their greatest ever, for they beat the full might of Ferrari and Maserati with what was virtually a brand-new car on the most demanding circuit in the world. However, the Testa Rossa was then only a prototype and not yet Ferrari's front-line sports racer.

So how do they compare as driving machines, these two classic sports racing cars of the 1950s? Roy Salvadori knows the DBR1 inside out, of course, and although he never raced a Testa Rossa he has driven both the 1958 and 1959 cars to sample the opposition, so to speak. First, the 1958 car, with drum brakes, four-speed gearbox and live rear axle:

"After a few laps I noticed a great difference between the two: the steering on the Testa Rossa has much less 'feel' and is heavier, and the back of the car hops about, you line up for a corner and suddenly the back starts to hop away from you, which was unpleasant even at the speeds I was doing. If you were racing, it would throw you right off line. That's not too bad because you've got more steam and a good gearbox, but you don't half pay for it with that rear end!

Opposite: back in the old routine. Aston Martin DBR1/2 (Roy Salvadori) and Ferrari TR 0774 (Paul Pappalardo) are reunited at Goodwood. Right: Roy samples the 1958 250 TR (0752), which is owned by Sir Anthony Bamford.

"By comparison the Aston was superb, we really had a good thing going for us there. In retrospect I reckon that all the Aston Martin drivers should have been treated to a few laps in a Testa Rossa in 1958. We were always complaining about the DBR1's lack of power and the lousy gearbox, but after a few laps in the Ferrari we would have shut up, because we were compensated by the wonderful roadholding of the Aston and the disc brakes, which were fabulous. Mind you, the drum brakes on the Ferrari aren't too bad, with a nice firm pedal, although the pedals themselves are very close together. I was wearing thin racing boots and even so, I was catching my foot on both throttle and brake.

"The Ferrari has that sweet V12 engine with substantially more power than the Aston's straight six, but it feeds it in so well you don't notice the extra oomph. Even in a high gear, it takes it very nicely on a light throttle and you can just pull away. With the DBR1 you've got to come right back off the throttle and feather it for a long time; if you boot it out of a corner it just spits at you, but you don't get any of that with the Ferrari, the power comes in so nicely.

"On the 1959 Testa Rossa the engine and gearbox are still in another world, compared with the Aston's. You have a wide range of usable revs and obviously, it's better to keep them fairly high, but I would say that you can work within 3,500 revs,

Roy found the 1958 TR much more of a handful than the Aston.

whereas on the Aston it's got to be only 2,200. You might stretch it to 2,400, but that's a very narrow range to drive in, so you pick up the lower gears.

"At Goodwood the only way I could get out of Lavant corner with the DBR1 was in third gear (you'd tear the wheels off in second), turning in and trying to get the back wheels on the grass and then booting it, in the hope of getting the back wheels spinning. Then, as the car started to drift, instead of putting my foot down I'd lift off until I had equated the revs, lost the wheelspin and was past the Aston's spit-back period, which was at about 3,500-3,700rpm. What a thing to have to do, to get wheelspin just to keep in the power range!

"On a purely fast circuit it was easy to keep within that range, but you had to have the right corners and the right gearing for every corner. At Le Mans, for example, where all the other cars were taking Mulsanne in first gear, on the DBR1 you had to take second and come out on a trailing throttle, not daring to floor it until you had about 3,800rpm on the clock. If you took first gear there you weren't going to last the 24 hours, you were going to tear the wheels off. With the Ferrari you've always got the right range of revs, and it must be bliss in the wet. That Aston chassis must be bloody good to make up for the engine's deficiencies."

(Mauro Forghieri makes an interesting point regarding the Aston's engine: "I think the 95° cylinder head was a big mistake, because it gives power, but not torque. The maximum torque was at 5,500rpm, 1,000 revs lower than the maximum power, which makes the car very difficult to drive, as you have a very narrow rev band to work with. Ferrari was much better with maximum power at 7,200rpm and maximum torque at 4,000. This gave greater elasticity and allowed us to use a four-speed gearbox until the drivers insisted on a five-speed, but that was only because the Aston had one!")

"That five-speed gearbox is a real pleasure on the 1959 Ferrari," continues Roy. "I have to criticise the Aston's gearbox because when you changed down the revs always went sky-high. That's when I used to get my maximum revs – if ever I had 6,2 or 6,3 on the maxi-hand I thought 'How can this be?' because I *never* went over 6,000, but it was always on the change-down. I always found it very difficult to make clean changes on the Aston. If I got the revs absolutely right sometimes the gear went in as smooth as butter, but then it seemed that I would do exactly the same thing next time and come up against a barrier, I just could not get it in.

"I've never known anybody make consistently perfect changes on the R1. We tried the Maserati gearbox in practice for the 1959 TT and every driver was so much quicker with it! It was known to be reliable and lighter than the David Brown gearbox and with a faster action.

"The de Dion rear end on the 1959 Ferrari is a great improvement on the 1958 car, but I still found the steering very heavy coming out of corners. It's nice and light going in, and you've got too much understeer, so you start to wind the wheel round and suddenly it seems to click and becomes terribly hard. I'm used to changing gear with one hand and steering with the other. It would be bloody hard work on that Ferrari, but I think in the course of a race the Testa Rossa would take less out of a driver than the DBR1 because we had to drive the Aston so hard.

"To sum up, the Aston had by far the better chassis and brakes, and the Ferrari by far the better engine and gearbox – though the Maserati gearbox was better still. The DBR1 powered by the Testa Rossa's V12 through the Maserati box would have been fantastic – and unbeatable!"

BIBLIOGRAPHY

FINN, Joel - Ferrari Testa Rossa (Osprey Publishing, Ltd., 1980);
FRÈRE, Paul - Starting Grid to Chequered Flag (B.T. Batsford, Ltd.,1962);
HAWTHORN, Mike - Champion Year (William Kimber, 1959);
MOSS, Stirling and BOYD, Maxwell - Le Mans 1959 (Cassell & Co, Ltd.,1959);
NIXON, Chris & WYER, John - Racing With The David Brown Aston Martins (Transport Bookman, Ltd., 1980);
NIXON, Chris - Mon Ami Mate (Transport Bookman, Ltd., 1991).

PERIODICALS

Autosport; The Autocar; The Motor; Motor Sport; Road & Track; Car and Driver; Sports Cars Illustrated; Automobile Year.

PHOTO CREDITS

Cliff Allison: 118 (left);
Aston Martin: 50;
Walter Bäumer/The Nürburgring Collection: 29 (top right); 38 (right); 97;
Bernard Cahier: 13; 18; 26 (top); 81; 83; 85; 91 (right); 103; 117; 124; 126; 127; 128; 131; 133 (right);
John Colley: 189; 190;
Corsa Photo Archive: 66; 71;
Ted Cutting: 12; 15;
DaimlerChrysler: 147 (top left);
Yves Debraine/Archives l'année automobile: 22 (both); 36; 40 (both); 44 (lower); 54; 134; 140 (both); 141 (both); 147 (lower); 156 (left);
Deutsche Wochenschau: 94 (all); 96 (both); 99 (lower); 100 (both); 101 (both); 105 (both lower);
Ferret Photographic/Ted Eves: 62; 64; 86; 88 (right); 90; 91(left); 118 (right); 132; 133 (left); 182 (upper right);
GP Photographic: 25; 29 (lower right); 41; 42 (left); 44 (top); 46; 47; 55 (lower left & right); 60 (right); 61 (top & bottom); 110 (both); 113 (top); 14; 153; 154; 155 (both); 158; 163; 164; 170 (both); 172 (top); 173; 183 (both); 187;
Brian Joscelyne: 56; 57 (both); 58; 59 (top); 60 (left); 108; 122 (left); 136 (both); 139 (lower); 150; 151; 152; 160; 162 (both); 165; 167; 178;
The Klemantaski Collection/Peter Coltrin: 39 (left); 43; 137; 139 (top); 143;
LAT: 27; 31; 34; 35; 52; 53 (left); 55 (top); 61 (centre); 74 (both); 75; 77; 82; 84; 92; 104; 111; 113 (lower); 142; 144; 147 (top right); 156 (right); 159; 174; 182 (lower left); 184;
Tony Matthews: 123;
Martin McGlone Collection: 38 (left); 39 (right); 42; 95; 98 (both); 99 (top); 102 (top); 105 (top); 120;
Motor Presse: 11 (lower left); 166;
Richard Newton: 48; 53 (right); 70; 72; 73;
Chris Nixon Collection: 11 (top & lower right); 16; 19; 20; 21; 23; 24; 27; 29 (top left); 75 (both); 109 (both); 122 (right); 171; 172 (both lower); 175; 186;
Maurice Rowe: 188; 191;
Michael Turner: 5; 168; 177; 180; 182 (lower right); 185;
Pablo Vignone: 79 (both); 80 (both).

PAINTINGS

Graham Turner: cover; 89; 106; 148; 157; 176.
Michael Turner: 45; 76; 102.

GOODWOOD GLORY
by Graham Turner

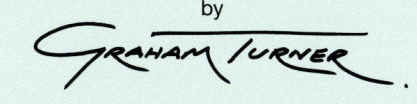

Stirling Moss slides his DBR1 out of Goodwood's chicane during one of his legendary drives, to win the 1959 Tourist Trophy and clinch the Sportscar World Championship for Aston Martin. Graham Turner's evocative painting of this historic achievement is available in a **LIMITED EDITION OF 500 PRINTS,** each one individually signed and numbered by the artist.

Overall print size 53cm x 43cm (21"x 17").

Product Code **MOSS-50**

£50 each   Plus £5.50 per order p&p in the U.K., £7 Europe & £9 the rest of the World.

Goodwood Glory is just one of Studio 88's extensive range of prints and cards, reproduced from original paintings by Michael Turner and Graham Turner. For details of the complete range, send for a copy of our **FREE COLOUR CATALOGUE** or visit the Studio 88 Web-site.

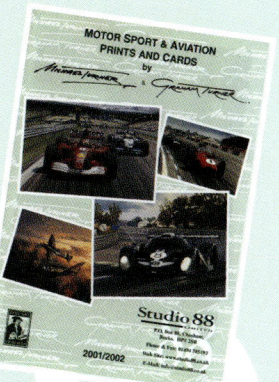

ORIGINAL PAINTINGS
by MICHAEL TURNER & GRAHAM TURNER

Michael Turner and Graham Turner, whose paintings are reproduced throughout this book, are two of today's best known motorsport artists. They have a constantly changing selection of original paintings for sale, covering many different eras of the sport.

If you would like to receive an up to date list of available originals or discuss commissioning something special, Michael and Graham can be contacted through Studio 88 at the address on the right. If you have internet access, many of these originals can now be viewed on the Studio 88 web-site -

www.studio88.co.uk

HOW TO ORDER
By Phone, Fax, Post or On-Line, giving full details of your requirements. We accept payment by cheque (payable to Studio 88 Ltd.), postal order or Mastercard, Visa, Eurocard or Switch. Please remember to include the credit card expiry date and Switch issue number. Overseas payments by the listed Credit Cards or I. M.O. only please.

Studio 88 LIMITED

P.O. Box 88, Chesham, Bucks. HP5 2SR.

Phone & Fax:
01494 785193

Web Site:
www.studio88.co.uk

Index

Adenau *38, 55, 142, 146, 147.*
Adenau Bridge *51, 52.*
Adenauer Forst *51.*
Aintree *13.*
Alfa Romeo *10.*
Allard *10.*
Allard, Sydney *14.*
Allison, Cliff *108, 117* (joins Scuderia Ferrari), *118, 120, 125, 127, 128, 129, 130, 131, 132, 135, 139, 140, 145, 149, 154, 161, 166, 167, 170, 171, 175, 177, 178, 181.*
Alexander, Jesse *161.*
Amarotti, Mino *142, 167.*
AMOCO *126.*
Arciero, Frank *117.*
Aremberg *50, 104.*
Argentine GP *78.*
Ascari, Alberto *24.*
Aston Martin DBR1/1 *12, 15, 16, 17, 18, 20, 26, 31, 41, 52, 60, 65, 82, 83, 84, 95, 108, 114, 120, 125, 126, 129, 136, 138, 145, 147, 170.*
  DBR1/2 *8, 11, 34, 35, 46, 49, 52, 60, 61, 64, 65, 67, 70, 71, 82, 84, 92, 95, 96, 98, 100, 108, 109, 145, 149, 151, 158, 164, 168, 170, 171, 175, 186, 189.*
  DBR1/3 *86, 87, 88, 90, 92, 95, 96, 108, 109, 145, 147, 149, 151, 154, 155, 164, 170, 171, 173, 174, 175, 185.*
  DBR1/4 *26, 149, 151, 164, 171, 177, 183.*
  DBR1/5 *130, 138, 149, 164, 171, 175.*
  DBR1 Specification *26.*
  DBR2 *56, 57, 59, 63, 65, 88, 89, 95.*
  DBR4 *120.*
  DB2 *10.*
  DB3 *10, 13, 183.*
  DB2/4 *15, 78.*
  DB3S *10, 13, 14, 17, 19, 20, 24, 55, 104, 107, 111, 112, 130, 146.*
Aston Martin Race Reports *52, 125.*
Autosport *32, 41, 63, 100, 116, 135, 142, 154, 169, 175, 178, 187.*
Automobile Club de Belge *64.*
Automobile Club de l'Ouest *17, 130.*
Auto Union *13, 38, 145.*
Ayto, Frank *14.*
Avus *167.*

Bamford, Sir Anthony *189.*
Barth, Edgar *47, 78, 87, 90, 96, 98, 100, 102, 112, 114, 118, 126, 127, 129, 131, 132, 133, 138, 151, 155, 156, 170, 171, 173, 175, 178, 182.*
Bauer, Erik *104, 107.*

Behra, Jean *22, 28, 30, 34, 37, 49, 57, 59, 60, 64, 68, 78, 80, 82, 85, 87, 89, 90, 91, 96, 98, 100, 102, 108, 112, 114, 118, 119* (joins Scuderia Ferrari), *120, 125, 127, 128, 129, 131, 132, 135, 138, 139, 140, 141, 142, 151, 153, 154, 155, 160, 162, 164, 165, 166, 167* (dies at Avus), *181.*
Belgian GP *64, 70, 107.*
Bentley, W.O. *12.*
Bergwerk *51, 142.*
'Beurlys' (Jean Blaton) *107, 112, 158, 161.*
Bianchi, Lucien *107, 112, 151.*
Blanchimont *70, 73.*
Blond, Peter *151, 173.*
Bolster, John *39, 22, 154.*
Bonnier, Jo *40, 41, 57, 64, 68, 118, 126, 127, 128, 129, 131, 132, 133, 138, 140, 151, 155, 156, 166, 170, 175, 177, 178, 182.*
Borrani wheels *31.*
Boyd, Maxwell *41.*
Brabham, Jack *95, 98, 100, 101, 108, 110, 114, 171, 173, 187.*
Brero, Lou *30.*
Bristol *15.*
Bristol Aeroplane Company *10.*
Bristow, Chris *170.*
British Automobile Racing Club *185.*
British Empire Trophy Race *31.*
British Grand Prix *13, 65, 113.*
Brooks, Pina *120, 121, 166.*
Brooks, Tony *11, 17, 19, 20, 25, 26, 34, 35* (wins at Spa), *36, 37, 38, 39, 40, 41, 42, 44, 46, 47* (wins Nürburgring 1000 Kms), *49* (describes a lap of the Ring), *50, 52, 53 55, 57, 58, 59, 60, 61* (crashes at Le Mans), *63, 64, 65, 67* (wins at Spa), *68, 70* (describes a lap of Spa), *80, 81, 82, 84, 87, 88, 89, 90, 92, 93, 95, 98, 99, 100, 101, 103, 104, 108, 109, 110, 111, 112, 114, 116, 120* (signs for Scuderia Ferrari), *121* (refuses to drive at Le Mans), *130, 131, 132, 133, 135, 138, 139, 142, 145, 151, 166, 167, 168, 170, 171, 173, 175, 177, 178, 180, 181, 182, 183, 186, 187.*
BRM *24, 119, 186.*
Brown, David *10, 12, 13, 14, 15, 24, 30, 44, 47, 65, 78, 95, 114, 120, 130, 149, 158, 159, 175, 181, 182, 187* (withdraws Aston Martin from sportscar racing).
Brünnchen *139, 142.*
Bueb, Ivor *19, 30, 57, 59, 60, 61, 65, 82, 108, 110, 111, 112, 126, 127, 151, 153, 158.*
Buell, Temple *63, 68.*
Buenos Aires 1000 Kms *10, 28, 76, 78, 79, 80, 112, 125* (cancelled).
Burnenville *67, 72, 73.*
Bussell, Darcey *49.*

Cabianca, Giulio *89, 90, 130, 131, 132, 170, 171, 173.*

Cacciari *10.*
Cahier, Bernard *87, 88, 111, 142.*
Campo Felice *132.*
Canestrini, Giovanni *29.*
Carrera Panamericana *10.*
Carrozzeria Touring *10, 17.*
Carveth, Rod *126, 129, 145, 151.*
Castellotti, Eugenio *17, 28, 37.*
Champion Year *79, 89.*
Chapman, Colin *32.*
Chinetti, Luigi *107, 117, 118, 125, 126.*
Chiti, Carlo *77* (joins Scuderia Ferrari), *116, 119, 122, 170.*
Clayton, Bryan *39, 129, 171, 175, 183, 184, 185.*
Coca Cola *159, 166.*
Collins, Peter *17, 19, 20, 24* (joins Scuderia Ferrari), *30, 33, 34, 37, 38, 39, 40, 41, 42, 44, 46, 47, 53, 57, 58, 59, 61, 63, 64, 68, 78, 79* (wins Buenos Aires 1000 Kms with Phil Hill), *80, 81* (wins Sebring 12 Hours with Phil Hill), *82, 84, 85, 86, 87, 88, 89, 90, 91, 96, 97, 98, 100, 101, 104, 107, 110, 112, 113* (dies at the Nürburgring), *116, 117, 120, 130, 135, 144, 145, 166, 181.*
Collins, Louise *39, 78, 86, 120.*
Colotti, Valerio *119.*
Connaught *10, 25, 37.*
Cooper *10, 95, 108, 110.*
Cooper-Jaguar *34.*
Cooper-Monaco *171, 173.*
Costin, Frank *57.*
Crawford, Ed *82.*
Crystal Palace *25.*
Cunningham *10.*
Cunningham, Briggs *82, 126.*
Cunningham-Reid, Noel *25, 31, 32, 37, 38, 39, 41, 43, 44, 46, 47* (wins Nürburgring 1000 Kms), *49, 51, 53, 54, 59, 60, 61, 64* (crashes at Spa), *65, 80* (retires from racing) *81.*
Cutting, Ted *10, 12, 14, 15, 26, 27, 49, 51, 52, 55, 57, 77, 125, 151, 171.*

da Silva Ramos, Nano *151, 153, 154, 164, 170.*
Daigh, Chuck *125, 127.*
David Brown CG537 Gearbox *15, 125, 170, 191.*
David Brown Gear Company *15.*
Davis, Colin *87, 89.*
DB Panhard *131, 158.*
Dei, Mimo *118.*
Delageneste *158.*
de Beaufort, Count Carel *96, 101, 112, 138, 151, 155, 156.*
de Changy, Alain *65, 99, 101, 107, 112, 151.*
de Portago, Fon *17, 19, 30, 32, 33, 34, 37, 120.*

de Tomaso, Alessandro *87*.
Döttinger Höhe *51, 139*.
Drivers' World Championship *89, 116*.
Drogo, Piero *78, 80, 107, 112*.
Dubois, René *101*.
Duncan, Dale *68*.
Dundrod *13*.
Dunlop disc brakes *116, 117, 119, 156*.
Dunlop Bridge *19, 59, 108, 111, 112, 153*.

Earl's Court Motor Show *117*.
Eau Rouge *64, 67, 71, 72, 73*.
Eberan-Eberhorst, Professor Robert *13, 14*.
Ecurie Ecosse *19, 34, 57, 60, 61, 65, 82, 101, 108, 109, 114, 151, 176*.
Ecurie Francorchamps *19, 60, 64, 65, 98, 107, 112, 114, 151*.
Eifel Sportscar Race *146, 147*.
'Elde' (Leon Dernier) *158, 161*.
Elva *10*.
England, Lofty *58*.
Englebert tyres *67, 117*.
Erickson, E. *107, 112, 151*.
Ex-Muhle *51*.

Fairman, Jack *19, 108, 130, 131, 135, 138, 140, 141, 142, 145, 149, 151, 154, 171, 173, 175, 182*.
Fangio, Juan Manuel *14, 17, 21, 22, 23, 24, 28, 30, 37, 38, 39, 41, 42, 46, 47, 53, 55, 57, 58, 67, 76, 78, 79, 85, 135, 144, 145, 146, 147*.
FIA Calendar for 1958: *78*.
FIA Sportscar Regulations for 1957: *21*; for 1958: *67*.
Fantuzzi, Medardo *10, 119*.
Feltham *12, 13, 15, 17, 169, 171*.
Feeley, Frank *10, 15, 17, 56, 77*.
Ferrari, Enzo *10, 17, 21, 24, 29, 30, 32, 64, 67, 68, 77, 78, 84, 85, 93, 97, 114, 117, 118, 119, 120, 121, 126, 129, 165, 166, 167, 181, 186*.
Ferrari Testa Rossa 0666 (1st prototype) *37, 38, 41, 46, 47, 56, 63, 64, 68, 78, 82, 87, 88, 91, 107, 112, 126, 129, 151*.
    0704 (2nd prototype) *56, 58, 60, 61, 62, 63, 64, 68, 76, 77, 78, 79, 82, 84, 85, 86, 87, 88, 91, 94, 96, 97, 101, 104, 107, 109, 110*.
    0710 *77, 78, 79, 82*.
    0714 *78, 79*.
    0716 *78, 79, 82*.
    0718 *49, 70*.
    0720 *126*.
    0722 *107, 112*.
    0726 *82, 87, 88, 91, 94, 96, 98, 100, 107, 109, 117*.
    0728 *82, 83, 87, 88, 89, 91, 96, 107, 110, 111, 126*.
    0730 *82, 107, 112, 126, 151*.
    0732 *82, 107*.
    0736 *99, 107, 151*.
    0746 *94, 96, 98, 100*.
    0748 *104, 107*.
    0752 *189*.
    0754 *107, 112*.
    0766 *119, 127, 128, 131, 136, 138, 142, 151, 154, 157, 164, 171, 178, 183*.
    0768 *11, 127, 128, 131, 135, 139*.
    0770 *127, 131, 132, 135, 137, 139, 151, 164, 171, 173, 177, 178, 187*.
    0772 *130*.
    0774 *151, 154, 155, 164, 171, 178, 189*.
Dino V6 *94, 116, 119, 131*.
Dino F2 *77*.
F1 *156* (sharknose), *70*.
290MM *17, 30, 37, 87*.
410S *79*.
290MM *17, 30, 37, 87*.
860 Monza *17, 135*.
500 Mondial *17*.
TR500 *17*.
315S *28, 30, 32, 37, 38, 39, 56, 58*.
500TRC *30*.
335S *32, 33, 37, 38, 39, 41, 56, 58, 64, 68, 80*.
250GT *32, 37, 116, 158, 161*.
TR58 *91, 94*.
TR59 *119, 121*.
296S *119*.
750 Monza *165*,
Fitch, John *82, 126, 127, 129*.
Flockhart, Ron *19, 31, 32, 57, 58, 60, 61, 82, 101, 151, 153, 176*.
Florio, Count Vincenzo *87, 89*.
Flugplatz *50, 55, 102, 104, 136, 138, 139, 144, 146*.
Flynn, Chet *82*.
Fordwater *178*.
Forghieri, Mauro *94, 119, 190*.
Fraschetti, Andrea *74, 75, 77* (killed at Modena).
Frazer Nash *10*.
French GP *23, 113, 165, 166*.
Frère, Paul *19, 26, 60, 61, 96, 104, 112, 130, 149, 151, 153, 154, 158, 164, 171, 175, 177, 178, 183*.
Fuchsröhre *50, 51, 52, 55, 138, 146*.

Gaisberg Mountainclimb *131*.
Garnier, Peter *116, 117*.
Geitner Gil *126, 129, 145, 151*.
Gendebien, Olivier *17, 20, 32, 34, 37, 38, 39, 41, 46, 47, 52, 57, 58, 59, 60, 63, 64, 65, 67, 68, 78, 79, 80, 82, 85, 87, 88, 89, 90, 91, 94, 96, 98, 100, 104, 107, 108, 110, 111, 112, 113, 114, 117, 120, 125, 127, 128, 131, 132, 138, 139, 140, 141, 142, 144, 151, 153, 154, 155, 156, 157, 158, 163, 166, 170, 171, 173, 176, 181*.
German GP *38, 49, 64, 95, 114, 118, 135, 144, 145, 167*.
Gilby Engineering *25*.
Ginther, Richie *82, 85*.
Girling disc brakes *31, 84, 116*.
Godia, Francesco *37, 40, 46, 78, 79*.
Gomez-Mena, A *107, 112*.
González, José Froilán *108, 110*.

González, Sergio *78, 80*.
Goodwood *114, 165, 169, 171, 173, 178, 180, 183, 189, 190*.
Goodwood Fire brigade *175*.
Goodwood Nine Hours *114, 165, 169, 171, 183*.
Gould, Horace *37, 46*.
Grand Prix de Spa *34*.
Grant, Gregor *116*.
Greene, Keith *144*.
Greene, Sid *25*.
Guelfi, André *118*.
Guiraud *158*.
Gurney, Dan *107, 110, 117, 118* (joins Scuderia Ferrari), *125, 127, 128, 129, 130, 131, 132, 135, 138, 139, 142, 145, 151, 154, 155, 156, 161, 164, 165,* (tests GP Ferrari at Monza), *166, 167, 169, 170, 171, 173, 175, 176, 177, 178, 180, 181, 182, 186, 187*.

Halford, Bruce *151, 154, 158, 172*.
Hamilton, Duncan *17, 34, 35, 57, 58, 60, 61, 106, 108, 110, 111, 112*.
Hampton Court Maze *52*.
Hansgen, Walt *82, 151*.
Hatzenbach *50, 103, 105, 144*.
Hawthorn, Mike *17, 19, 23, 24* (early career), *30, 37, 38, 39, 40, 41, 42, 46, 47, 53, 57, 58, 59, 60, 61, 63, 64, 68, 78, 79, 80, 82, 83, 84, 85, 87, 88, 89, 90, 91, 94, 96, 98, 100, 101, 102, 104, 107, 108, 109, 110, 112, 114, 116, 117* (wins World Championship), *118, 119, 120, 124, 125* (dies in road crash), *127, 130, 135, 145, 181*.
Hansgen, Walt *82, 151*.
Herrmann, Hans *37, 41, 42, 68, 112, 118, 131, 133, 138, 145, 151, 170*.
Hill, Graham *108, 171, 173*.
Hill, Phil *17, 20, 28, 30, 37, 57, 58, 59, 63, 64, 68, 70, 76, 78, 79* (wins Buenos Aires 1000 Kms with Peter Collins), *80, 82* (wins Sebring 12 Hours with Peter Collins), *84, 85, 86, 87, 88, 89, 90, 91, 94, 96, 97, 98, 100, 104, 106, 107* (wins Le Mans with Olivier Gendebien), *108, 110, 111, 112, 113, 117, 118, 120, 125, 126, 128, 130, 131, 132, 134, 136, 138, 139, 142, 143, 144, 151, 154, 155, 156, 158, 161, 162, 163, 164, 165, 166, 170, 171, 173, 175, 177, 178, 181, 182, 183*.
Hind, Eric *39, 87, 88, 162, 165, 171*.
Hocheichen *103*.
Hodkinson, Harold *116, 117*.
Höhe Acht *51, 100*.
Holbert, Bob *129*.
Hollywood *169*.
Holmes, Jerry *184*.
Hotel de France *15, 57, 108, 112*.
Hugus, Ed *82, 107, 112, 151*.
HWM *10*.
HWM-Jaguar *25*.

Indianapolis 500 *171*.
Indianapolis Corner *112*.
Ireland, Innes *151, 152, 153*.
Italian GP *116, 186*.

Jackman, Paul *30*.
Jaguar *10, 23, 24, 84*.

Jaguar C-type *10*.
Jaguar D-type *10, 19, 30, 34, 35, 57, 60, 61, 65, 82, 104, 106, 108, 109, 110, 111, 112, 114, 117, 151, 153, 176*.
Jaguar XK150 disc brakes *116, 117*.
James, Bill *81*.
Jenkinson, Denis *34, 38, 46, 47, 89, 90, 132, 138*.
Johnston, Jim *126, 129*.
Juhan, J *107, 112*.

Kallenhard *51, 147*.
Karussell *51, 55, 99, 100, 145*.
Keift *10*.
Kesselchen *47, 51*.
Kessler, Bruce *107, 110, 112, 117*.
Kimberly, Bill *151*.
King, John *39, 87, 88, 156*.
Klemantaski, Louis *32, 33*.
Kling, Karl *147*.
Kochert, Gottfried *104, 107*.

La Chartre *159*.
Lagonda *10, 14*; V12 *13*; saloon *13*.
LB6 (Lagonda-Bentley) engine *12*.
L'Action Automobile *23*.
Lallement, Henri *166*.
Lancia *10*.
Lancia-Ferrari *135*.
La Source *35, 65, 67, 70, 72, 73*.
Lavant Corner *173, 190*.
Lawrence, Jock *34, 57, 60, 61, 65, 151, 153, 154*.
Le Mans *10, 13, 14, 15, 17, 20, 24, 72, 93, 107, 108, 110, 121, 126, 130* (Test Day), *146, 149, 170, 182, 186, 187*.
Le Cheval Blanc *112*.
Les Combes *71, 72*.
Les Hunaudieres *130*.
Leston, Les *37, 38, 39, 41, 43, 47, 60 , 81* (retires from racing).
Lewis-Evans, Stuart *57, 61, 92, 95, 98, 100, 101, 108, 110, 111, 114, 125*.
Linge, Herbert *112*.
Lister *10*.
Lister-Jaguar *31, 32, 82, 114, 126, 127, 151, 154, 173*.
Lucas, Jean *61*.
Lunken, Eb *126, 129*.

Madgwick *173, 183*.
Maglioli, Umberto *38, 40, 47, 61, 131, 133, 138, 142, 145, 151, 170, 175, 178*.
Mairesse, Willy *98, 99, 101, 107, 112*.
Malmedy *70, 72, 73*.
Mantovani, Sergio *87*.
Martin, E.D. *82, 107, 112, 126, 129, 151*.
Maranello *17*.
'Mary' (M. Brousselet) *61, 112*.
Maserati *10*; 250S *30*; 300S *10, 17, 21, 28, 30, 32, 34, 37, 41, 46, 47, 57, 63, 67, 76, 78, 79, 135*; 300S V12 *68*; 450S *10, 21, 28, 29, 30, 34, 37, 38, 41, 42, 58, 59, 63, 67, 68, 82, 85, 96*; 450S

Berlinetta 57, 60, 63; 250F *37, 65, 67, 78, 145, 166*.
Maserati gearbox *170, 191*.
Masta Straight *73*.
McCluggage, Denise *145*.
McLaren, Bruce *171*.
Menditeguy, Carlos *28*.
Mercedes-Benz *10, 14, 145*.
Mercedes-Benz W196 *14*; 300SLR *14, 34, 87, 90, 146*.
MIRA *15, 149*.
Mières, Roberto *78*.
Mille Miglia *10, 14, 22, 24, 28, 32, 37, 68, 78, 87, 105, 120*.
Modena Autodrome *28, 77, 117, 118, 119*.
Monaco GP *37, 108*.
Mon Ami Mate *116*.
Monthléry *19*.
Monza *17, 120* (Aston Martin testing), *165, 186*.
Morocco GP *116, 117*.
Morolli, Olindo *39, 41, 46, 47*.
Moss, Katie *89*.
Moss, Stirling *14, 17, 19, 20, 21, 22, 24, 28, 30, 34, 37, 38, 39, 41, 42, 45, 46, 47, 51, 53, 57, 60, 64, 65, 68, 76, 78, 79, 80* (joins Aston Martin), *81, 82, 84, 85, 87, 88, 89, 90, 91, 92, 93, 95, 96, 98* (wins Nürburgring 1000 Kms), *99, 100, 101, 102, 104, 105, 108, 109, 114, 116, 117, 120, 121, 126, 127, 128, 131, 132, 134, 135, 136, 138* (wins Nürgurgring 1000 Kms), *139, 141, 142, 144, 145, 146* (talks about the Ring, Astons and Mercedes), *147, 149, 151, 152, 153, 154, 155, 159, 164, 168, 170, 171, 172, 173, 175, 176, 177, 182, 183, 185, 186, 187*.
Motor Sport *38, 46, 47, 89*.
Mr Magoo *49*.
Mulsanne Straight *19, 20, 60, 61, 108, 109, 126, 130, 161*.
Munaron, Gino *87, 88, 89, 90, 96, 104, 107*.
Murray, C *34*.
Murray, Ian *171*.
Musso, Luigi *28, 30, 32, 37, 57, 60, 63, 68, 78, 79, 80, 82, 85, 87, 88, 89, 90, 91, 96, 98, 100, 104, 107, 113* killed at Reims, *117, 166*.

NART *107, 110, 117, 126, 151*.
Naylor, Brian *32, 65, 138, 139, 140, 149, 154, 164*.
Nelson, Ed *34*.
Neubauer, Alfred *24, 146*.
New York Motor Show *17*.
News of the World *173*.
Nixon, Chris *172*.
North Turn *42, 50, 55, 100, 101, 144*.
Nostradamus *169*.
Nürburgring *11, 49, 50, 63, 70, 72, 80, 81, 97, 101, 105, 108, 114, 118, 120, 126, 133, 135, 145, 149, 165, 167, 169, 182*.
Nürburgring 1000 Kms *10, 12, 32, 37, 87, 93, 107, 131, 177, 186, 189*.

O'Connor, Pat *82*.
Officine Maserati *10, 37, 78* (withdraws from racing).
OSCA *10, 87, 89, 90, 118*.

O'Shea, Paul *126*.

Pabst, Augie *126, 129*.
Pappalardo, Paul *189*.
Parnell, Reg *17, 19, 24, 30, 35, 37, 39, 54, 57, 59, 60, 61, 64, 65, 67, 72, 81, 82, 87, 88, 95, 96, 98, 100, 101, 108, 120, 125, 127, 135, 138, 141, 146, 149, 152, 154, 156, 158, 162, 164, 165, 173, 175, 181, 185*.
Parnell, Roy *15, 19, 20, 26, 39, 59, 67*.
Pavarotti, Luciano *49*.
Perdisa, Cesare *17, 28*.
Pescara 12 Hours *10*.
Pescara GP *64*.
Peugeot 403, *101, 104*.
Pflanzgarten *45, 51, 100, 114, 139, 142*.
Picard, Francois *107, 112*.
Pininfarina *10, 17, 30, 119*.
Piper, David *144*.
Porsche *10, 38, 40, 61, 76, 85, 119, 182, 183*.
Porsche, Professor Ferdinand *13*.
Porsche RSK *87, 89, 90, 93, 96, 98, 100, 102, 104, 108, 125, 127, 129, 131, 133, 138, 145, 151, 155, 156, 170, 178*.
Porsche Spyder RS *87, 90, 167*.
Porsche Carrera *87, 131*.
Portuguese GP *116*.
Potton, Jimmy *165, 184*.

Quiddelbacher-Höhe *50, 144*.

Rabelovsbana circuit *63*.
RAF School of Aeronautics *149*.
Reims *165, 166*.
Reims 12 Hour race *10, 17*.
Reventlow, Lance *126, 129*.
Road & Track *87, 111, 142*.
Rocchi, Franco *77, 119*.
Rodriguez, Don Pedro *126*.
Rodriguez, Pedro *126, 127*.
Rodriguez, Ricardo *126*.
Rosemeyer, Bernd *38*.
Rouen GP *15*.
Rouselle, Freddie *19, 34, 35, 60, 61*.
Rowe, Maurice (Dunlop) *116*.

Salvadori, Roy *17, 19, 25, 31, 32, 34, 35, 37, 38, 39, 40, 41, 42, 43, 47, 52, 54, 57, 58, 59, 60, 63, 64, 67, 81, 82, 83, 84, 95, 96, 98, 99, 108, 110, 114, 120, 125, 126, 149, 151, 152, 153, 155, 156, 158, 159, 162, 164, 171, 173, 174, 175, 182, 189* (tries the cars).
Salvarini, Walter *77*.
Sampras, Pete *49*.
Sanderson, Ninian *19, 34, 35, 40, 43, 57, 60, 61, 82*.
Sayer, Malcolm *10*.
Scaglietti, Sergio *10, 17, 30, 37, 56, 75, 77, 87, 94, 95, 119*.
Scarfiotti, Ludovico *87, 170*.
Scarlatti, Giorgio *30, 34, 37, 41, 57, 64, 68, 87, 90, 96, 131, 170*.

197

Schell, Harry 23, 30, 40, 41, 42, 60, 64, 68, 85, 96, 98, 104.
Schell, Monique 23.
Schwalbenschwanz 42, 43, 51, 92, 101, 102.
Scott-Brown, Archie 31, 32, 82, 87.
Scuderia Ferrari 13, 17, 30, 37, 38, 82, 91, 94, 107, 114, 116, 117, 118, 121, 129, 138, 151, 161, 164, 165, 169, 186, 187.
Scuderia Centro Sud 118.
Scuderia Sudamericana 78.
Sculati, Eraldo 30.
Sebring 12 Hours 10, 28, 81, 87, 114, 121, 125, 126, 140.
Segrave, Sir Henry 25.
Seidel, Wolfgang 63, 64, 68, 78, 85, 87, 88, 89, 90, 91, 96, 104, 107, 110, 111, 112, 117, 131, 133, 151, 155, 156.
Sessler, Don 129.
Severi, Martino 57, 61, 118.
Shelby, Carroll 25, 30, 81, 82, 84, 95, 108, 114, 125, 127, 130, 140, 149, 151, 153, 154, 155, 156, 158, 159, 162, 164, 165, 173, 175, 178, 182, 184, 185, 186.
Shell fuel 126.
Sieff, Jonathan 173.
Silver City Airways 15.
Silverstone 13, 14, 94, 95, 149.
Simon, André 17, 20, 57, 60.
Smith, Reg 126.
Smith's 'Jackall' system 171.
Sopp, Jack 59.
South Turn 42, 49, 50, 147.
Spa-Francorchamps circuit 10, 11, 64, 70, 169, 186.
Spanish GP 23, 25.
Sportscar World Championship 10, 12, 13, 17, 63, 64, 114, 125, 135, 169, 178, 181, 182, 183, 187, 189.
Sports Cars Illustrated 161.
Stanguellini 158.
Starting Grid to Chequered Flag 151.
Stavelot 65, 73.

Steed, Dick 43.
Stephens, Alex 'Steve' 12, 15, 171.
St Mary's 171, 176, 177, 178, 180.
Sunbeam 25.
Supercortemaggiore 1000 Kms 10, 17.
Swaters, Jacques 19, 34.
Swedish GP 21, 62, 63, 108.
Syracuse GP 23, 25.

Talbot 10.
Targa Florio 10, 11, 22, 24, 87, 95, 100, 107, 114, 131, 135, 146, 165, 170.
Taruffi, Piero 32, 34.
Tavano, F. 107, 112.
Tavoni, Romolo 29, 30 (becomes Team manager of Scuderia Ferrari), 38, 39, 62, 63, 67, 78, 85, 96, 101, 118, 119, 121, 126, 127, 129.
Taylor, Henry 34, 35, 40, 162, 173, 175.
Tertre Rouge 61.
The Autocar 109, 111, 116, 162.
The Motor 104.
Thinwall Special 24.
Titterington, Desmond 19, 35.
Tojeiro-Jaguar 114, 151, 153, 154.
Tour de France 78, 130.
Tour of Sicily 10, 24, 32, 37.
Tourist Trophy 10, 13, 22, 24, 93, 108, 113, 114, 165, 169, 170, 173, 178, 181, 182, 186.
Trimble, Max 34.
Trintignant, Maurice 17, 20, 28, 30, 37, 38, 39, 41, 46, 47, 52, 57, 60, 63, 64, 68, 79, 108, 110, 111, 149, 152, 153, 158, 162, 164, 171, 173, 175, 177, 178, 183.
Triumph TR2 127.

Ugolini, Nello 30, 46, 64.

Ulmann, Alec 125.
USAC 126,
US GP, Sebring 186, 187.

Vandervell, Tony 24, 120, 121, 182.
Vanwall 23, 37, 65, 70, 84, 95, 114, 135.
Venezuela GP 21, 63, 67.
Volvo 444 101.
von Hanstein, Huschke 78, 87, 114, 131.
von Neumann, John 77, 78, 79, 80, 82, 85.
von Trips, Wolfgang 'Taffy' 30, 32, 34, 37, 38, 68, 78, 79, 80, 82, 85, 87, 88, 89, 90, 91, 96, 98, 100, 101, 104, 109, 110, 111, 114, 117, 126, 127, 128, 129, 131, 133, 138, 139, 151, 155, 156, 167, 170, 173, 175, 178, 182, 183, 187.

Walker, Peter 17, 19, 24.
Walker, Rob 25, 198, 125.
Walkerley, Rodney 104.
Washer, Jacques 32, 34.
Watkins, Martyn 135, 142.
Watson, Willie 12, 13, 14.
Wehrseifen 51, 147.
Westhampnett Airfield 169.
Wharton, Ken 19.
White House 154.
Whitehead, Graham 32, 34, 37, 47, 59, 104, 107, 111, 112, 113, 130, 138, 139, 140, 149, 152, 154, 171, 173, 175.
Whitehead, Peter 34, 37, 40, 47, 104, 107, 111, 112, 113, 130 (dies during Tour de France).
Wippermann 51, 104.
Wisdom, Tommy 86.
Woodcote 178, 182, 187.
Wyer, John 10, 13, 14, 15, 17, 19, 20, 25, 30, 44, 49, 52, 54, 59, 60, 81, 87, 112, 120, 121, 135, 152, 182, 185.
Wyer, Tottie 60, 112.